PATTON: A STUDY IN COMMAND

PATTON

A STUDY IN COMMAND

BY

H. ESSAME

CHARLES SCRIBNER'S SONS • NEW YORK

Contents

Maps and Illustrations

PHOTOGRAPHS BETWEEN PAGES 152–53 AND 168–69

FRONTISPIECE: General Patton and General Roosevelt in Sicily.

Prologue

This seems to me to be the record of a man who was devoted to war. He could have lived in peace without incurring any reproaches or any harm, but he chose to make war. He could have lived a life of ease but he preferred a hard life with warfare. He could have had money and security, but he chose to make the money he had less by engaging in war.

All this shows how devoted he was to war. As for his great qualities as a soldier, they appear in the facts that he was fond of adventure, ready to lead an attack on the enemy by day or night, and that when he was in an awkward position, he kept his head, as everyone agrees who was with him anywhere. It was said that he had all the qualities of leadership which a man of his sort could have. He had an outstanding ability for planning means by which an army could get supplies, and seeing that they appeared; and was well able to impress on those who were with him that Clearcus was a man to be obeyed. He achieved this result by his toughness. He had a forbidding appearance and a harsh voice. His punishments were severe ones and were sometimes inflicted in anger. . . . With him punishment was a matter of principle, for he thought that an army without discipline was good for nothing; indeed it is reputed that he said that a soldier ought to be more frightened of his commander than of the enemy if he was going to turn out one who could keep a good guard, or abstain from doing harm to his own side, or go into battle without second thoughts. So it happened that in difficult positions the soldiers would give him complete confidence and wished for no one better. On these occasions they said his forbidding look seemed positively cheerful and his toughness appeared as confidence in the face of the enemy, so that it was no longer toughness to them, but something to make them feel safe. . . . Once they began to win victories with him, one could see how important were the factors which made his men into good soldiers.

Xenophon of Clearcus the Spartan his first general
in about 360 B.C.

PATTON: A STUDY IN COMMAND

1

Flying Start

Favouritism is the secret of efficiency

attr. Admiral of the Fleet
Lord Fisher

Early on 20 July 1917 General John J. Pershing, Commander-in-Chief American Expeditionary Force, accompanied by Colonel Harbord, his Adjutant-General, Colonel Alvord, his Chief of the General Staff, and his aide-de-camp Captain G. S. Patton Jr, left Paris and motored northward on the *Route Nationale* which leads to Beauvais, Montreuil and the English Channel. It was harvest time. On either side of the almost empty road stretched cornfields cultivated for over two thousand years. Tall poplars fringed the highway; age-old villages, farms and small woods dotted the landscape. This indeed seemed to be one of the loveliest and most peaceful lands in the world. Soon however the scene changed: they had reached the rear areas of the zone of the British armies. Long columns of marching men in khaki with heavy packs on their backs sweated their painful way, all in step, over the cobblestones; lorries with iron tyres and horse-drawn guns and limbered wagons threw up great clouds of dust. About noon they reached the little walled town of Montreuil which housed the British GHQ. Here they were welcomed by Lieutenant-General Fowke, the British Adjutant-General and a friend of Pershing since the days when they had both been observers with the Japanese forces in Manchuria. A very smart guard of honour from the oldest military unit in the British Army, the Honourable Artillery Company, stood ready for Pershing's inspection. After luncheon he and his party toured the headquarters and delved into the British organisation, surprised to find that it differed very little from their own. It was almost dusk when eventually they arrived at an old *château* half-hidden in a magnificent grove of chestnut trees at Blendecques. Here the British Commander-in-Chief, Sir Douglas Haig, who lived here when not in the forward zone in his headquarters train, made them welcome. Only the rumble of distant gun fire faintly wafted from the east by the evening breeze disturbed the calm of an almost perfect summer evening. No effort was spared to make them feel at home and that they were more than welcome guests. That night the Field-Marshal recorded in his private diary:

> Friday July 20. . . . I had a talk with General Pershing before and also after dinner. I was much struck with his quiet gentlemanly bearing—so unusual for an American. Most anxious to learn, and fully realises the greatness of the task before him. He has already begun to realise that the French are a broken reed.
>
> His AG and CGS are men of less quality and are quite ignorant of the problems of modern war. The CGS is a kindly, soft-looking fellow with the face of a punchinello. The AG having served long in Manila and other hot places seems to be less mentally alert than the others. The ADC is a fire-eater and longs for the fray.

Thus in a flash one cavalry general sized up Patton—as Pershing had already done—as a young officer after his own heart who would go far.

It would be flattering to modern popular sentiment in the Western World, the USSR and China to be able to record that the future commander of America's most glamorous army was born amidst the dregs of society and raised himself by his own efforts on sheer merit to high command. This is not possible. George Smith Patton Jr was in fact born, on Wednesday 11 November 1885, in affluent circumstances to a wealthy Californian rancher and lawyer who owned the 1,000-acre Wilson-Patton ranch in San Marino, just outside Pasadena, and whose family originally came from Scotland as Jacobite refugees. Neither was he, like Wellington and Montgomery, deprived of his ration of mother love and feminine affection in his tender years. In fact he may well have had an overdose of the latter from his aunt. Slick comment in accordance with current concepts of psychology and pediatrics is thus ruled out. Neither was he like Churchill condemned to the society of servants. The boy in fact adored his father who on his part was only too happy to give up his own time to teach him the basic male accomplishments: how to ride, swim, shoot, hunt and fish. Although living in California, the elder Patton had remained at heart a Virginian landowner. His own father had been killed in action as a colonel at the battle of Cedar Creek. Seven uncles had served as officers in the Confederate Army.

He and his son visited the Civil War battlefields; they were proud of their pedigree and their military tradition. From his earliest days the boy seems to have had no doubt that his destiny was to lead his country's armies, that the greatest privilege of citizenship is to be able freely to bear arms under one's country's flag and that courage is the highest of the virtues. His father was an original and cultured man who held what were then unorthodox views on the subject of education. His theory was that the child should first be exposed from the very early days to all the best that has been said or thought in the world, read to him by his elders, little attention being given to formal reading and writing. Much of this spate of culture apparently passed over young George's head; what did stick were legends, heroic verse, the *Iliad* in Pope's translation, Macaulay's *Lays of Ancient Rome,* Kipling and above all the Bible which so far as the Old Testament is concerned is as good a guide as any to the development of the offensive spirit in battle and the maintenance of morale. Throughout his life he retained his love of verse and the ability to recite long passages of it by heart. In the long term these early impressions did much to mould the man he would one day be. In the short term when he eventually went to school at Pasadena at the age of 11 he could neither read, write nor calculate, a handicap so far as academic studies were concerned which dogged him all the way to manhood. Although he soon learned how to express himself fluently and forcibly on paper he never learned to spell; he was weak too in mathematics. In due course he followed his father and grandfather to the Virginia Military Institute where one of his heroes had been Professor of Artillery—Stonewall Jackson. Appointment to West Point followed almost automatically in 1904.

From the day he joined he was determined to reach the highest rank a cadet could hold—that of Cadet Adjutant. Owing to his poor performance in mathematics this took five years instead of the normal four. From start to finish however he was top in military discipline and deportment. Military historians being students by nature have tended to depict their heroes as endowed with the intellectual aptitudes they think they themselves possess. Unfortunately the theory that great commanders must be high-level intellectuals is not borne out by the records of Patton at West Point and Montgomery and Alexander at Sandhurst. Their academic performance in fact never rose above the level of mediocrity. The secret of success in high command in World War Two would therefore appear to lie elsewhere. All three however had this in common: they were ardent players of violent games. Patton in particular drove himself hard to excel in individual sports—swimming, riding, pistol shooting, cross-country running and track events. He had less interest in team games: it is doubtful whether he ever visualised himself as a 100 per cent cooperative member of a team. In 1909 he was commissioned as a 2nd lieutenant in the 15th Cavalry. He was over six feet in height, well developed, self-confident and good to look at. A year later he married Beatrice Ayer, the daughter of a rich and influential industrialist and financier.

It proved to be a supremely happy marriage. His wife was a highly intelligent and cultured woman who, although coming from a luxurious background, was nonetheless prepared to follow her husband wherever he was posted, to endure cheerfully the discomforts and boredom of remote and primitive stations and to pull her weight as an army wife. She was a woman of outstanding personal courage: although she hunted all her life and in the end died from an accident in the hunting field it is probable that she hunted only to please her husband. She was an accomplished yachtswoman and spoke French well. From the very first day of her marriage she made the furtherance of her husband's career her main object in life. They were blessed like Mangin, whose fiery temperament and love of the dramatic Patton shared, with happy and intelligent children. She had great social gifts and soon became expert in shielding her husband from the social complications in which his exuberant and ardent temperament inevitably involved him. There is a striking similarity in their relationship to that between Mountbatten and his wife Edwina. No woman other than his wife ever cut any ice with Patton. By virtue of their wealth and influential connections the two from the first were able to move socially in more affluent and sophisticated circles than most of their contemporaries in the United States Army. They entertained lavishly and maintained a fine stable of polo ponies and racehorses. In 1912 Patton almost inevitably was appointed ADC to General Leonard Wood, the Chief of Staff and thus gained an early insight into the inner workings of the Army hierarchy. It was at this time that he made a friend of Secretary of War Stimson, with whom he used regularly to go riding in the early morning. He would badly need his aid in later years when Stimson once more in World War Two returned to hold the same office in Franklin Roosevelt's administration.

To some extent these early years resembled those of rich young officers in the British Brigade of Guards and cavalry before 1930 which both provided a useful outlet for their energies and incidentally curtailed at the minimum expense to the Treasury, overstocking at the wealthier levels of society.

They were happy days. Patton, however, did not allow a hectic social life to interfere with his determination to outshine all his contemporaries in physical achievement and skill at arms. In 1912 he was chosen to represent the United States at the Olympic Games at Stockholm—naturally at his own expense—in the military pentathlon. This consisted of a long steeplechase, pistol shooting, a gruelling swimming race, fencing and a cross-country run of 5,000 metres. Overall he finished fifth out of 43 of the military athletes of the world. On his way home he stopped at the French Cavalry School at Saumur to take a course in fencing from Adjutant Cléry, the French Army's expert. The two soon became friends. On return to United States he was posted to the Mounted Service School at Fort Riley, Kansas and was soon selected for a second-year advanced equitation course. France and her Army's long history had caught Patton's imagination. The following summer he and his wife went back once more to the French Cavalry School at Saumur for further study at his own expense. From this visit dated the close friendship with Lieutenant Houdemon (later General Houdemon) one of the instructors in equitation. At this time the vogue of the *Memoirs* of Baron General de Marbot, one of Napoleon's ADCs was at its height in the French and British armies. Though sometimes misleading in detail Marbot does recreate the spirit of the Emperor's campaigns and of life in the inner circle of his headquarters: he certainly captured the imagination of Patton who with the help of his wife struggled to read them in French. He and Houdemon spent hours together eagerly discussing the great campaigns and what it was that enabled Napoleon to dominate both his own armies and his enemies so completely and for so long. Houdemon convinced him that war with Germany was not now far off. Patton had no doubt where his own sympathies would lie and even contemplated fighting for France if his own country refused to become involved.

Whilst based at Saumur he found time to tour Normandy and Brittany in company with his wife and on return home submitted a report on his reconnaissance to Washington where it lay unnoticed until 1944. Prophetically it emphasised the mobility a force would achieve by moving on the high ground.

At Fort Riley his outstanding skill at arms had already gained him the honorific title of 'Master of the Sword' and an instructorship. That year his design for a new sabre to replace the existing pattern of curved cavalry sabre was accepted; significantly it had runnels to facilitate the free flow of blood. The official manual on the use of this weapon, revised by him at this time, characteristically contains no reference to the parry. *'L'attaque, toujours l'attaque'* would for ever be his doctrine. He found time too to revise the pistol regulations.

The autumn of 1915 brought with it a transfer to the less sophisticated atmosphere of Sierra Blanca, Texas, for cavalry border-patrol duty. Here Mexican bandits were an ever-present menace and life was lived to some extent on lines made only too familiar by the movies: hard-faced men wearing boots and spurs and long guns on their hips, dashing cowgirls with hearts of gold, flashy saloons, and rough justice lavishly meted out. The Pattons found no difficulty in adapting themselves to this invigorating society. Both indeed seem to have found it stimulating, to have made many friends and to have gained the approval of the 'grizzled old-timers' endemic in those parts.

Whether Pancho Villa was a mere bandit or a Che Guevara-type champion of the poor and oppressed is debatable. So far as President Woodrow Wilson's government was concerned he was an intolerable nuisance. Early in 1916, hoping to embarrass President Carranza's government, Pancho Villa perpetrated a night raid on Columbus, New Mexico and the camp of regular troops stationed there. This forced Wilson to mount a punitive expedition under Brigadier-General John J. Pershing which eventually rose to 15,000 men and came very close to involving the United States in all-out war with Mexico at a time when Wilson was telling the Allies and the world at large that there was such a thing as being too proud to fight. As soon as he heard that this force was being assembled Patton was quick to present himself at Pershing's headquarters and press his claims to be allowed to go with him. After several refusals Pershing relented and took him as Headquarters Commandant and acting aide.

The expedition penetrated some 400 miles into Mexico: as Pershing advanced, Villa withdrew. As in all guerilla warfare, the operations were about as rewarding as nailing jelly to a wall. Nevertheless the Americans did succeed in forcing Villa to break up his forces into small parties. It was with one of these that a patrol under Patton, consisting of six soldiers, an interpreter and some army cars, clashed on 14 May. He had in fact come upon Cardenas, a bandit 'general' on Villa's staff. They were in a house. No sooner had Patton deployed his men than three horsemen appeared on the scene. They fired first. Patton promptly shot one out of the saddle and with a second shot brought the horse of another to the ground and, as this one was raising his pistol, shot him dead. By this time the first bandit had recovered. He held up his left hand in token of surrender, fired and missed. Patton promptly shot him too: it was 'General' Cardenas. A further bandit having been similarly eliminated, Patton drove back to the American camp with the bodies of the men he had shot tied to the running board to show to Pershing. Thereafter the relationship with Pershing was close. It would only end with death in World War Two.

When the Expedition had penetrated some 400 miles into Mexico Wilson's government decided that the bandits had been taught an adequate lesson and that in the light of Mexican disapproval it would be wise to order Pershing to withdraw to a position 150 miles short of the border. Pershing promptly complied.

This minor campaign had far-reaching results. It made two reputations: firstly that of Pershing, whose handling of a situation complicated by extremely difficult political factors had enabled Wilson to avoid all-out war with Mexico at a most inconvenient moment and at the same time to proclaim publicly that the aim of the campaign had been achieved; and secondly that of his ADC Captain Patton who had spectacularly proved his worth as a fighting soldier in the close-quarter rough and tumble of battle. When Pershing in April 1917 almost inevitably was selected to command the American Expeditionary Force, one of his first decisions was to ask for Patton as his ADC and Headquarters Commandant.

From the very moment when Pershing and his staff landed at Liverpool from the British steamship *Baltic* on 10 June his mind had been made up on two vital issues: he would have his own all-American army and his own sector of the Front. In no circumstances would he tolerate the dispersal of his raw and virtually untrained armies as cannon fodder to plug gaps in the Allied front or to bolster up Allied morale. From the American point of view this constitutes the main theme of their campaign in World War One.

By September 17 it had been finally agreed that the American sector would be in Lorraine. Pershing therefore moved his GHQ to the four-storey barracks at Chaumont, a little town on the Upper Marne. Here he and his staff at once plunged into high-pressure planning for an army two million strong and the build-up of a transportation system to sustain it based on the Atlantic ports of Bordeaux and St-Nazaire and the railways thence to eastern France. The staff faced a gigantic task—all the long hours at the desk, the frustration, the intrigue and the overwork almost inevitable in a newly formed GHQ in a theatre overseas. In these circumstances the close association Patton had enjoyed with Pershing was now no longer possible. He soon decided that he had not come to France to wear out the seat of his well-cut riding breeches on a chair in his little office at the gate of the barracks. The juggling with statistics, the persuading, cajoling, exercising tact, registering charm, interminable conferences, suffering fools gladly, checkmating Allied machinations which go with this type of exercise, were not for him. The logistic side of planning indeed would never be his line of country. In September therefore he went to Pershing and asked to be posted to a fighting unit. Pershing understood: he would have done the same thing if he had been in his ADC's place. He gave him a choice: the command of an infantry battalion or posting to the Tank Corps now about to be formed under Brigadier Samuel D. Rockenbach. At a time when tanks were regarded by many in all the armies as expensive toys whose value had still to be demonstrated and when tanks of American design and manufacture did not exist, Patton had the vision to stake his future career on service with a corps which literally had to be created from the very beginning. Rockenbach handled the higher policy and provision for the new corps; Patton, now promoted to major, was given the task of training and commanding the first two battalions which would form the first brigade. Recruitment was no problem: the prospect of service with the new corps had a natural appeal to the best men in the new levies. All officers and men were volunteers and their quality was high. Patton knew little about tanks and had no doctrine to guide him. He therefore set off for the British Tank School at Bovington in Dorset and the French school at Chaplieu to pick up what he could. Wherever there was tank action of any size on the whole front there went Patton to observe and learn.

The Battle of Cambrai on 20 November 1917 is generally regarded as the birth of armoured warfare as understood in the first half of the twentieth century. Haig's great offensive starting on 31 July east of Ypres and continuing throughout the late summer and autumn had by this time irretrievably ground itself into the mud of Flanders; the Cambrai battle on the good tank area of the rolling chalk downs of the Somme was almost an afterthought. In it three brigades of tanks, some 476 in all, supported by 1,000 guns and six divisions of infantry attacked without preliminary artillery registration and achieved complete surprise. Within four and a half hours the leading troops advanced seven and a half miles and the whole of the Hindenburg defences on the front of attack were in British hands. For the moment it seemed that the 'Cavalry Gap' for which the armies had been seeking ever since 1914 had at last been created. In London the church bells were rung to salute the victory. Soon however all hopes were dashed: inadequate provision had been made for the exploitation of success, momentum was lost and time given to the Germans to recover. A week later a brusque counter-attack sent the British reeling back practically to their original start line.

In this battle Patton had what amounted to a ringside seat and a roving commission. He came away convinced that even the primitive tanks then available, acting in conjunction with the air, artillery and infantry arms, could restore mobility to the battle and that the scale had at last been tipped in favour of the man against the machine-gun. This conviction Pershing would soon share, even going so far as to offer 'anything in the AEF for 500 additional tanks'. Unfortunately none were forthcoming from American resources and the British and French, now casualty-conscious, understandably placed their own needs first.

On offer to the American Tank Corps were the British Mark V, a cumbrous 30-ton tank with a speed of 5 mph, with two 57mm. guns and four machine-guns, and the French Renault. The latter was a light two-man tank mounting a 37mm. cannon or two Hotchkiss machine-guns with a somewhat better cross-country capability. This was Patton's choice. Accordingly 22 were allotted for training purposes to his brigade, now established at a training centre a few kilometres south of Langres with billets in the little villages of Bourg and Brennes. When they arrived Patton was the only man who knew how to drive them. Companies were organised on a basis of 24 tanks each; a captain's tank and three platoons of five tanks each, the remaining eight being held in reserve under brigade control. Each company used the 22 tanks available in rotation for training purposes. Patton sent some of his officers to a French tank school to learn tactics; to others he gave actual battle experience in minor operations with the French Tank Corps for whom they soon developed a sincere esteem. The emphasis was almost exclusively on close cooperation with infantry following a rolling artillery barrage.

In his brigade Patton insisted from the very start on the highest standards of dress and deportment and saluting—even amongst the manure heaps which surrounded the troops' billets. Soon the super-correct salute which he expected and got became known throughout the American Army as a 'George Patton'. Punishment for laxity was prompt but humane and impartial. To the actual training he imparted the incomparable drive and enthusiasm which would characterise every unit he ever commanded. By mid-July 1918 the brigade had gained the reputation of being the smartest in the AEF. Neither he nor his men ever failed to advertise the fact.

The collapse of Russia and her withdrawal from the war in the late autumn of 1917 had temporarily tipped the strategic balance of power against the Allies. No one saw more clearly than Ludendorff that, if Germany was to win, he must defeat the British and the French before the arrival of American divisions on a large scale from the United States once more gave the advantage to the Allies. This he rightly estimated would come in July. In the event, thanks to the Bruchmüller technique of annihilating artillery bombardment, brilliant staff work, and the superior training of his assault divisions he came very near to success in the terrible and costly battles of March and April on the Somme and south of Ypres, on the Aisne and Marne in May and on the Matz in early June. Finally, on 15 July his last great blow misfired in the face of the skilful defensive tactics of Gouraud. Mangin on 18 July east of Villers Cotterets, using all the available French tanks, the 1st and 2nd US Divisions and the best French colonial troops at heavy cost—no less than 80 per cent of the tanks were destroyed—finally forced the Germans to start a slow withdrawal from the Marne salient.

When, a week later, the Allied Commanders-in-Chief assembled at Foch's headquarters at Bombon 25 kilometres south-east of Paris, Pershing sensed for the first time that year an atmosphere of optimism. The initiative, said Foch, who revelled in platitude, must not be lost. The Americans were now arriving at the rate of a quarter of a million a month. At long last it seemed that his doctrine of 'l'offensif à l'outrance' was the right solution to all their afflictions. The immediate need for the British and French was to straighten out the great salients created by the German spring offensives and for the Americans to attack at St-Mihiel. Here he requested Pershing

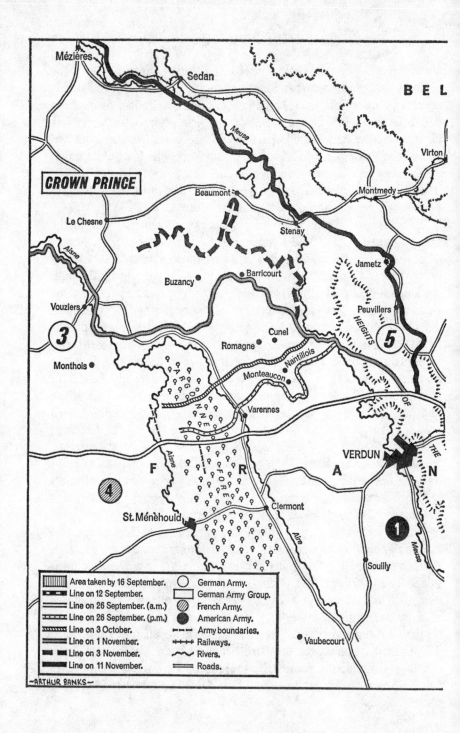

Mézières

Sedan

BEL

Meuse

Virton

CROWN PRINCE

Beaumont

Montmedy

Le Chesne

Stenay

Aisne

Jametz

Barricourt

Buzancy

Peuvillers

HEIGHTS

Vouziers

3

Cunel

5

Romagne

Monthois

Nantillois

Monteaucon

OF

Varennes

VERDUN

A

N

THE

F

Aisne

R

1

4

FOREST

St. Ménèhould

Clermont

Aire

Souilly

Meuse

~ARTHUR BANKS~

Vaubecourt

Area taken by 16 September.	○ German Army.
Line on 12 September.	◨ German Army Group.
Line on 26 September. (a.m.)	⊘ French Army.
Line on 26 September. (p.m.)	● American Army.
Line on 3 October.	Army boundaries.
Line on 1 November.	+++ Railways.
Line on 3 November.	∿ Rivers.
Line on 11 November.	═ Roads.

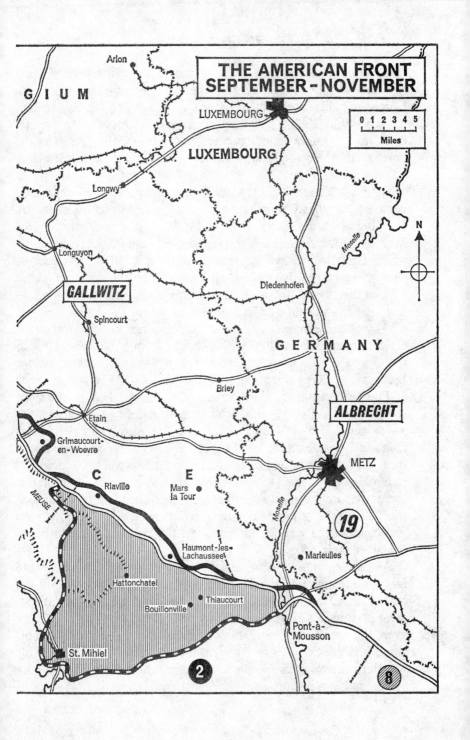

THE AMERICAN FRONT
SEPTEMBER - NOVEMBER

0 1 2 3 4 5
Miles

N

Arlon

LUXEMBOURG

LUXEMBOURG

G I U M

Longwy

Longuyon

Moselle

GALLWITZ

Diedenhofen

Spincourt

G E R M A N Y

Briey

ALBRECHT

Etain

METZ

Grimaucourt-
en-Woevre

C

E

MEUSE

Riaville

Mars
la Tour

Moselle

19

Haumont-les-
Lachaussee

Marieulles

Hattonchatel

Thiaucourt

Bouillonville

Pont-à-
Mousson

St. Mihiel

2

8

to chop off the salient so that the use of the railway from Paris to Nancy could be regained. To this end he placed the 2nd Colonial Corps under his command and promised to supply sufficient Renault tanks to bring Patton's two battalions up to strength. By the end of August the unexpected spectacular success of the British in the north enabled Foch to issue what would in fact be his last strategic directive of the war.

Haig was to attack in the north in the general direction of the complex of railway junctions about Aulnoye to meet a thrust by Pershing towards Mezières from his 90-mile front between the Meuse and the Argonne. The German rail communications on the whole front would thus be shattered. Foch insisted, despite Pershing's objections, that the St-Mihiel operation should not advance beyond the base of the salient. American plans for exploitation into Lorraine had therefore to be dropped. In outline the American main effort was to be made against the southern face under cover of an artillery bombardment by 3,000 guns and 2,000 Allied aircraft with I Corps on the right under Liggett and IV Corps on the left under Dickman. V Corps were simultaneously to attack the western face and II French Colonial Corps to make a holding attack on the town itself. Patton's 304th Tank Brigade consisting of two battalions, the 344th and 345th—174 tanks in all—was detailed to support Dickman's 1st Division on the left flank of the main effort on the southern face. The attack went in at 5 a.m. on 12 September in drizzling rain and mist. Trained teams of pioneers and engineers with bangalore torpedoes preceded the infantry through dense forests of barbed wire. The tanks of the 344th Battalion chugged ahead, cutting wire and clearing the way for the infantry; the tanks of the 345th followed in their wake.

As the commander of a tank brigade, Patton in this first battle faced a dilemma which would not be satisfactorily solved until the advent of radio in World War Two. He could go forward and at great personal risk direct the deployment of his tanks by orders delivered in person: the insuperable drawback to this method of command and control was that it placed him out of contact with his superiors, his reserves and the supporting artillery. Alternatively he could establish a static command post with good communications to the rear; if he did this he would be able to keep contact with his superiors and incidentally enable them to visit him with the minimum of inconvenience and personal risk. His personal influence on the battle itself, however, would be minimal. Characteristically Patton chose to face the certainty of a reprimand and fight his battle from the front.

It was a dramatic day. The tanks fanned out as they cleared the German first line of defence in front of the battle-hardened 1st Division. Many broke down; others bogged themselves in the mud. In the front line Patton on top of a tank urged his men forward like an MFH; his officers led their tanks on foot. He was in the front line all day under intense shell and machine-gun fire. At the little village of Essey he came upon the only other officer above the rank of major in the forefront of the battle. It was Brigadier-General Douglas MacArthur of the Rainbow Division. By early afternoon the Americans had gained most of the objectives of the day and captured 15,000 prisoners and 450 guns. Tank losses due to enemy action had not been great but by the late afternoon the brigade was virtually immobilised by lack of fuel and mechanical breakdown. Patton therefore had to go back to organise refuelling and repair and recovery and to face the reprimand he expected from his superior General Rockenbach. When it came it rolled like water off a duck's back. Rockenbach's vividly expressed disapproval of what in the Second War would be called 'swanning' in the forward area did not deter Patton on the 14th from leading a reconnaissance in force down a ridge running from the little village of Nonsard and penetrating the Hindenburg Line. Rockenbach peremptorily ordered him to return. On this day too MacArthur made an equally daring reconnaissance towards Metz. Then and later both he and Patton were of the opinion that, if Foch had allowed Pershing to exploit his victory, far-reaching results might have been achieved. The recollection of this lost opportunity would profoundly influence the imagination and plans of Bradley and Patton in this very same part of France a quarter of a century later.

Pershing now switched his weight 60 miles to the west to the Argonne front. Here, virtually unimpeded by the French, the Germans had built a defensive system as elaborate and ingenious as any in

France. It was a veritable labyrinth 12 miles deep bristling with barbed wire and mutually supporting machine-gun posts in concrete emplacements in great depth. It would have been difficult in First War terms to have found a position offering greater advantages to the defender, or less favourable to the use of armour. The heights of Montfaucon, Cunel, Romagne-sous-Montfaucon and Barricourt rising to 1,000 feet gave the Germans natural strong-points with all-round observation over bottomless woods, dense thickets and deep ravines. Pershing's plan envisaged the punching of two corridors through this devil's garden on either side of the Montfaucon feature. Patton's tank brigade was allotted to the left thrust by I Corps towards the village of Varennes down the Aire valley. Incredibly, thanks largely to the brilliant staff work of Lt-Colonel Marshall, later to become CGS in World War Two, when the 2,700 guns supporting the attack opened up at 2.30 a.m. on 26 September, all was ready.

By all-out effort, improvisation and ingenuity, Patton somehow or other managed to muster 189 Renaults. Owing to the haste with which the operation had to be mounted time did not permit him to arrange for the infantry of I Corps and his own tank crews to get to know each other and have a trial run. In the event they were to fight what amounted to independent battles. After three hours' intense bombardment by the massed artillery, three corps and Patton's tanks lunged forward into the chaos of the mist and smoke ahead. What happened now on the American First Army front baffles description. This at least is clear: Patton and his tanks had by 9 a.m. advanced five miles and captured the little town of Varennes. The infantry he was supposed to be supporting were nowhere to be seen; in fact they would not appear upon the scene for another four hours. Patton therefore proceeded to round up other bewildered infantrymen who happened to be in the neighbourhood and led them forward behind his tank urging them towards the hamlet of Chepy. In the vivid language for which later he would become celebrated he conveyed to them that they must close with the German machine-guns which had now sprung to life and that, to use the words of Frederick the Great on a similar occasion, they could not expect to live for ever. In a short time he and his runner found themselves attacking on their own; the infantry were nowhere to be seen. A machine-gun bullet then hit him in the leg. He fell into a shell hole from which stretcher-bearers later carried him back. Before losing consciousness he found time to give out his orders for the further conduct of the battle and to dictate a short report on the situation. He was then evacuated to a makeshift hospital train and on to a base hospital about 14 miles south of Dijon. The wound was severe, leaving a hole in his hip about the size of a teacup.

The Battle of Meuse–Argonne lasted 47 days and cost the Americans 26,227 dead and 95,788 wounded—that is 6,000 more dead and more wounded than the Battle of the Hedgerows in 1944. In the bottomless morass of the Argonne Forest in almost incessant rain the First Army plumbed depths of misery equalled only by the nightmare battle in the Hürtgen Forest in November 1944. On 1 November however, Liggett now commanding the First Army, carried the formidable Heights of Barricourt and thrust forward towards Sedan. Here on the hills above the town he paused for a moment to prepare for a further advance on Montmédy. In the Woeuvre the Second Army too was in motion towards the Briey iron basin. The whole Allied front at long last was surging forward.

Patton, although his wounds were not yet healed, could no longer endure the suspense of waiting in hospital to get fit again. The Army was advancing: he must get back to it at once. Together he and Lieutenant Harry H. Semmes broke out of hospital, appropriated a car and in flagrant defiance of authority took the road to Montmédy. The roads were crammed with troops of the American armies, now two million strong, pressing forward to the kill. The two absentees reached Verdun. It was 11 November. The war was over.

If ever a man since joining the Army had filled 'the unforgiving minute with sixty seconds' worth of distance run' it was George Patton. Before the war his ample means could have enabled him to lead a life of luxury and expensive idleness; instead, uncorrupted by inherited wealth, he had chosen to spend his time and money in the service of his country. He had followed the Greek ideal of excellence in whatever he undertook whether it was fencing, pistol shooting, equitation or athletics. His wealth and family influence had made it possible for him to move in social circles in Washington closed to the majority of his contemporaries in the American Army. He had not hesitated for one moment to use these advantages for the promotion of his own career, whether as an ADC to General Leonard Wood, the Chief of the General Staff, or to General Pershing. He had travelled in Europe and broadened his mind by contact with some of the best elements of the French Army. All this he had done without sacrificing unduly his capacity for the enjoyment of the good things of life. In the process he had made many useful friends. In Mexico he had shown that he had all the qualities of an outstanding junior officer in the field. In France he had personified the offensive eagerness and enthusiasm which the Americans had brought to the jaded French and the encouragement they had given to the British to fight on almost alone for nearly a year. It could be said that no officer of the American Expeditionary Force had seen more of the war at all levels than he had: first in close personal contact with the Commander-in-Chief himself and later as the young commander of America's first brigade of tanks with the freely exercised right to go anywhere on the whole front to collect ideas for the development of the new arm. In battle with his tanks he had shown, to use the actual words of his citation, 'conspicuous courage, coolness, energy and intelligence': never was the DSC more worthily earned. The DSM would follow later and be equally well deserved. He had got the feel of battle and seen how men react to fire. He could speak on tactical questions with the authority of personal experience and full knowledge of their implications in terms of human life. He was 33 and a temporary colonel. Now that the war was over he must revert to his permanent rank of captain. Eighteen years would elapse before he regained his highest wartime rank.

2

'Othello's Occupation's Gone....'

For the majority of soldiers the end of the fighting had brought a feeling of surprise that they should be still alive and of relief from operations which had combined the maximum possible physical discomfort with profound boredom and unrewarding personal risk. Patton was not among them. By July 1919 he was back with his 1st Tank Brigade in the United States at Fort Meade, Maryland. Although he and all the other regular army officers had now been reduced to their substantive rank he had lost none of his enthusiasm for the development of mechanised war. The tanks which had taken part in the campaigns of 1918 had been clumsy and primitive machines designed to meet a temporary need. Patton with his vivid imagination was convinced that, provided their mechanical defects could be overcome, their potential was great. At Fort Meade therefore he at once plunged with unabashed zeal and vigour into new schemes for research, development, experiment and training in the new arm. To say that the reception of his proposals by his immediate superior, General Rockenbach, was chilly would be an understatement. Congress was in no mood to vote the necessary funds. In fact for the next 17 years, when considering the allotment of money for the Army, their attitude would be well expressed by the tag:

> Tanks is tanks, and tanks is dear:
> There shall be no tanks this year.

Patton was undeterred. Although now only a mere major, he would continue the campaign on his own.

It was at this time that he got to know a remarkable New Jersey mechanical engineer named Walter Christie who had invented the tank chassis with sprocket wheels which bears his name. Christie was a man after Patton's own heart. His invention, with its rear engine and wheels as well as removable tracks, was the very type of machine for which Patton was looking: he even went so far as to lend Christie money. Furthermore he managed to persuade seven generals to come to Fort Meade for a demonstration.

When the day of the test arrived, Mrs Patton, fashionably dressed, for she was to be the hostess of the generals at luncheon after the display, accompanied her husband to the spectators' stand. Patton opened the proceedings by announcing that the odd-looking machine now on show, which in fact was little more than a platform mounted on sprocket wheels, had a speed of 30 mph over good going, could knock down small trees and buildings and slide down steep banks of sand. He then suggested that one of the generals should take it on a trial run; there were no offers. Patton therefore turned to his wife and told her to put the model through its paces. Somehow or other she survived the course but not without considerable damage to her summer outfit. Such is the penalty of marriage to high-grade obsessionals. He then suggested that one of the generals should repeat her performance. They had however seen enough. They would, they said, recommend the adoption of the Christie tank. Sad to relate in the end the Ordnance Department turned down this particular model.

The mood of the country in fact had completely changed. At the Peace Conference which produced the monstrous Treaty of Versailles in July 1919, Woodrow Wilson, hoping to save his scheme for the League of Nations, cost what it might, was forced to watch his dreams of a 'just and honourable peace' blown to the four winds. His celebrated Fourteen Points were virtually ignored. Rapturously received by the crowds of Europe, he lost sight of political realities not only among the Allied politicians but also in the US Senate. He returned home to find that he had no authority to speak for the American people and that the Senate would not ratify the Treaty, which contained the League Covenant. In September came mental and physical collapse. So far as the majority of Americans were

concerned the war was now regarded as having been a mere interruption of normal life: they were no longer interested in 'making
the world safe for Democracy': it would be far more congenial to
tackle their own internal social and political problems and to seize
the vast new opportunities now opening before them for growing
rich. Therefore, they reasoned, there was no need to provide for
a large army for operations against a first-class enemy outside the
American continent. Accordingly in 1920 the National Defence Act
settled for only an army of 280,000: two years later it would be
reduced to 125,000. War experience showed that tanks had been
successful in supporting the infantry by crushing wire and machine-
guns. That tanks could be employed in any other way was dismissed
as the pipe dream of a few eccentric enthusiasts such as Patton.
It was a strange conclusion for a nation more obsessed by mechanical ingenuity than any other. What remained of the Tank Corps
in 1920 was therefore dispersed as independent companies on the
basis of one company to each division and made the responsibility
of the Chief of Infantry. For the next 12 years the Tank School
would remain at Fort Meade under his control. Clearly there was
no place for Patton, a cavalryman, in this organisation. After a final
effort to secure Pershing's support for his ideas had failed, he
reached the conclusion that the times were out of joint. He had done
his best: he would go back to serve with the horses he loved. He
would nonetheless retain his seat on the Tank Board—until posted
to Hawaii in 1925—and maintain a lively interest in the controversies
concerning future mechanised warfare.

In consequence, the development of armour in the US Army between the wars came to be associated with the name of Major-
General Adna R. Chaffee rather than that of Patton. The official
doctrine that the tank's primary task was infantry support had a
marked effect on their development, implying as it did that they
should be slow moving, have great crushing power and be capable
of standing up to the weapons of the day. Nothing therefore was
produced to take the place of the cavalry which in the past by virtue
of its speed, power of manoeuvre and shock had enabled commanders to reap the fruits of victory. The machine-gun in fact had made
horse cavalry obsolete, as Fuller, Martell and the brilliant military

journalist Liddell Hart left no stone unturned or wire unpulled to demonstrate. Regrettably some influential officers in both the British and American armies still saw a future for 'the well-bred horse on the battlefield'. First to move to fill the gap were the British who, in spite of financial stringency and widespread pacifist feeling, assembled in 1927 the 'Experimental Force' on Salisbury Plain which was in fact to be the prototype of the armoured divisions of the Second War. This impressed the Secretary of War, Dwight F. Davis when he saw it on a visit to England. On return home he issued instructions that steps should be taken to develop an adequate tank force in the American Army. Some trials were accordingly carried out at Fort Eustis but got nowhere owing to the fact that the National Defence Act of 1920 laid down that tanks should be part of the infantry. It was not until 1933 that Colonel Daniel van Voorhis and his Executive Officer, Lt-Colonel Adna R. Chaffee, were allowed to start experiments with the 1st Cavalry Regiment at Fort Knox on lines independent of the infantry. In the mid- and later thirties this small force was gradually built up to become the 7th Cavalry Brigade (Mechanised) with the role of exploitation and making wide flanking moves designed to strike deep into the enemy's rear areas—the historic task in fact of Napoleon's great masses of cavalry. All the elements needed in modern warfare—tanks, infantry, artillery, air, engineers and signals—were visualised as playing their part in future operations to be characterised by surprise, shock and speed.

As in British military circles there was no shortage of ideas, particularly amongst ambitious junior officers: what was lacking was the money to implement them. Ironically, all the British—who had invented the tank, thought out its implications and talked more about it than anyone else—could produce for their Expeditionary Force in 1939 would be one under-strength brigade of Matildas to be followed nine months later by an incomplete armoured division. As late as July 1941 there were only 66 medium tanks in the United States by which time Guderian's panzer divisions, created on lines advocated by Fuller, Liddell Hart and Chaffee had knocked both Poland and France out of the ring and penetrated deep into Russia.

It is against this background of frustration, the heyday of the timeserver and the sycophant, that Patton's career between the Wars must be judged. Unshaken in his conviction that he was destined for greatness, he found peacetime army routine uninspiring, trivial and irritating. Herein to some extent lies the explanation of his habitual lurid language and petulance on obviously inappropriate occasions. Suvorov, the great Russian general, used to behave in a very similar manner. Inevitably Patton qualified with distinction at the Command and General Staff School at Fort Leavenworth and the Army War College, the forcing house for potential higher commanders. With war experience second to none in the American Army, his forceful personality and his influential connections, it would have been surprising if he had not passed out well. Apart from two tours in Hawaii he managed to put in three tours with the 3rd Cavalry at Fort Meyer, no great distance from Washington, and a period in the office of the Chief of Cavalry.

The qualities essential in a commander and those in a good staff officer are as the poles apart. It is the duty of the latter to take all detail and as much other work as possible off the shoulders of his commander so as to leave him time to think and plan ahead. He is expected to be tactful, patient, reticent and diplomatic. He must be industrious, unselfish and, above all, happy to subordinate himself to another man. For good or ill, Patton was no Berthier, Bedell Smith or de Guingand. The senior officers under whom he served in Hawaii deserve some sympathy. Indeed it would have been difficult to find any officer in the United States Army less qualified temperamentally to exercise these delicate functions. It is not surprising therefore that his two tours in Hawaii from 1925 to 1928 and from 1935 to 1938 failed to gain the palm of official approval.

The first tour in fact culminated in an adverse report by his divisional commander, Major-General W. R. Smith. As in the British Army, reports of this type before despatch to higher authority must be shown to the victim. Patton's read: 'This officer would be invaluable in time of war but is a disturbing element in time of peace.' (This did not go quite as far as the legendary annual confidential report on an officer of the Indian Army, who subsequently rose to high rank. In his case the reporting officer, after forecasting that he would go far in war, is said to have added: 'In peace he is a

pestilential nuisance owing to his persistent attempts, not always un-
successful, to seduce the wives of his seniors.') A smaller man than
Patton would have taken his report as adverse: he took it as a com-
pliment. It cast no reflection on his personal character and indeed
contained an element of truth. He had his own unorthodox ideas
on such trivial matters as dress which always loom large in military
communities when they have nothing more important with which
to occupy their minds.

His second tour in Hawaii in a chair-bound job as G2 to General
Drum from 1935 to 1938 was equally unrewarding. This involved
the collection and collation of intelligence. As usual in those days
funds provided for these purposes were miserably inadequate. According to his son-in-law, he endeavoured to run a section at his
own private expense only to be told for his pains that he was a
fool for doing so. Ironically, one of his reports at this time which
got nowhere forecast an attack on Pearl Harbor as a feasible operation by the Japanese and recommended that steps should be taken
to meet it if it came. Incidentally, at this time he and his commanding general had a full dress row in the blatant publicity of the polo
ground, which arose from his lurid language in the excitement of
the game.

Thus condemned between the Wars to an irksome life of routine
unworthy of his talents, he sought release in almost inordinate
equestrian activity. He seldom missed a horse show, a steeplechase
or a foxhunt. Altogether he amassed 400 ribbons and 200 cups.
To keep his weight down he resorted to running for miles in heavy
clothes, drastic doses of citrate of magnesia and Turkish baths.
Miraculously these drastic measures seem to have damaged neither
his heart nor his digestion: he could claim with justice that he had
the constitution of a horse. In the late thirties he and his wife were
joint masters of the Cobbler Hunt which covers some of the stiffest
country in Virginia. It was to polo however that he preferred to
devote as much as possible of his off-duty time, rising to captain
the Army team. He thought, and many other generals have held
and still hold similar views, that polo is the ideal recreation for aspir-
ing higher commanders. It demands speed, split-second tactical decision and perfect team work. It enables men to continue playing a

violent game long after the deadline which comes to the majority at about 35. Above all it demands intense concentration, good judgement and a high standard of physical fitness. There is the spice of danger in it too. It is also expensive. Patton put into it almost fanatical drive and energy. To many he seemed to be the epitome of the traditional hard-riding, foul-mouthed cavalryman and expert swordsman with a fine record in sport and war and little more.

To this period belongs his voyage across the Pacific from the west coast of the United States to Hawaii in the *Arcturys,* an old 40-ft schooner. Although, owing to his weakness in mathematics, he had had to put in an extra year at West Point, his navigation was perfect. In this as in everything else he seems to have sought out difficult physical and mental tasks for the sheer joy of overcoming them. In these years he also wrote a good deal of poetry. It is unfortunate that like Churchill, Alexander and Eisenhower he did not choose painting instead as an outlet for his surplus creative urge. He should have taken note of the elder Mr Weller's aphorism on this subject: 'Poetry's unnatr'l no man ever talked poetry except a beadle on Boxing day, a Warren's blacking, or Rowland's oil, or some of them low fellows.' It would not have been difficult for him to produce results as good as Eisenhower's in this particular branch of art.

There was in fact an inner side to his life, of which few were aware, represented by his library of over 500 books: furthermore he read them. According to his son-in-law he had read more history than any man he ever knew. Little-minded men live entirely in the present; the minds of big men with historical imagination, such as Patton and Churchill, range not only into the future but into the past. Patton's choice of books and his markings on them show wide reading and sometimes penetrating comment. He could visualise himself marching along the great roads, standing in front of the impressive buildings and mingling with the crowds of the Roman Empire. He could imagine himself on campaign in Gaul with Caesar and the Tenth Legion. He had studied French so that he could see the campaigns of Napoleon through the eyes of Marbot. In spirit he could ride with Murat in the great battles in Italy, Egypt and Germany. He knew the broad topography of Europe, the river lines, the ridges and the defiles like the back of his hand, why invasions had followed the routes they actually took, why armies had stood and fought where they did. In his own country he rode again with J.E.B. Stuart and the other great cavalry leaders of the Civil War. At times throughout his life he would disconcert his hearers by claiming that he had been actually present at some battle or other hundreds of years ago. This type of departure from normal behaviour is commonly called *déjà vu,* sometimes expressed in the words 'I have been here before'. There are various psychological explanations for it none of them entirely satisfactory. The fact is that some individuals of high intelligence and exceptional historical imagination can convince themselves that they have lived in another age. A glance into any University senior common room, political convention or cultural assembly should convince even the most sceptical that men, when they wish to do so, can make themselves believe almost anything—that is the basic theme of the comedy of the human race.

The late twenties and thirties were a particularly acrimonious period of controversy in England and amongst junior officers in United States. Fuller, Liddell Hart and Hobart were all proclaiming that a new era in war had dawned, that battles in the future would be like naval engagements with armour fighting armour and the infantry degraded to the role of 'land marines'. None of them was either tactful or tolerant: in fact they damaged their own case by sheer bad manners and intrigue. Fuller left the Army in a huff; Liddell Hart manipulated the Press and the politicians against the Army hierarchy. Patton followed these controversies and also those started by de Gaulle in France without getting on the wrong side of the higher authorities of the day. In Berlin, the American military attaché kept Washington and the United States Army well posted with developments associated with the name of Guderian. Patton's own contributions to the *Cavalry Journal* (now *Armor*) at this time are obviously endeavours to clear his own mind in the dust raised by the more extreme protagonists for mechanical war at all costs and the atavistic worshippers at the shrine of the horse. Sometimes, it must be admitted, he led himself and others astray as for instance when he attempted to justify combinations of horse cavalry and armour in an article in the *Cavalry Journal* in 1933. Trials soon proved that mechanised infantry could perform most of the orthodox cavalry tasks in half the time, as Chaffee had maintained from the start of the argument. What is significant, however, is the angle from which, unlike most of the military prophets, he approached the problems of future war. Whilst others immersed themselves in technicalities, Patton saw that the fundamental problem concerned not merely weapons, mechanics and electronics but men as well: 'The Roman sword was only 18 inches long and yet it conquered the World.' Two papers he wrote in 1927 and 1931 reveal the line of thought which in days to come would inspire his own particular contribution to the art of war and the history of his country.

In the first paper he asked himself what it was in the past that had given men the courage to fight and risk death or mutilation in battle. From his own personal experiences in action he knew something of the nature of fear and recognised the fact that its basis is awareness of danger. This he regarded as healthy, for a man who is aware of danger automatically takes steps to provide against it. This led him to examine the factors which in the past had enabled men in battle to fight fear with courage, to advance or stand firm and not bolt in panic.

His studies of Marbot and other writers on the Napoleonic Wars led him to the conclusion that the French soldier had often been moved by intense emotional inspiration. Faith in abstractions such as *La Patrie, Liberté, Le Peuple Souveraine* and *La Gloire* had been amongst the motive springs of their greatest feats of arms. In sharp contrast concepts such as these had never had any apparent appeal to the British and their descendants in Canada, Australia and New Zealand. Here he found himself faced by an enigma—the built-in inarticulate and unemotional obstinacy of the race which in the past had saved the world from Napoleon and would do the same again from Hitler in 1940. Surprisingly he did not consider the special case of the Irish concerning whom Montgomery, one of the six field-marshals produced in the Second War by Ulster, remarked with truth: 'The Irish love fighting; when they have no one else to fight, they fight each other.'

The record for heroism on the battlefield of his own people, particularly in the Civil War, was second to none. Patton was steeped in its history. He knew that morale was never stable. Sometimes it had risen to sublime heights: at others it had slumped. One factor however was crystal clear: for high morale the American soldier must have faith in the cause for which he fights. In the end, Patton argued, all would depend on the ability of their leaders to capture the imagination of their men. In the next war, the armies of the United States must inevitably consist not of seasoned regulars but of young men fresh from civil life—little more than boys in fact. Life in the Army at any rate tended to be an extension of boyhood: many men remained mentally adolescent throughout life. Therefore, argued Patton, the leader must appeal to the vanity of the youthful male—the fondness for bizarre clothing, the strange hair styles and weird whiskers which are, in fact, the human equivalent of the sexual displays of the peacock and both the blue- and red-bottomed baboons. Highly coloured uniforms, flamboyant hats, sophisticated haberdashery all had their appeal: he strongly approved of the wide variety of military millinery affected by the British Army. In this sphere in the future he would show himself to be no mean innovator. There must also be a variety of decorations readily available for prompt reward and display. To these boyish foibles, he decided, the leader must appeal. Whatever their nationality it was clear that the performance of troops in battle had ultimately depended on the quality of the leadership given to them.

Here Patton felt that historians, being scholars themselves, had tended to overstress the importance of great intellectual capacity on the battlefield. Here he was on firm ground. As a general rule the men in the senior common rooms of Universities or at the higher levels of industry and political parties are not those whom a soldier would trust as leaders in a tight corner or a rough house. The secret of leadership he therefore decided must lie elsewhere.

He found it in history. The nature of man has altered little in recorded time. Whether he considered the campaigns of Scipio and Hannibal in North Africa or those of Allenby in Palestine, as described by Wavell, one fact was clear as daylight. All the great commanders of the past had had a thorough grasp of the technique of their job, outstanding personal courage and the knack of being at the right place at the right time. All, too, had had the ability not only to make a sound and simple plan, which all could understand, but also to convince the troops that provided they played their part they must succeed. This had been the secret of Caesar when he rallied the Tenth Legion in Gaul, of Joan of Arc when at a time that all seemed lost she led the French armies to victory at Orléans, of Napoleon when he rode five horses to death at Rivoli. Patton deduced what his own experience at the sharp end of battle confirmed: that leadership above all must be personal, dynamic and direct, that the 'living presence' of the commander must infect every man of his command. Napoleon and Stonewall Jackson seemed to have possessed this unique quality to a supreme degree—the capacity to make men go beyond the limits of endurance, to take great risks and to face with equanimity the possibility of mutilation and death. This is the theme of the article he wrote in 1931 called 'The Secret of Victory'. In it he said that the leader himself must be the very epitome of self-confidence, enthusiasm, abnegation and courage; he must so fascinate the men under his command that they each and every one become, to a greater or less degree the embodiment of the leader's own eager and aggressive personality. This obviously demanded some of the arts of the actor. Napoleon himself had realised this and had not disdained taking lessons from Talma, the idol of the Paris stage—hence the celebrated stance, the threadbare greatcoat in sharp contrast to the glittering uniforms of the surrounding staff, the white charger Marengo, Rustam, the colourful Mameluk orderly, and the rest of the Imperial circus. Hence too the flamboyant uniforms and panache of Murat. Patton made up his mind to build up his own intrinsically histrionic personality and take the risk. He therefore created the Patton stance by rehearsing in front of a mirror and increased the volume of his high-pitched voice by constant practice, the method used by Demosthenes two thousand years ago on the sea shore and in a high wind—with admittedly somewhat different results. It would in due course become a great act, all the more effective from being sincere, so convincing indeed that he himself, like some of the giants of the stage, would never be able to escape from it. Having brought down the house and hit the headlines he would find himself, like Montgomery, Mountbatten and MacArthur, condemned for ever to endless repetition of what was in principle their one and only act. Inevitably the performance would provide the sensational press with exactly the type of news they wanted and bring upon him the jealousy of rivals unable by virtue of their very mediocrity to perceive the true quality of the man behind the tinsel and the motley. The lurid language, allowing for the coarse vocabulary affected by the fanciers of horse and hound the world over, was to some extent part of the act. His aphorism 'Never be obscene or use profanity unless the obscenity is so splendid or the profanity so outstanding that people will be so interested that they will forget to be shocked' betrays the motive behind the startling effusions to which the world would in due course be treated.

In those days promotion in the United States Army, like the mills of God, ground very slowly. He had to wait to the age of 49 before becoming a Lieutenant-Colonel. It seems that by 1937 he was facing the possibility of retirement, for, while serving in Hawaii he decided the time had come to establish a permanent home. He therefore bought an old-established farm in South Hamilton near Boston. The farmhouse itself was over a hundred years old and of great charm, set as it was amongst splendid trees and with a lovely vista stretching down to the Ipswich River. There were ample outbuildings. It was the kind of home of which many a professional soldier since Xenophon has dreamed for his retirement. He called it 'Green Meadows'. The passage of time to 1 July 1938 almost automatically brought his promotion to full Colonel and posting to the 5th Cavalry at Fort Clark in the Texas Panhandle, a military backwater generally regarded as providing a dignified climax to a meritorious career pending departure to that bourne from which their successors ensure that few ever return. The talk in the Army was all of the need for youthful generals. In England, Hore-Belisha, advised by Liddell Hart, had sacked the whole Army Council and reduced its mean age by 11 years. It had become an article of faith that 50 should be the ceiling for major-generals in mobile war. Patton was 53: there seemed to be nothing ahead beyond the joys of country pursuits backed by ample means. In fact, however, changes in the Army Higher Command were at long last moving in Patton's favour.

In 1937, after years in eclipse, Marshall, a good friend who had long since appreciated Patton's unique qualities, had become Deputy Chief of Staff. In Europe events were already in train which it was evident would sooner or later compel the United States to re-arm. Marshall was quick to decide that Patton would be needed. He therefore arranged his posting to Fort Meyer so as to have him near at hand. On 1 September the Germans with forces including ten armoured divisions and supported by 1,600 close-support aircraft invaded Poland. Within 17 days the brave, but obsolete, Polish Army had been wiped off the map. The heyday of armoured forces had dawned.

In May 1940 came the great German breakthrough at Sedan by von Rundstedt's Army Group A, the crossing of the Maas and the thrust over the rolling downs north of the Somme by seven armoured divisions and three motorised divisions supported by three air fleets to the sea at Abbeville, thus forcing the British Expeditionary Forces to evacuate via Dunkirk and creating the situation which in three weeks precipitated the fall of France. At the very moment when the Panzer divisions were heading towards Paris, Marshall, now Chief of Staff, ordered General Frank Andrews of the War Department General Staff to draw up plans immediately for the organisation of two armoured divisions, their logistic support and for their future expansion. A War Department Order of 10 July created the Armoured Force under General Adna Romanza Chaffee. Two days later Colonel George S. Patton Jr was appointed to command the 2nd Armoured Brigade at Fort Benning. As the Sunday papers said there were to be 'Panzers for the US' too.

3

The Foundations

Great God, who through the ages,
Has braced the bloodstained hand,
As Saturn, Jove and Wodan,
Hast led our warrior band,
Again we seek Thy council,
But not in cringing guise;
We whine not for Thy mercy—
To slay: God make us wise.

G. S. Patton Jr in
The Women's Home Companion

Chaffee's plans for the armoured force envisaged as a first step the formation of the I Armored Corps consisting of the 1st Armored Division at Fort Knox, under Magruder, the 2nd Armored Division at Fort Benning under Scott and the 70th Reserve Tank Battalion. In the last week in June, Patton, well aware of what was in the wind, had sought a meeting with Chaffee and failed to get one. He did however see Scott. The result was a letter to Chaffee dated 24 June which betrays Patton's fears at this time that he would be passed over for a command in the new force as being over age or out of favour. Its wording is significant.

My dear General (Adna),
  I was unfortunate in being unable to connect with you for a meal while you were here. I did see Scott, who told me that you were good enough to mention me in connection with a command in mechanization. I certainly appreciate your kindness and want to assure you, if it is necessary, which, knowing me, it probably is not, that I am always willing to fight and am enthusiastic in whatever job I have. I will always

do my best to give satisfaction should I be fortunate enough to be selected.

Chaffee replied:

I put you on my preferred list as a brigade commander of an armored brigade. I think it is a job you can do to the queen's taste . . . I hope things work out favorably for you. I shall always be happy to know that you are around close in any capacity where there is fighting to be done.

It was not the least of Chaffee's services to his country—and they were great—that at this crucial moment in Patton's career, when the cry was all for men under 50, so great was the physical and mental strain of mobile warfare alleged to be, that he saved from relegation to the scrap heap the future commander of the armoured force which would move farther and faster than any other in the Second World War. Without Chaffee's help at this time to secure for him the command of one of the tank brigades at Fort Benning, Georgia, thus ensuring his promotion in due course to command 2nd Armored Division, Patton's life might well have been almost a tale of 'sound and fury signifying nothing'; his heartfelt gratitude reveals the inner warmth and sincerity of the man. Furthermore the incident raises doubts whether in war, as in other human activities, there should be arbitrary casting ages, the ratio of stupid to clever being about the same in both young and older age groups. It may be true that there is 'no fool like an old fool' but historically the young ones have always run them close.

Chaffee had barely another year to live but in that time he laid not only the foundations of an American armoured force which would eventually rise to 16 divisions but also profoundly influenced the design and production of the tanks required for them and, on a lend-lease basis, for their allies. The difficulties to be surmounted would have daunted any man not built on the grand scale. The first conscripts to fill the ranks would not begin to arrive until October 1940; the problem of officers for this vast expansion was equally baffling. Understandably the other arms of the service were reluctant to let their best officers go to the armoured force; the temptation to send those who would be least missed was great. The majority would require considerable retraining. Merely to provide shelter for the huge new influx involved building construction at high pressure on a fantastic scale.

The greatest difficulty however was the shortage of medium tanks. Fortunately experience gained by the British in North Africa was becoming available. Chaffee was quick to grasp the need for superior gun power and thicker armour without the sacrifice of speed and cross-country capacity. This, largely owing to his insistence, was met by the M3 and later by the M4. The British in particular had reason to be grateful for the M3, known to them as the 'General Grant'. It was this tank and the M4, called the 'Sherman' and the M7 self-propelled 105mm. howitzer, called the 'Priest' which would in due course provide a high proportion of the armour in Montgomery's armies to the end of the war. Incidentally, the light-tank version of the M3, called the 'Stuart', after the great Confederate cavalry leader J.E.B. Stuart, would in the very near future play a conspicuous part in the North African Campaign. The British affectionately called it the 'Honey'. As the American automobile industry geared itself for war production, Chaffee flew from factory to factory to get to know at first hand the manufacturing problems involved and in due course by direct personal pressure on the Chief of Ordnance in Washington ensured that the fighting men got the tanks and vehicles they wanted. Meanwhile he had set up the Armoured Warfare School to train the vast number of specialists required and a Replacement Centre (motto: 'Kill or be killed') to hold the reserves which would inevitably be required to meet future wastage and expansion. When, worn out by driving himself beyond the limit, Chaffee died on 18 August 1941, four months before Pearl Harbor, he left behind foundations well and truly laid. What Carnot, the organiser of victory, was to Napoleon's armies, Chaffee in the matter of armour was to those of Eisenhower and MacArthur.

The material difficulties to be surmounted however were as nothing compared with the problem of morale. The Americans were not at war and would not be until the Japanese gave them no alternative at Pearl Harbor on 6 December 1941, two years and four months after the British. The recruits coming into the Army had little of the enthusiasm of their fathers who had flocked to join the colours in 1917. They were not professional soldiers and they never wanted to be. There was little apparent sense of dedication. Profoundly civilian at heart they read the newspapers where the advertising industry fawned upon them, inciting them towards the soft life and self-indulgence in all its forms. They read at least the headlines of the newspapers; the radio and the movies had profoundly coloured their outlook. All these influences had tended to stress their so-called democratic rights rather than their obligations to their country. Their attitude to authority was often critical. Some, unaware of the offence-oriented optimism and will to fight which comes from exercise and simple diet, were physically soft and morally flabby. Many were resentful at being deprived of some of the comforts which they had come to regard as their democratic right. The regulars were far too thin on the ground to influence them to any great degree. Time was short. Patton realised that in a none-too-distant future these raw levies would have to face some of the most highly professional, battle-hardened and blood-thirsty soldiers the world has ever known; men Spartan in outlook, united by a discipline of steel and with a fanatical faith in the Nazi creed for which they were ready to fight and if necessary to die.

In south-east England at this time Montgomery, commanding in succession the v Corps, the xii Corps and the South-Eastern Army was facing a by no means entirely dissimilar problem. To contrast and compare his approach with that of Patton at virtually the same stage of the war is therefore an intriguing exercise.

The mood of the British conscripts before Dunkirk, even allowing for that normal British phlegm which has always enabled the race to face the prospect of being less frequently alive without unseemly drama, had been little more enthusiastic than that of their American counterparts. Even after Dunkirk, despite Churchill's speeches, some were slow to realise the peril they were in.

Montgomery, on taking over the v Corps in Hampshire and Sussex in the late summer, had already diagnosed the disease and was ready with the remedy. He faced the fact that they were in the main civilians in uniform who could read, listen and to some extent, if appropriately stimulated, think for themselves. As he himself said later what they needed was 'not only a guiding mind but a point of focus or to put it in another way, not only a master but a mascot'. He therefore deliberately set about producing the latter. He would exploit his own austere Protestant beliefs, his Spartan personal life—for he neither smoked nor drank—and above all his own remarkable ability to dominate an audience, looking them straight in the eye and driving home what he had to say in simple words of biting clarity which all could understand. He would be the first British general to wear battledress; he would live on a private soldier's rations and see that everyone knew he was doing so. All must see and hear him. He would in fact create his own legend: he must be talked about. Above all he must make an ally of the Press. Here he was quick to grasp the kind of news the correspondents wanted and their point of view. Generals, whatever their nationality, seldom provide good press copy. They all seem to come out of the same box and to use the same clichés. They know from bitter experience that it is seldom wise for a general to bare his heart to a pressman; nearly all realise that it is impossible to be a good journalist and a gentleman at the same time. They therefore tend to reveal as little of themselves and their plans as possible. Montgomery saw that although it was often hard to see the necessity, the correspondents had to live and that what they wanted was human interest, colour and anecdote, the more eccentric and bizarre the better. He would see they got it and in the process enlist them on his side and whet their appetite for more in his campaign to raise his soldiers' morale to the highest pitch and his personal reputation too, if possible, to the skies.

In stature, bearing and physique Patton had an immense advantage over Montgomery and he exploited them to the full. In a drab age in the matter of uniform he was a law unto himself. His superbly cut riding breeches and English-made riding boots outshone those of all other generals in any army. His helmet, later to be adorned with the insignia of his former commands, sparkled in the sunlight so thick was the varnish on it. Wherever he went he took with him a large and varied wardrobe skilfully packed by his Negro orderly, Sergeant Banks. Of his many uniforms, the most amazing was one of his own design aptly described as the 'Golden Hornet'. It consisted of a soft green leather cadet jacket with two long rows of gold buttons slanting downward towards a gold belt buckle, tight jodhpur breeches and short soft boots. He carried his heavy Colt Model 1873 .45-calibre revolver in a shoulder holster under his left arm: its stocks were of ivory. On his head he wore a glittering gold plastic helmet. His arrival therefore in this outfit at a unit, announced by the steamboat trombone on his scout car, said to be audible for eight miles on a still day, was shattering. Staff officers came all the way from Washington to see it: the Press suitably reacted to its designer's complete satisfaction. Never since the days of the Prince Regent, who revelled in designing fantastic military uniforms had anyone had the courage to indulge in such a magnificent sartorial lark. On training and in battle however his dress, though always elegant, was more practical.

It is not surprising that Patton and Field-Marshal Alexander, the very epitome of the Brigade of Guards, should have held each other in high esteem. In the vital matters of discipline, deportment and saluting whatever the circumstances their views were as one. His insistence on shaving, cleanliness and the wearing of neckties at all times would become proverbial. For a whole year from April 1941 the 2nd Armored Division sustained the full blast of the Patton drive. In the process he made every man in the division to some extent the image of himself. No one damned by Patton for failing to salute ever forgot the reprimand. Rightly he pointed out in blistering words that an officer who cannot get his men to salute when they should do so is unlikely to carry much weight with them when he has to order them to place their lives in his hands. He was everywhere. He would even swoop down in his light aircraft over a traffic jam and in his shrill penetrating voice blast everyone for the breach of discipline. He had an uncanny knack of turning up where anything had gone wrong on an exercise—when a tank broke down as a result of bad maintenance or incompetent driving, when a unit was late at a rendezvous or when an order had gone astray. At Fort Benning he had an amphitheatre constructed and here he first delivered some of the lurid orations which would later become part of the Patton legend. Their effect was all the more stunning because many of his words were not those which anyone would expect a senior officer to include in his vocabulary but it would be wrong to damn him to flatter the prejudices of a later more sophisticated generation. Once or twice a week he assembled all his officers for lectures on tactics and related subjects. It was at one of these that he delivered himself of the aphorism that the war would be won by 'Blood and Guts alone'. It had an electric effect on his hearers and the phrase stuck.

With no clear guidance from above or for that matter from the British in the Western Desert, Patton trained his division on his own lines at high pressure and without respite. In fact he was working out by trial and error under practical conditions the techniques of rapid grouping, regrouping and deployment which in due course would make the Third Army the most flexible and quickly responsive force in the Allied armies. Patton's motto was the same as that of Catherine the Great's equally unorthodox General Suvorov: 'Hard in training: easy in battle'. Not without suffering did the 2nd Armored Division earn its sobriquet 'Hell on Wheels'. As a result, when it had its first opportunity to demonstrate its quality on a large scale in the Tennessee Manoeuvres of September 1941, so aggressive were its tactics and so sure was the grip of its commander that it finished several exercises 12 to 24 hours ahead of the time the directing staff had expected them to last. In the following month therefore in Louisiana, determined not to allow Patton to romp all over the countryside as he had done in the exercises in Tennessee, they staged a situation giving him no option other than frontal attack over ground made impassable by three days' torrential rain. Patton and Scott protested and were eventually allowed to move around a flank. Within a couple of hours Patton had regrouped, issued fresh orders and set off on a 100-mile sweep into Texas which, if the umpires had not arbitrarily ruled otherwise, would once more have finished the manoeuvres ahead of time. Next month in a further exercise in North Carolina, Patton and 2nd Armored Division completely outshone all others and, when all was over, as a final demonstration of their high state of training, at once hit the road for Fort Benning 300 miles away. They got there with only one halt of two and a half hours—a feat which up to that time had never been equalled in United States. Patton knew too, when to give a word of praise. He now told them that they had successfully met 'every test short of war'. That was all they wanted to know from him for by now he had infected them all with his own exuberant efficiency and thirst for battle.

In April 1942 having been promoted to command the I Armored Corps he set out from Fort Benning in his own private aircraft, a Stimson Voyager, to select a site for the Desert Training Centre near Indio in California. He soon found one after his own heart 180 miles long and 90 miles wide, covering some 162,000 square miles in the Great American Desert including parts of California, Nevada and Arizona.

It was a training area calculated in every way to delight a keen soldier's heart. There were no civilians whatever in it to raise objections to training or get in the way of practice with live ammunition: the only living things were coyotes and rattlesnakes. The terrain included many concealed approaches and abounded in surmountable and insurmountable obstacles. There were lots of volcanic cones, barren mountains and dry and dusty lakes. In summer the temperature rose to 120 degrees; there was absolutely no water. Patton took four days over the reconnaissance under combat conditions, allowing himself and his companion, Lt-Colonel Ennis, only a gallon of water each per day. No better area could have been found anywhere for the training of America's armoured forces. As troops arrived for training Patton allowed them only a canteen of water a day and insisted on every officer and soldier, himself included, running a mile in ten minutes every 24 hours. He also laid down that they should be able to march eight miles in two hours. In his eyes, the fact that they belonged to mechanised units was no excuse for them to forget how to use their legs. Sometimes the temperature inside the tanks rose to 150 degrees: men fainted and machines broke down as Patton drove them on. At night they learned to sleep beside their tanks or under trucks and how to go without sleep for at least 36 hours at a stretch. Tests for the prevention of heat exhaustion with salt tablets were rewarding: engines which overheated were discarded. All learned how to navigate by the sun and stars. He did all this, not because he was a sadist—in fact he loved the wholesome pleasures of life as much as any man—but because he knew from his own experience the violent shock they would soon have to face and overcome when they came to grips with Hitler's fanatical, tough and super-efficient soldiers. At least at Indio he could reproduce many of the horrors of war without the killing and thus, when in due course the trial came, steel their hearts.

The aims of both Patton and Montgomery were in fact the same: both sought to convince their men that they had a great and noble object, the overthrowal of the vile Nazi and Japanese tyrannies which threatened to destroy the liberties which were their birthright and that this could only be done by bold offensive action in battle. They were out to convince each and every man that provided he individually pulled his weight victory was certain. They were engaged in proving to all that they were part of an organisation which was 100 per cent efficient, that their leaders knew their job and that their own lives would not needlessly be thrown away. Above all they stressed the fact that every man would get a square deal and that every possible effort was being made to provide the best weapons and equipment. Of the two commanders probably Montgomery, in the setting of wartime England with its towns under nightly air attack and its civil population subsisting on four ounces of meat a week and an egg a fortnight, to accompany the lowest grade of pig's belly bacon from Chicago, may well have had the easier task. Patton had to harden his troops for battle in a country remote from the actual fighting, with little conception of the realities of war and still enjoying many of the luxuries of peace. Furthermore he had to do this in the teeth of lively and at times malicious criticism. The difference in fact between the aims of the two generals was one of style rather than intention.

There would be a marked resemblance too in their mode of life when they took the field. Montgomery lived in his caravans in the company of his small group of liaison officers, hand-picked for their ability and courage, at some distance from his main headquarters. He thus avoided becoming immersed in the details which he regarded as the province of his Chief of Staff. He thus secured time to reflect, concentrate on essentials and to plan. Patton too, would live apart from his staff in reasonable personal comfort and dignified isolation like the captain of a British battleship. In this respect he ran counter to the cult of extreme simplicity popular with some American commanders, to the embarrassment of their British allies. The sight of a major-general or colonel carrying his own bedding, or lining up on the chow lines with their soldiers or digging their own fox-holes lowered their prestige in the eyes of British NCOs and privates who saw them. How could, they said, a senior officer who wasted his time and energy on tasks any moron could do quite as well, really concentrate on his real job?

For the Allies the month of July 1942 was the nadir of the war. The Japanese had driven the Americans out of the Philippines and the British out of Hong Kong, Malaya, Singapore and Burma. On the Eastern Front it seemed that Hitler's armies could not now be far from a resounding triumph over the forces of Stalin who in almost insulting terms was demanding the opening of a Second Front to take the pressure off his apparently disintegrating armies. On 21 June Rommel had captured Tobruk; by the end of the month he and the Afrika Korps had reached the Alamein Line a bare 80 miles from Cairo. Ever since Pearl Harbour Churchill had been pressing the claims of an Anglo-American landing in North-West Africa to re-open the Mediterranean to Allied shipping and, he hoped, bring the French forces in Algeria and Morocco into the war on the Allied side. Roosevelt was quick to grasp the political and strategic advantages of Churchill's proposals; his strategic advisers, Marshall and King, were less enthusiastic, seeing in them a dispersion of force away from the decisive strategic point, that is, North-West Europe. They therefore urged instead a landing in the Cotentin peninsula that very summer. For this the British were not ready, pointing out that a Second Front prematurely opened up in North-West Europe to please Stalin would at best become a barely tenable beach-head and place an intolerable strain on the Royal Navy and Royal Air Force. The argument continued throughout the summer to the ever-increasing exasperation of all concerned. Rommel's threat to Cairo in July finally decided the issue. Churchill categorically refused to stage a cross-Channel operation in 1942. There remained therefore only two feasible Anglo-American operations for 1942: either the despatch of American troops to serve under British command in

Egypt or 'Torch' as Churchill now called it, the landing in Algeria and Morocco under American supreme command. Obviously in American eyes the latter was the lesser of the two evils.

On 25 July the Chiefs of Staff, having been ordered to agree on one operation or the other, plumped for Torch under the command of Eisenhower. At this stage the form the operation would take was vague in the extreme: the British urged a landing well inside the Mediterranean to be followed by a quick advance in Tunisia; the Americans favoured a landing on the Atlantic coast in Morocco in the vicinity of Casablanca. They said they had to get a base port on the Atlantic in case the Germans countered with a move through Spain via Gibraltar to isolate the forces in the Mediterranean. So wherever else the Allies were put ashore, a landing in Morocco there had to be. All realised that it would be a gamble of the first order rather than a straightforward military operation. At any rate there was available a commander who even if ordered to storm the gates of Hell would be prepared to take it on rather than let anyone else do it.

Eisenhower wanted Patton for the Moroccan landing but hesitated to ask for him as he was five years junior to him in rank. Marshall therefore stepped in and on 30 July summoned Patton to Washington. Nine days later he flew to England to confer with Eisenhower at Claridges and in Norfolk House, St James' Square. At this stage everything was in a state of flux. It was still in this state when Patton flew back to United States on 20 August at the top of his form having assured Eisenhower that so far as he was concerned, after studying the problem, his mind was at ease. Writing to Marshall at this time Eisenhower assured him that Patton had shown definite capacity to cope with the problem and was enthusiastic.

Meanwhile the inter-Allied debate continued. It was not until 5 September that Churchill was able to put an end to what was aptly called the 'Trans-Atlantic Essay Competition' by cabling to Roosevelt: 'We agree to the military lay-out you propose.' Roosevelt answered 'Hurrah' and well he might for no inter-Allied planning in the whole war was bedevilled by more complications, intangibles, uncertainties, misunderstandings, frustrations, amendments, alterations, compromise, snags and hitches than Torch. One of the senior British planners, a brigadier of very great ability, dropped dead with cerebral hemorrhage outside Norfolk House in the process. The fact emerged that the American Army and Navy were scarcely on speaking terms. At one stage so strained did the relations become between Patton and Hewitt, the admiral with whom he had been paired off, that King, the Chief of the Naval Staff, went so far as to say that unless the Army sacked Patton, he would have to recommend that the Navy withdraw from the unequal contest. It would have been to the advantage of both services if Patton's planning staff had been with the Navy in Hampton Roads instead of in Washington. Later they got on well together.

The final plan envisaged three task forces: the first a descent on the Atlantic coast by an all-American force to capture Casablanca with 24,000 troops under Patton, sailing direct from America in 102 ships of which 29 were transports of the Western Naval Task Force under Rear-Admiral H. Kent Hewitt; the second the Centre Task Force of 18,500 American troops from Scotland and Northern Ireland under Fredenhall, sailing from the Clyde escorted by a British naval force to land at Oran; the third the Eastern Task Force under British Command scheduled to land at Algiers but including 9,000 American troops for the initial landing. It was hoped with good reason that they would receive a more cordial welcome from the French than the British, memories of what had happened to the French Fleet in 1940 being still fresh. Within North Africa the American diplomatic representative, Robert Murphy, and others were deeply immersed in secret, highly complex and slightly shady negotiations which it was hoped would ease the way of the invaders.

Patton proposed to make his main landing at Fedala, 15 miles north of Casablanca with subsidiary ones at Mehdia, 50 miles further north to capture the Port Lyautey airfield, the only one in Morocco with a concrete runway, and at Safi, 150 miles south of Casablanca to ward off the strong French garrison at Marrakesh. The harbour here was also suitable for the landing of medium tanks. No one could say with certainty how the French would react. There were at least 60,000 good colonial troops in Morocco, the coast defences were well developed and the Navy embittered by memories

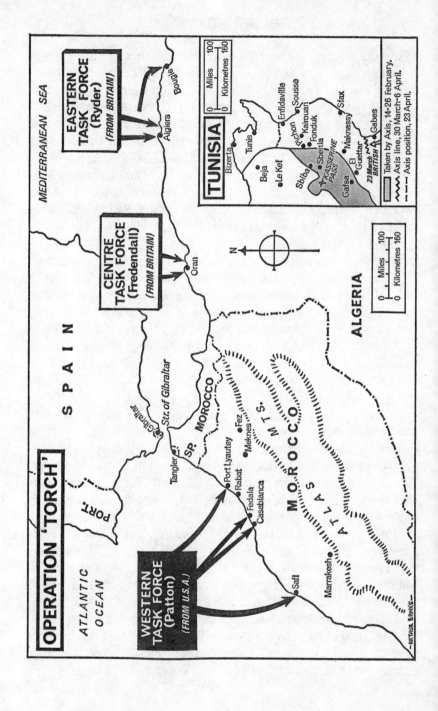

OPERATION 'TORCH'

ATLANTIC OCEAN

PORT.

SPAIN

MEDITERRANEAN SEA

EASTERN TASK FORCE (Ryder)
(FROM BRITAIN)

Bougie

Algiers

CENTRE TASK FORCE (Fredendall)
(FROM BRITAIN)

Oran

Str. of Gibraltar

Gibraltar

Tangier

SP. MOROCCO

Port Lyautey

Rabat

Fedala

Casablanca

Fez

Meknes

Safi

Marrakesh

M T S.

A T L A S

M O R O C C O

ALGERIA

WESTERN TASK FORCE (Patton)
(FROM U.S.A.)

N

0   Miles   100
0   Kilometres   160

TUNISIA

Bizerta

Tunis

Beja

Le Kef

Sbiba

Sbeitla

Gafsa

Enfidaville

Sousse

Pichon

Fonduk

Kairouan

KASSERINE PASS

El Guettar

Maknassy

Sfax

Gabes

23 March BRITISH

0   Miles   100
0   Kilometres   160

☐ Taken by Axis, 14–26 February.
∿∿ Axis line, 30 March–6 April.
— — Axis position, 23 April.

ARTHUR BANKS

of Dakar and Mers el Kebir. No one knew what the attitude of the eight million Arabs and Berbers would be.

On 24 October the cruiser *Augusta* with Hewitt and Patton aboard left Hampton Roads off Norfolk, Virginia, to join the rest of the task force assembling at sea. In the autumn sunshine the invading fleet presented an impressive sight:

Thirty transports and cargo vessels protected by a screen of forty to fifty destroyers milling around like polo ponies; the cruisers *Augusta, Cleveland* and *Brooklyn* compact, business-like—and in the dim distance the reassuring presence of the big battle-wagons, *Texas, New York* and, last but not least, the newly-commissioned *Massachusetts*. On the converted Esso oil tanker's decks, clusters of Army P 40s straining at their leashes, and from the *Ranger*'s flight deck, Navy dive bombers and Wildcat fighters roaring and zooming over the convoy.

Now the troops could be told without loss of security whither they were bound and what they were going to do. Patton's message to them had the Napoleonic touch:

Soldiers:

We are now on our way to force a landing on the coast of North West Africa. We are to be congratulated because we have been chosen as the units of the United States' Army to take part in this great American effort.

Our mission is threefold. First to capture a beach-head, second to capture the city of Casablanca, third to move against the German wherever he may be and destroy him. . . .

We may be opposed by a limited number of Germans. It is not known whether the French Army will contest our landing. . . . When the great day of battle comes, remember your training and remember that speed and vigor of attack are the sure roads to success. . . . During the first days and nights after you get ashore you must work unceasingly, regardless of sleep, regardless of food. A pint of sweat will save a gallon of blood.

The eyes of the world are watching us. . . . God is with us. . . . We will surely win.

No one knew better than Patton that the operation was a gamble. By resisting, the French might see a chance to restore the tarnished

military reputation of France. The odds were against a landing in
early November on the exposed coast of Morocco, so heavy is the
Atlantic swell. There was a distinct possibility that the surf would
overturn the landing craft and drown all aboard. Even if the troops
could be landed successfully they might have to wait for several
days before they could be supplied or reinforced. In fact at the final
inter-service conference before embarkation he had caustically told
the naval members that their elaborate landing plans would break
down in the first five minutes. He had added: 'Never in History has
the Navy landed an Army at the planned time and place . . . But
if you land us anywhere within 50 miles of Fedala and within one
week of D-Day, I'll go ahead and win.'

Characteristically, and appropriately, during his fortnight at sea
he chose to read the Koran—a work which stresses the fact that whatever happens is the will of God and that worry about the future
is therefore a waste of time. Death in battle according to the Prophet
brings a glorious reward in a Paradise likely to appeal to most young
Americans. What was uncharacteristic was that on his visit to the
British Combined Operations Headquarters in London the previous
August he had failed to see the point when Mountbatten told him
the sad story of what had happened to the British General Irwin
on the ill-fated expedition to Dakar in 1940. Now he, like Irwin,
was going into a battle fraught with imponderable hazards in an
admiral's flagship.

4

Morocco

War is a pretty dirty business, but politics—by gum!

Field-Marshal Viscount Montgomery

'Command in war,' said Napoleon in one of his sincere moments, 'is a fine career.' It has however, even to the most dedicated professional, this drawback—personal success involves the expenditure of the lives of one's fellow men. No commander was ever more conscious of this moral conflict than Patton—a conflict in his innermost heart which he shared with Montgomery who like him believed in God. As the *Augusta* and the rest of the great fleet neared the Moroccan coast he attended the last communion service before D-Day in company with his staff, all fully conscious that it might be their last.

During the voyage a feeling of complete understanding and sympathy had developed between him and Hewitt. For the moment the latter exercised overall command of the Western Task Force. No one realised more fully the grave risk of landing troops on beaches exposed to all the vagaries of the Atlantic in November: if attempted in bad weather a disaster on a gigantic scale would be almost inevitable. On 6 November, 48 hours before D-Day, the forecasts from Washington and London were ominous: 'Surf fifteen feet high and landings impossible.' Hewitt's meteorologist however gave his opinion that the storm was moving too swiftly to affect the breakers on the beaches and predicted that the weather would improve: the landing, after all, stood a reasonable chance of success. He thus placed Hewitt on the horns of a dilemma. If he ignored the forecasts from Washington and London and decided to stick to the plan of landing at Casablanca he must deploy his forces on 7 November, the eve of D-Day. If he drowned a large number of soldiers he would, at

best, do irreparable damage to the prestige of the Navy in the Army's
eyes. If, on the contrary, he adopted the approved alternative plan
of entering the Mediterranean and landing the troops on the small
strip of French Morocco between Oran and Spanish Morocco it was
highly probable that he would have to deal with a large number
of enemy submarines and the beaches here were largely unsur-
veyed. Furthermore if he landed here he would have to leave a large
part of the French Army and Navy in North Africa still at large
and, indeed, free to act if they saw fit against the Centre and Eastern
Task Forces at Oran and Algiers.

In the tradition of the great admirals of history Hewitt took the
bolder course and at midnight on 6 November headed for Casablanca. Almost at once the wind dropped and on 7 November the
vast fleet drew near the coast of Morocco in fair weather with an
easterly breeze and a smooth sea.

Meanwhile the military situation within Morocco can appropriately be described as Byzantine—that concatenation of circumstances
in which politics and intrigue have been allowed to sap the morale
of an army and defeat has undermined the loyalty and self-respect
of a nation. Having induced Roosevelt to intervene in Algeria and
Morocco Churchill, although he preferred de Gaulle to the American nominee Giraud for the role of liberator, was content to leave
the task of softening up the French from within to Robert Murphy,
the American chief diplomatic representative in North Africa who
was in touch with at least three factions of French officers known
to be sympathetic to the Allied cause. His intrigues with them and
those of Mark Clark have all the fascination of high-grade sensational fiction. Murphy relied particularly on General Mast, the commander of the troops in the Algiers sector and on General Béthouart,
the commander of the Casablanca division. Within Morocco power
was in the hands of General Noguès, the Resident-General at Rabat,
who was known to be likely to remain loyal to Pétain's government.
French plans for the defence of Morocco were elaborate, well understood and had recently been brought up to date. Responsibility for
the defence of the coast was divided into three sectors: the northernmost about Port Lyautey under General Dody, the Casablanca
sector under Admiral Michelier and the southernmost, responsible

for the port of Safi, under General Martin with his headquarters at Marrakesh. General Lascroux exercised overall command under the Resident-General.

Béthouart was a gallant and most intelligent soldier, the only general to come out of the ill-starred Allied operations in Norway in 1940 with even a vestige of distinction. Unfortunately although he commanded the troops at Casablanca, his immediate superior, Admiral Michelier, was also stationed there, a fact of which the Americans were unaware. When the Western Task Force approached the Moroccan coast on 7 November their friends ashore were by no means ready to receive them. Incredibly Hewitt's huge fleet was not spotted by the French Air Force. Late that evening Béthouart, to his astonishment, received a message that the landing would take place at 2 a.m. on the morrow. He therefore jumped to the conclusion that they would land on the undefended beach at Rabat, 50 miles north of Casablanca and posted troops there at the water's edge to welcome them ashore. He then surrounded the Army headquarters at Rabat with a battalion of infantry, arrested Lascroux and then informed Noguès and Michelier that the Americans were about to land in Morocco and Algeria, that Giraud would take over command in North Africa and that he, Béthouart, was now in charge in Morocco. Unfortunately he overlooked the fact that Noguès had a secret line to the other commanders in Morocco. For the moment he played for time. Michelier in Casablanca however acted quickly. His air and sea patrols on the previous evening had failed to spot the Western Task Force within cruising distance of the shore. He therefore jumped to the conclusion that Béthouart was bluffing. Even when the first reports of the landings reached him about 5 a.m. he dismissed them as mere commando raids, ordered all land, sea and air forces to resist and arrested Béthouart for treason.

At Safi 140 miles south of Michelier's headquarters at Casablanca orders reached Major Douve, the commander of the garrison, to man the defences as early as 3.20 a.m. He had about 400 men in defensive positions covering the port. On the Pointe-de-la-Tour a battery of 130mm. coast-defence guns commanded the approaches. At this very moment eight miles out to sea the beach-landing teams of 47th Infantry were in the process of climbing down the scrambling nets of the transports into the landing craft; owing to lack of training, the darkness and the heavy swell they were finding this extremely difficult and were soon behind schedule.

Safi is a small town with an artificial harbour which the French had constructed for the export of phosphates. As no LSTs could be provided for the tanks of 2nd Armored Division Patton had ordered Harmon, its commander, to land here, seize the docks, establish a bridgehead, disembark his tanks, hold off French forces likely to advance from Marrakesh and as soon as possible hasten along the coast road to join the troops landing at Fedala in attacking Casablanca. As the landing craft neared the shore at 4.38 a.m. the guns of the battleships opened up. Despite enemy fire three of the five waves of about 200 men each of 1/47th Infantry touched down in the right place and, with all the *élan* to be expected from troops Patton personally had trained, pushed on to their objectives. Two others followed at dawn. Within an hour the harbour, all the port facilities and the southern part of the town were under American control. After an abortive attempt to land in the dark, 2/47th Infantry successfully got ashore soon after daylight. By 9 a.m., despite sporadic fire from French troops established in buildings on the waterfront, on the hillsides and in the barracks, disembarkation of the tanks was in full swing.

Fifty miles north of Casablanca at Mehdia and Port Lyautey Truscott with Force Z faced an assignment of greater difficulty and complexity—to seize on D-Day the only airfield in Morocco with concrete runways for the use of the P 40s in the aircraft carrier *Chenango* and other aircraft to be flown in from Gibraltar to support the main effort at Casablanca. It lay five miles inland, was dominated by high ground to the south-west and cut off in the north, east and north-west by a loop in the Sebou river. Truscott planned to land in darkness at five separate points, two north of the river and three south, establish beach-heads and then thrust inland towards the airfield. On landing he intended to send a party to parley with the French commander: if his reply was unfavourable the airfield would be taken by an attack from three sides supported by the guns of the supporting ships and the aircraft on the *Sangamon*. As the transports with all lights out drew near the coast in the early hours they lost formation. As a result there was delay in transferring the assaulting waves to the landing craft. Small French steamers in the area were quick to report the presence of the invading fleet by signal to the troops ashore. At 4.30 a.m. the coast-defence guns opened up: obviously the arrangements made with agents ashore to sabotage them had gone astray. Surprise had been lost. Nevertheless Truscott decided to press on with the landing. Last-minute alterations had to be made. As a result only two of the five landing teams succeeded in getting ashore as originally planned. All were late, all were soaked to the skin, and all had to struggle ashore in the teeth of small-arms fire. Many of the landing craft foundered in the foaming Atlantic surf. Little parties of bewildered men roamed the beaches. Low-flying attacks by French aircraft added to the delay and confusion. With the advent of daylight the transports had to be withdrawn 15 miles out to sea, so accurate was the fire of the coast-defence artillery. Meanwhile Colonel Craw, accompanying Truscott's emissary Major Hamilton under a white flag to the French headquarters at Port Lyautey, was shot dead. Hamilton on arrival was made a prisoner. When at 8 a.m. Patton in the *Augusta* off Fedala was about to go ashore he knew little of what had happened to Truscott's force and what little he knew was disquieting.

Here Patton's main effort by the 3rd Division had had better but almost equally chequered fortune. Their task was to land immediately east of the little port of Fedala, establish a bridgehead around it and then swing south to capture Casablanca 12 miles away. Two batteries of coast-defence artillery at Cap de Fedala and two at Cherqui completely enfiladed the four selected beaches. To these could be added the 15-inch guns of the battleship *Jean Bart* and other ships, including five submarines. In Fedala there were about 2,500 troops with some field artillery. At Casablanca there were a further five battalions of infantry and two of field artillery. There were also 14 coast-defence guns in concrete emplacements and a number of anti-aircraft guns. At Meknes there were five more battalions and some tanks.

Shortly after midnight the battleships and transports arrived off Fedala in intermittent rain. The lights of Casablanca and Fedala could clearly be seen. Suddenly they went out. The transfer of the troops from the transports to the landing craft began; it was then discovered that an unexpected current had carried all the ships 10,-000 yards away from their planned position. Delay was thus inevitable. Nevertheless the run-in got going at 04.45 hours with an hour of darkness still in hand. On touching down some of the troops, heavily burdened with their equipment, were rolled over and drowned in the undertow. On one beach 18 landing craft were lost out of 25. Many were landed in the wrong place. Machine-gun fire swept the beaches. Nevertheless the leading waves with the coming of the dawn reorientated themselves and pressed forward to their objectives. The guns of the *Jean Bart* and the coast-defence batteries opened up on the fleet, to be answered by withering fire from the *Massachusetts,* the heavy cruisers and the destroyers, which temporarily silenced them. By 06.00 hours the 1st Battalion 7th Infantry had captured Fedala and was pressing on with the attack on the coast-defence batteries at Cap de Fedala. With equal gallantry and enterprise the beach-landing teams of 15th Infantry carried the batteries on the other flank at Cherqui at 07.30 hours. By now the leading troops of 15th Infantry were also coming ashore. Despite the chaos on the beaches and the heavy losses in landing craft all three regiments were now approaching their D-Day objectives. Overhead the fighters and bombers from the *Ranger* and the *Swannee* dominated the air from Port Lyautey to Casablanca.

At 08.00 hours the landing craft containing Patton's baggage was swinging from the davits of the *Augusta* ready for lowering into the sea. He himself impatiently awaited the moment to go ashore. Suddenly from behind a smoke screen seven French destroyers burst out of the harbour of Casablanca and opened fire on the American transports and landing craft. The *Augusta* abruptly accelerated to 20 knots and returned the fire. A highly complex naval battle now developed in the course of which the muzzle blast of the *Augusta*'s rear gun turret blew the landing craft containing Patton's kit to smithereens. For the rest of the morning, a prisoner in the *Augusta,* he was treated to a close-up demonstration of a battle at sea such as few soldiers are ever privileged to enjoy. All Hewitt's ships closed in on the French and forced them to withdraw into Casablanca.

About an hour later they broke out once again, this time supported by the cruiser *Primaguet,* and succeeded in luring the covering group to a point within range of the coast-defence batteries at Casablanca. In the *Augusta* Patton found himself in the midst of salvoes from the French guns at El Hank and torpedoes from the French submarines. Aircraft from the American carriers now joined in the fray. The *Primaguet* fought it out to a finish: tragically its captain, a sympathiser with the Allied cause, was killed on his bridge. The battle was an unforgettable demonstration of the courage of the men of the American and French Navies. At any other time no one would have enjoyed the spectacle more than Patton. On this particular morning however he had other matters on his mind. Not until 13.20 hours could Hewitt spare the time to put him ashore at Fedala with some of his staff, all now firmly convinced that in any future amphibious operations the army commander must have a command ship of his own as Mountbatten had advised.

Once ashore, he found himself confronted by that strange arrest of action which is liable to descend upon the best of troops when suddenly decanted by a navy on a hostile shore. Apart from desultory fire from the guns of Casablanca all was quiet. According to Major Henriques, Mountbatten's liaison officer with Patton and the only British officer with the Western Task Force who, disguised in American uniform out of consideration for French susceptibilities, had landed with the first waves and who now reported to him on the beach, the leading waves and those immediately following them had behaved with vigour and resolve. What the British call 'Beach Groups' and the Americans 'Shore Regiments' had also landed. Instead however of operating the recovery organisations, aid posts, report centres and signal installations for which they were designed, all were busily engaged in digging their own fox-holes, through sheer ignorance placing their personal safety before their real duty. Meanwhile the sea had risen and as the troops continued to disembark many more of the landing craft were being swept broadside on in the surf and abandoned. An atmosphere of muddle, inertia and bewilderment pervaded the beaches. Patton quickly sized up the situation and going from group to group stirred them into action, ordered landing over the beaches to stop and diverted all incoming craft into the small port of Fedala. Nevertheless when night closed in, although all the assault battalions had reached their objectives for the day, less than a fifth of their essential transport and guns had been landed and practically no supplies. On the suggestion of the French commandant at Fedala Colonel Gay had been sent to Casablanca under a flag of truce to try to persuade Admiral Michelier to stop fighting and had met with an indignant refusal. The news from Harmon at Safi was good: 2nd Armored Division had a bridgehead 5,000 yards deep and their tanks were being rapidly disembarked. At Port Lyautey however confusion still reigned despite Truscott's personal intervention. Short shooting by the Navy had not helped. Stranded crews and troops who had lost their units roamed the beaches. Fire from the French coast-defence guns had forced the transports 15 miles out to sea. The surf was rising in waves 15 feet high. Hardly any heavy weapons had been put ashore. Eisenhower's headquarters at Gibraltar was out of radio contact. There was no news of the landings at Oran and Algiers. Patton, determined to return to the beaches at first light to flay the idle, rebuke the incompetent and drive the timid, established himself for the night, a far-from-welcome guest in the Hôtel Miramar in the rooms from which the German commissioners had hurriedly decamped in the morning. It now seemed that there could be no alternative to a full-dress assault on Casablanca. Until more transport, guns and ammunition could be landed this, in the face of French resistance, was not for the moment a practicable proposition—certainly not on the morrow.

At dawn he descended on the beaches and the harbour like the wrath of God and stayed there till well after noon; none who met him that morning ever forgot the encounter. Much of what has been written of his behaviour then can be written off as myth. The truth is that he was justifiably angry at the lack of grip being displayed by some of his officers and non-commissioned officers. In extenuation of their behaviour it should be realised two-thirds of them had been civilians less than a year before and were still civilians at heart. Amphibious operations were in their infancy. Patton showed his displeasure by personally taking charge of one party after another as if he had been a master-sergeant. Obviously in doing so he stepped outside the province of a higher commander. Patton realised this but on reflection at a later date still considered his behaviour in every way justified. At any rate by the afternoon the unloading of the ships in the harbour was in full swing, landing craft were being salvaged, local transport was being requisitioned, the beaches were being cleared and the orderly build-up of stores was proceeding with ever-accelerating speed. Henriques thought at the time that Patton's personal intervention had 'a touch of magic'. Later when he had more experience of Americans he learnt that 'All Americans are like that. Like everyone else they can make a mess of things; but they are unlike anyone else in the speed with which they put things right—if and when they are ordered, persuaded or led to do so'— as they were in no uncertain terms on this occasion. This incidentally was the impression throughout the war made on many British officers who witnessed American troops in action.

Throughout 9 November radio communication with Gibraltar was still fragmentary and confusing. The 3rd Division still short of transport, heavy weapons and radio equipment advanced four miles towards Casablanca against light opposition on the ground and low-flying air attacks. From Safi, Harmon reported a vicious French air attack during the morning but that a column of troops on the road from Marrakesh was showing little eagerness for battle. He proposed to hold them off with a squadron and advance with the rest of his division on Casablanca by the coast road in the morning with all speed. There was more reassuring news too from Truscott in the north. Soon after first light a column of two battalions with artillery and 18 Renault tanks had advanced from Rabat against his southern flank held by Semmes with seven light tanks, thus precipitating the first American tank-versus-tank battle of the war. The French fire failed to penetrate the frontal armour of the American tanks; Semmes' tanks on the contrary soon had four French tanks in flames and then proceeded to shoot up the infantry with deadly effect. Obstinate resistance, particularly in the Kasbah at Mehdia, continued throughout the day. By nightfall however Truscott could report that he had the situation well under control.

For all the influence he could exert on the operations in Morocco, Eisenhower in the damp tunnels of Gibraltar might well have been in Abilene so bad were his communications with the Western Task Force. In fact the Army had swamped the Navy's signal communications: in consequence their messages had been given the lowest priority. It was now discovered that the two services had widely different ideas on the subject of procedure.

Fortunately at Algiers the landing of the Centre Task Force, thanks to the helpful attitude of the local French commander, General Mast, had followed a smoother course than at Casablanca. French resistance at the worst was sporadic. At Oran too by the evening of the 9th operations were nearing their end: French resistance had been at most fitful and half-hearted. Giraud however had proved a broken reed. By chance Admiral Darlan happened to be in Algiers visiting his sick son in hospital. Eisenhower, finding that he could command the obedience of the majority of French officers and officials, decided, with the powerful support of Admiral Cunningham, the Allied Naval Commander-in-Chief, and the approval of Roosevelt and Churchill, to deal with Darlan. He took this decision on military grounds. The British, primarily backing their own nominee de Gaulle, and those elements in United States and Great Britain who are always friends of every country but their own and, having no personal responsibility, expect their governments to give a moral lead, cost what it may, would have to put up with it. The whole operation had been designed to ensure the quick capture of Bizerta and Tunis before they could be reinforced by Hitler. The over-riding immediate need was to push on with all speed towards Tunisia. Great difficulties lay ahead. Algiers to Tunis is 560 miles by two roads and an indifferent railway. Only one division was available for this vital thrust.

On the 10th Eisenhower had leisure to send a sharp message to Patton concluding with the words: '. . . the only tough nut left is in your hands. Algiers in bag for two days: Oran now in: crack it open quickly and ask for what you want.' This in fact was exactly what Patton was engaged in doing.

During the 10th the 3rd Division had swung forward to the southeastern outskirts of Casablanca. Despite the fact that there was no apparent prospect of support from XII Air Support Command and little hope of Harmon's tanks arriving till late on the 11th, Patton decided in the early afternoon to mount a full-scale ground assault on the city next morning, 11 November. The French ground forces in fact outnumbered his own and included tough troops such as the Goumiers and the Foreign Legion: nevertheless he felt that he could count on naval gun fire and air support to redress the balance. His orders reached units in ample time for the necessary reconnaissances to be carried out in daylight and for all his inexperienced troops to be committed to battle fully briefed and backed by all possible fire support. Late in the day Truscott reported that the 60th RCT had captured the airfield at Port Lyautey and that some of the *Chenango*'s P 40s were already using it. At a cost of 79 killed he had secured a vital air base for the support of the Allied navies in the Battle of the Atlantic and at the same time given Patton command over the air in Morocco. At nightfall Harmon's tanks were approaching Mazagan 50 miles to the south. Patton, reluctant though he was to expose the civil population to the horrors of bombardment, could therefore count on almost certain success on the morrow. By midnight all was ready for the assault at 7.30 a.m.—not at dawn. Patton wanted no mistakes in the dark. Thirty years later it is hard to see how, given the Army and Navy's comparative ignorance of each other's capabilities and needs, the virtual collapse of the Army's communications, the raw character and lack of training of some of the troops, the administrative muddle on the day of the landing and the unpredictable and equivocal behaviour of the French, a full-dress attack on the defended city of Casablanca could have been mounted in a shorter time.

At 2 a.m. on 11 November—it was Armistice Day and Patton's birthday as well—a car carrying two French officers, heralded by the blowing of a bugle, with lights on and white flags flying, drove into the bridgehead. They were conducted to Patton's headquarters in the Hôtel Miramar. Here they explained that they were carrying orders from General Lascroux to the Casablanca Division to cease firing. Colonel Gay promptly wafted them on to Casablanca telling them to come back quickly to negotiate an armistice. On Patton's orders he made it quite clear that a full-dress attack had been ordered for daybreak and that if they did not return by then it would go in on schedule supported by all the guns of the fleet and every available aeroplane in Morocco. As H-Hour drew near the ships moved to their battle stations, the aircraft, bombed up, engines running, stood ready to take off, the field gunners standing by their pieces glanced at their watches as the last minutes ticked by. The party with the agreement to stop fighting and parley got back only just in time for Patton to radio to Hewitt and all concerned 'Cease firing'. It had been a near thing. He then ordered Anderson, the commander of the 3rd Division, to move into the town and if anyone tried to stop him to attack. In his diary he recorded: 'No-one stopped him but the hours 7.30 to 11 were the longest in my life.' The Casablanca garrison surrendered to Anderson shortly before noon at their headquarters in the town. It was thereupon agreed that the Americans should occupy key positions in the area and that the French troops should remain in their barracks retaining their arms. 'Their resistance had cost the American Army and Navy 337 killed, 637 wounded, 122 missing and 71 captured. French casualties had been much heavier.'

The formal cessation of hostilities came at 3 p.m. when at Patton's request Noguès, a smart, rather Spanish-looking man arrived from Rabat at the Hôtel Miramar in a black limousine with outriders. Here he was met by General Keyes and a guard of honour. After inspection of the guard, Keyes conducted him to the smoking room where Patton received him with great dignity. Michelier, the French Naval Commander-in-Chief, was already there and Hewitt had therefore come ashore to join the conference. With Noguès were Lascroux commanding the ground forces, a well-nourished figure, and Lahoulle commanding the air force. Patton opened the proceedings by cordially congratulating the French on their gallantry during the past three days' fighting. He then ordered the draft armistice terms which had been approved by the Chiefs of Staff before the landing to be read. There were two versions. One assumed only token resistance: this was clearly irrelevant. The other presupposed prolonged French resistance ending in their total defeat: this prescribed the complete disarmament and disbandment of the French armed forces. On hearing this Noguès icily pointed out that this meant the end of the French Protectorate in Morocco. Who then, he asked sarcastically would maintain order among the eight million

Arabs, Berbers and Jews, defend the frontier against the Spaniards and protect the Allies' long lines of communication with Algiers and Tunisia? He thus raised political issues of great complexity on which Patton had no brief: he was in fact out of his depth. Inevitably he reacted like the good and generous soldier but politically naive man he was. He loved France—the romantic France of his youth which no longer existed and probably never had. He gave a snap decision, a decision which would soon involve him in dubious company. As soldier to soldier they would have a 'gentleman's agreement' (one of those vague arrangements so called by the British because they are never made between gentlemen). The Americans would take over whatever they wanted for operations against the Axis, prisoners would be exchanged, the French troops would remain in barracks but would keep their arms. Finally no one would be punished for helping the Americans without Eisenhower's approval. In fact the final decision on all matters would be left to Eisenhower and Darlan to sort out in Algiers. He then invited the French to join him in a glass of champagne. Not surprisingly the conference ended in an atmosphere of profound relief on the part of the French and of mutual cordiality and esteem. As an impromptu theatrical display of military magnanimity in the grand manner of Napoleon it was magnificent: to describe it as a politically ham performance would be an understatement.

In sharp contrast to the British commanders of World War Two, traditionally accustomed to receiving tight and precise political direction, Patton—like Eisenhower in 1944—suffered from the lack of it. Broadly speaking he understood that his relations with the French should be based on the formula 'forgive and forget', that the Stars and Stripes and the *tricolore* should fly side by side and that all Morocco had to offer for the furtherance of operations against the Axis was at his disposal. An entirely new group of Americans at his headquarters now took the place of the diplomats who had previously been responsible for United States' interests in Morocco. It was a change for the worse: they certainly failed to protect some of the pre-invasion friends of the Allies and to shield their commander from political indiscretion. Patton seems to have thought that Noguès was an honourable man caught in a conflict of loyalties similar to that of Robert E. Lee at the outbreak of the Civil War. This he emphatically was not: in fact there is good reason to believe that he was still secretly maintaining contact with Pétain and even the Germans whilst at the same time overwhelming Patton with flattery and pompous parades. When he called at the Residency at Rabat on 16 November he was received by a battalion of Moroccan cavalry and the Governor-General's bodyguard, dressed in white uniforms with red leather equipment. Meanwhile two bands blared appropriate music. A week later in the cathedral at Casablanca he and Noguès attended a combined Franco-American religious service conducted by the Bishop of Morocco in full canonicals. There were two biers, one American and one French, each covered with their national flag and with a guard of six soldiers each. He and Noguès then proceeded to the cemetery and in the presence of an American battalion and a French battalion, formally placed wreaths on a tablet commemorating the heroic dead. At this very moment Noguès was doing his best to have Béthouart shot for treason. Fortunately the matter came to the ears of Patton and Eisenhower: Béthouart and Colonel Pierre Magnan, the commander of the troops in the abortive *coup* at Rabat on the night of the invasion, were released and flown in an American aircraft to Algiers. Despite this unsavoury incident Patton continued to trust Noguès. In his eyes there was no alternative to the Noguès–Darlan government: they and they only could be depended upon to keep the native population under control. Over-simplifying the issues he argued in good faith that the Allies' over-riding aim was to destroy the Axis forces in North Africa. There was a risk of an invasion of French territory by the Spaniards and of Franco allowing the Axis to use the airfields in Spanish Morocco. There were no Allied forces available to meet these threats. He was 4,000 miles away from United States and 400 miles from Oran. Therefore, he concluded, he must cooperate with Noguès and support his government to which de Gaulle and others could offer no plausible alternative. As a result considerable numbers of pro-Laval officers and civil officials remained in power and many who had served the Allied cause before the surrender languished in prison even after a political opponent obligingly assassinated Darlan in December. Inevitably the situation in Morocco raised strong protests not only in left-wing circles in United States and Great Britain but also in sober and well-informed quarters as well. Macmillan, Churchill's political representative in North Africa, certainly was shocked when he arrived in mid-January for the Casablanca Conference. Of Noguès he says:

> . . . he had brought General Patton, the American commander in the area, altogether under his sway. This eccentric and opinionated officer proved a cause of great trouble to Eisenhower, Murphy and myself. It seemed to me a monstrous thing that General Patton should be so easily impressed by the gay hunting parties and the lavish entertainments which Noguès gave in his honour, and show so little concern at the way Noguès was treating the friends of Britain and America.

For this momentous inter-Allied conference, Patton was the host. As on all occasions of this sort his arrangements were on a lavish scale and in every way worthy of his illustrious guests. Churchill, no mean judge of hospitality and the stage management of historic events, described them as 'beautiful'. Patton had reserved a large hotel in the lush suburb of Anfa with ample accommodation for all the American and British staffs and big conference rooms. Around the hotel were dotted luxurious villas reserved for the President, Churchill and Generals Giraud and de Gaulle. The whole area was wired-in and closely guarded by Patton's troops. Churchill, fresh from the gloom of an English wartime January, walking on the beach in the sunshine watched 'the wonderful waves rolling in, the enormous clouds of foam'. He marvelled that anyone had got ashore at the landing: 'Waves fifteen feet high were roaring up the terrible rocks. No wonder so many landing craft and ships' boats were turned over with all their men.'

When the President arrived the troops lined either side of the road for miles. Immaculately turned out from well-shaven chin to spotless shoes each man was the very epitome of discipline and self-respect. It was the first time since the Civil War that an American President had reviewed 40,000 troops fresh from battle. He was visibly moved.

With the actual business of this second great inter-Allied conference of the war, Patton, apart from his role as host and guardian,

was not personally concerned. It is important nevertheless to sum-
marise the decisions reached. Some sort of accord was patched up
between Giraud and de Gaulle. The fact was faced that the full-
scale Anglo-American invasion of North-West Europe demanded
by Stalin was not feasible for 1943. Instead Roosevelt and Churchill
decided to open up the Mediterranean by invading Sicily when the
operations in North Africa came to an end. They hoped thus to
release a large amount of Allied shipping, to get air bases for the
Bomber Offensive against Germany and to placate Stalin by attracting German forces in their direction away from the Russian front.
Perhaps even Mussolini's government might be overthrown. It was
at this conference that the unfortunate phrase 'unconditional surrender' was first used in this war. What would be done after the
conquest of Sicily was left to be settled later. King and Marshall
showed no inclination for further operations in the Mediterranean:
Churchill for the moment kept his own counsel. Now that the 8th
Army was approaching Tunisia the time was ripe for the appointment of a commander under Eisenhower for the land forces. Alexander, *persona grata* both to Churchill and the Americans, was the
obvious choice. For 'Husky', the Sicilian landing, there would be
two task forces, one American under Patton and one British under
Montgomery. Patton's sumptuous arrangements at the end of the
conference for the two-day picnic at Marrakesh for the President
and Churchill were unanimously voted by all concerned as the social
highlight of the war. There had been nothing to equal it in Africa
since Cleopatra entertained Mark Antony.

It would be wrong however to conclude that Patton's time in
Morocco was entirely devoted to spectacular calls on the Sultan,
reviews and grandiose junketings. He had been quick to open his
headquarters in the workman-like and modern office buildings of
the Shell Oil Company in Casablanca where his staff could operate
with all the convenience available to high-level business. Here his
staff worked all out to transform Casablanca into a first-class base.
The clearing of the ports presented a gigantic task: wrecked ships
had to be salvaged, damaged cranes and railways repaired, airfields
to be rehabilitated and modernised, rail and road accommodation
developed and the logistic services necessary for the support of a

large army installed. The fighting troops were speedily concentrated for further training: in the three days' fighting many mistakes had been made and many had been found wanting. Training for the whole force on the same Spartan lines which had characterised the preparation of the 2nd Armored Division was ordered and carried out. For at least one day a week the troops went for 24 hours without sleep. The strictest discipline was enforced. No soldier was left in doubt that he was an ambassador of his country and that at all times he must be smartly turned out, wearing his necktie, leggings and the rest and his helmet. Great emphasis was laid on the correct interchange of salutes whatever the circumstances. To all it was made clear that in the near future they would have to face a far more efficient and cruel enemy than the French. For Patton himself the time came soon. In the north the redoubtable Rommel had staged a come-back. American troops under the very noses of the British and French had sustained a humiliating reverse. In February Eisenhower called him forward to take over the command of the II Corps in Tunisia—a role better suited to his talents than that of commander of the forces of an occupying power in a defeated country and a fact which his masters would have done well to remember later on. For the moment something had gone badly wrong. Patton must put it right and with all speed.

5

Tunisian Spring

But if it be a sin to covet honour,
I am the most offending soul alive.
King Henry v

American prestige in the eyes of the British and French, sky high at the time of the landings in Algeria and Morocco in November, by late February 1943 had plummeted. In the race for Tunis and Bizerta the British spearheads had been beaten by a short lead by German reinforcements under Nehring flown into Tunisia and by December the front had congealed along the great chain of mountains which covers the frontier with Algeria. By Christmas Anderson, the commander of the so-called First Army, and Eisenhower faced stalemate. The reasons were many: long distances, congested roads, shortage of airfields near the front, the slow build-up of reserves and above all the unspeakable winter weather which had now set in.

Seldom in the history of war can an Allied commander have faced a more baffling political and military situation than Eisenhower at this time. The French, rent by political discord, lacked almost every necessity for war: inevitably the morale of their troops was low. They were clamouring for arms which for the moment Eisenhower was finding it difficult to supply. In no circumstances were they prepared to serve under British command. Giraud, the American choice, had turned out to be a politically imbecilic professional soldier of the old school. Anderson was a dour Scot who had never studied how to win friends and influence people nor apparently wanted to. Fredendall, the commander of II US Corps had taken a strong dislike to him and made no attempt to conceal it: Harmon thought he was disagreeable. He was certainly reserved and reticent: what he thought of his American allies is unknown. Although at Eisenhower's headquarters there was complete accord, this was by no means the case at the lower levels of command. The fact that the chain of supply was British and not American did not help. The squabbles of the French inevitably kept Eisenhower tied for much of the time 600 miles behind the line in Algiers. To coordinate the ragged front he had therefore set up an advanced coordinating headquarters at Constantine under Truscott. This was still 200 miles behind the front; furthermore its functions and authority were ill-defined and in consequence its rulings were often obscure.

On 22 January Montgomery and the Eighth Army, after an advance of 1,400 miles on the tail of Rommel and the Afrika Korps, had reached Tripoli to find the port completely wrecked. Like Marlborough 'he never fought a battle which he did not win nor besieged a town which he did not take.' He therefore did not contemplate a further thrust forward to link up with Anderson until he had built up the logistic backing he considered necessary to make victory as cheap as possible in terms of human life and absolutely certain. He accordingly announced that he would be ready for a further advance in the first week in March at the earliest. Never happier than with a blackboard and pointer, driving home often unpalatable truths he now characteristically organised a series of lectures, demonstrations and discussions for senior officers in Tripoli to ensure that his battle technique and particularly his arrangements for close and effective air support were understood. Patton flew over from Morocco to attend one of these performances. Horrocks, walking back with him after the opening lecture on 'How to make war', asked him what he thought of it. With a twinkle in his eye he answered, 'I may be old, I may be slow, I may be stupid but it just don't mean anything to me.' The world would soon see that he was neither slow nor stupid. What astonished Horrocks was the ease with which he could switch from two entirely different acts: one the fine old Southern gentleman and cavalry officer, the other the tough guy with steel helmet and pistols. His strong personality certainly fascinated Horrocks himself (later destined to be as much at home on the television screen as on the battlefield). It was from this time that stories about him began to circulate outside the American Army. Throughout their history which is studded with unusual and unorthodox men the British have delighted in eccentricity. At the moment, in Montgomery and particularly Churchill with his flamboyant eighteenth-century vocabulary, festive habits, boiler suits and comic hats they had two unique specimens already. Patton with his pistols and panache, apparently straight out of the mythology of Hollywood, their main cultural food, made an instant appeal. They loved the story of his description of one unit which had incurred his wrath as a 'bunch of bananas, some's green, some's yaller and some's plum rotten'. Few armies escape odd units to which this comment cannot be fairly applied. Meanwhile the Axis forces under von Arnim in Tunisia had become ominously offensive; furthermore their junction with those of Rommel, artfully dodging in front of Montgomery, was imminent.

The theatre in which the final operations in North Africa were to be played has been aptly described as a huge triangle. The northernmost side is the road 250 miles long from Constantine to Bizerta: on the eastern side another road follows the coast for about 250 miles to Tunis, Sousse, Sfax and Gabes. The south-west side of the triangle is the road from Gabes across the mountainous interior back to Constantine: it is 300 miles long. Within this triangle running due south from Ponts-du-Fahs one mountain chain known as the Eastern Dorsale stretches to the oasis of Gafsa and another, called the Western Dorsale, runs south-west to Feriana. The position of the passes in these mountain barriers and the roads running through them inevitably dictate the pattern of military operations. In the Eastern Dorsale they are the Pichon, Fonduk, Faid and Maknassy passes: in the Western Dorsale, the Sbiba and Kasserine passes. It is 50 miles across the flat and arid plain of Sbeitla from Faid to Kasserine. At the beginning of February the British First Army, which in fact consisted only of one corps of two infantry divisions plus a parachute brigade, held the northern flank between Bou Arada and the sea. Thence the line stretched southwards along the Eastern Dorsale with the French XIX Corps, responsible up to Fonduk, and the American II Corps under Fredendall holding a sector 100 miles long with the 1st Armored Division under Ward and Welvert's French Division to El Guettar. 1st Armored Division was formidable: it had over 15,000 men, 158 light tanks, 232 medium tanks, 100 armoured cars, 730 half-tracks and 2,100 trucks and other wheeled vehicles. It was designed to fight in two balanced forces of all arms: Combat Command A and Combat Command B. To posterity it seems odd that with a force as mobile as this at his disposal Fredendall should have chosen to establish his headquarters in underground shelters near Tebessa some 60 miles in rear of the forward troops in a gloomy canyon accessible only over a barely motorable track. In early February the 1st and 34th US divisions were in the process of moving into the corps sector, and the 168th Infantry Regiment had just relieved the French in the area of Sidi Bou Zid just west of Faid.

Fredendall at 58 was a prime specimen of the traditional overripe, over-bearing and explosive senior officer in whom the caricaturists have always delighted. He made no effort whatever to conceal his anti-British feelings or his supercilious impatience with the unfortunate French. Furthermore he had little use for Ward, the commander of 1st Armored Division. His utterances were couched in cryptic and homely words intelligible only to the initiated and confusing to everyone else. For example, his verbal orders on the telephone to an officer on the staff of CCB:

> Move your command, that is, the walking boys, pop guns, baker's outfit and the big fellow to M, which is due north of where you are now, as soon as possible. Have your boss report to the French gentleman whose name begins with J at a place which begins with D which is five grid squares to the left of M.

When in January the French on his northern flank had shown signs of collapse he had taken Combat Command B under Robinett away from Ward to stabilise the situation on their front. This they very effectively had done. Fredendall then proceeded personally to take charge of 1st Armored Division over Ward's head—every platoon of it—thus reducing its headquarters to the level of a post office and figuratively speaking emasculating Ward. It was on his personal orders that the 168th Regiment had been sited in defensive positions on two isolated features, Djebel Lessouda and Djebel Ksaira on either side of the road from Faid to Sbeitla near Sidi Bou Zid. Although on commanding ground they were outside supporting distance from each other. When therefore on 14 February von Arnim attacked with 10th and 21st Panzer Divisions at Sidi Bou Zid and Rommel with DAK thrust forward on Feriana and Thelepte airfield all the ingredients of the classic recipe for disaster were present— friction between allies, incompatible personalities, bad manners, over-centralised command by remote control, wide dispersion and unblooded troops.

There is little point in describing in detail the disasters of the next seven days which sent II Corps streaming back 50 miles to the Western Dorsale and culminated in the loss on 20 February of the Kasserine pass. That there was no breakthrough towards the rear areas of the First Army in the north, or to Tebessa and Bone, was primarily due to the resistance of the 34th Division and the British Guards Brigade at Sbiba, part of the 9th Division and the British 26th Armoured Brigade at Thala and the 1st US Division and what was left of the 1st Armored Division east of Tebessa. Close cooperation between Harmon, Robinett, Nicholson and Dunphie certainly contributed to the stabilisation of the front. Rommel's decision on 22 February, when at long last given full authority over the operations, not to proceed further with the offensive here but to fall back to the Eastern Dorsale and concentrate against Montgomery, also helped. American losses in round figures exceeded 3,000 killed and wounded and 200 tanks; the Germans claimed 3,721 prisoners. Vast quantities of supplies and equipment were looted by the local Arabs who also robbed the dead. That there was some panic is well attested by Harmon, sent up on 20 February by Eisenhower to bolster up Fredendall. He wrote:

It was the first—and only—time I ever saw an American army in rout. Jeeps, trucks, wheeled vehicles of every imaginable sort streamed up the road toward us, sometimes jammed two and even three abreast. It was obvious there was only one thing in the minds of the panic stricken drivers—to get away from the front, to escape to some place where there was no shooting. Two or three times Rooney and I were forced off the road into the ditch, and I began to worry that he and I might be wrecked, possibly killed.

There had been nothing like it in American history since the First Battle of Bull Run and for similar reasons. Alexander, arriving during the last days preparatory to taking over the Army Group to be formed from First and Eighth Armies on 20 February, toured the various Allied headquarters with McCreery his Chief of Staff. He was not impressed. Writing at the time to Alanbrooke, he summarised his impressions:

> The general situation is far from satisfactory. British, American and French units all mixed up on the front, especially in the south. Formations have been split up. There is no policy and no plan of campaign. This is the result of no firm direction from above. . . . We have quite definitely lost the initiative.

Three days later he cabled to Alanbrooke for Churchill's eye: 'Situation on battle front is critical and the next day or two should decide the issue. . . . My main anxiety is the poor fighting quality of the Americans.' Rommel's comments at this time were on similar lines but he added that they recovered quickly after the first shock and that their superiority in weapons and equipment was enormous.

The news of the disaster set off a wave of indignation and alarm in the United States. Encouraged by the Press and Radio to believe that their splendid youth, fighting in a noble cause, had only to appear on the battlefield to triumph, the populace overlooked the fact that they and their leaders lacked battle experience. They exaggerated the magnitude of the disaster. They did not realise that soldiers like babies have their teething troubles and have to be weaned from the cosy comfort of the breast feeding of civilian life to the harsh and less easily digested diet of war. At the worst they had lost only a minute proportion of their manpower and at most a few days of war industrial production. A bare nine months earlier the British in the Gazala battles leading to the fall of Tobruk had lost three times as many men and as great a build-up of supplies and equipment. In that very month of February 300,000 Germans had perished or surrendered at Stalingrad. Fortunately in Alexander, Churchill's favourite general, Eisenhower had a commander of vast experience in dealing with defeat as well as victory. As a young officer he had fought in the Retreat from Mons in 1914; he had been last out of Dunkirk and almost the last out of Rangoon and Burma. He therefore was quick to diagnose what was wrong with the command system and all three Allied contingents and to put it right. Like Marlborough, another Guardsman two centuries previously, 'he was always cool and nobody ever observed the least variation in his countenance; he could refuse more easily than others could grant, and those who went from him the most dissatisfied as to the substance of their business were yet charmed by his manner and, as it were, comforted by it.' His integrity was absolute; from the first, mutual trust and understanding between him and Eisenhower were complete and cordial.

It was clear to both that the front must be reorganised so that as far as possible troops would fight under their own commanders. The practice of fighting in penny packets and improvised groups must cease. The normal chain of command must not be disrupted as Fredendall had done. Divisions must fight as divisions: each must be given tasks within its capacity so that confidence could be revived. Cooperation with the air forces had been bad: Tedder and Spaatz must put this right. Inter-Allied friction must be ended: the French must smother their ruffled feelings and work with the British. There must be genuine partnership between the Americans and the British at all levels. Eisenhower's chief intelligence officer who had guessed wrongly with regard to Axis intentions must go and be replaced by Brigadier Kenneth Strong, a former British military attaché in Berlin who was believed, and rightly, to be more likely to guess right next time. Momentarily Anderson's fate hung in the balance but it was eventually decided to retain him. Montgomery is said to have described him as 'a good plain cook'. The boorish Fredendall was posted to the United States, promoted to the rank of lieutenant-general and given command of the Second Army 'so that his ability in training troops, especially after his recent battle experience, might be employed at home'. He thus achieved a graceful exit from a stage which he had not adorned. No arrangements were made for a formal handover of II Corps to Patton, called up from Rabat on 5 March to replace him: their mutual antipathy was well known.

Patton, according to Harmon, had not been Eisenhower's first choice: apparently he would have preferred Harmon who very wisely declined the offer when it was suggested to him. If he had accepted it at this time he would have given the impression that he had jockeyed Fredendall out of the job in his own interest. It proved to be a wise decision.

On 5 March Eisenhower and Patton flew into Maison Blanche airfield near Algiers, the one from the east and the other from the west. Without a moment's delay Eisenhower proceeded to leave him in no doubt that American prestige must be restored with all speed. He must prove, and quickly, that the men of II Corps were not too soft to be able to face the veterans of the Afrika Korps or to stand comparison with the men of the Eighth Army, a *corps d'élite* in the eyes of their own commander, the British Press and themselves. He must retrain, re-equip and reorganise the corps and give it back its self-respect. They must take the lessons of their lost battle to heart bearing in mind that there is often more to be learnt from defeat than from victory. In particular, everybody and not the Engineers alone, must be thoroughly trained in the detection, removal and handling of mines in defence. Their 37mm. anti-tank gun was a good gun if handled properly now that new ammunition had become available: faith in it must be restored. Whilst Eisenhower was briefing Patton, Bedell Smith close by conferred with Brigadier Hugh J. Gaffey the new Chief of Staff of II Corps, thus ensuring complete identity of view on the staff level as well as that of command. Eisenhower, fully aware of Patton's contempt for personal danger, concluded his orders with the warning: 'I want you as a Corps Commander, not as a casualty.' He added:

You must not retain for one instant any man in a responsible position when you have become doubtful of his ability to do the job. . . . This matter frequently calls for more courage than any other thing you will have to do, but I expect you to be perfectly cold-blooded about it. . . . I will give you the best available replacement or stand by any arrangement you want to make.

He would take his orders as the commander of an American formation from the commander of the Army Group, Alexander. Briefed in this frank and forthright manner, Patton knew exactly where he stood. He must get II Corps on its feet again with all speed or go.

Rommel had administered one form of shock treatment to II Corps: they were now to be subjected to another different kind but little less dramatic, this time from one of their own countrymen. On the morrow at 10 a.m. he arrived at Fredendall's old headquarters at Djebel Kouif.

That very morning roughly a hundred miles to the south, in the early mist, Rommel had launched the 15th, 10th and 21st Panzer Divisions in full array against the veterans of Alamein, the 51st Highland Division, the 7th Armoured Division (The Desert Rats) and the New Zealand Division. The Lord had indeed delivered them into the hands of his servant Montgomery. He had over 400 tanks and 500 anti-tank guns sited to kill tanks, not to defend the infantry but ordered, as at Alam Halfa, to stand at Medenine and if they could not stay there alive to stay there dead. Four times during the day the Panzer divisions advanced to the attack: four times they were driven back. Not a single soldier of the Eighth Army budged an inch. At the end of the day there were 52 German tanks left on the battlefield: British losses were negligible.

Time for Patton was short. Alexander expected him to take the offensive towards Gafsa on 17 March. He had 11 days to get his corps on its feet. From his own experience, confirmed by years of study, he knew that, no matter how high the intrinsic value of the men in their ranks, armies are useless without discipline and without faith in their leaders. In the next week, displaying the largest stars his aides could produce, escorted by scout cars and half-tracks bristling with machine-guns and to the accompaniment of screeching sirens, armed to the teeth, he swooped down on every single battalion of his four divisions like Moses descending from Mount Ararat. Moses brought with him the Ten Commandments; Patton brought the Army's traditional orders for maintenance of discipline: helmets worn at all times; neckties properly tied and leggings correctly threaded. The slightest errors in dress must be checked. Officers and non-commissioned officers must assert their authority by constant vigilance, example and voice. Their own turnout must be impeccable. Orders with regard to saluting and punctuality must be mercilessly enforced. Punishment for slackness in these respects must be prompt and severe. In these matters he shared the views of the cockney non-commissioned officer in Kipling's verse:

> The 'eathen in 'is blindness bows down to wood and stone;
> 'E don't obey no orders unless they is 'is own;
> 'E keeps 'is side arms awful; 'e leaves 'em all about;
> And then comes up the Regiment an pokes the 'eathen out.
> All along o' dirtiness, all along o' mess,
> All along o' doin things rather more or less.

Only too often dirty hair and dirty clothes betray a dirty mind—a fact painfully obvious in certain civilian circles in 1973. To punish the breach of these regulations he established a uniform system of fines running to $50 for officers and $25 for enlisted men. 'When you hit their pocket books', he said, 'you get a quick response.' Sometimes he would sally forth in person and round up a batch of offenders. He was certainly feared: whether he was loved is not so certain. There was never a dull moment for II Corps: no one was left in any doubt as to who was in command.

Wherever he went he proclaimed his gospel in his high-pitched voice in earthy words intelligible even to the least literate and stupidest soldier. Concurrently with this showmanship he set in motion an administrative drive which stretched his staff and services to the limit. Luckily Eisenhower's staff had achieved a build-up of supplies at Tebessa adequate for any operations the corps was likely to have to undertake. New equipment and clothing arrived like magic: men in the workshops worked round the clock to get vehicles back on to the road. Whenever humanly possible troops got properly cooked food as a change from K-rations cooked by boy-scout methods. The mails were speeded up; the need for recreation was not forgotten: there were concerts and popular radio programmes. Realising that soldiers, especially after a reverse, should never be allowed an idle moment to brood on their losses and future prospects he simultaneously stimulated an all-out concentration on training and preparation for the next battle now imminent. Next time, he insisted, they would go in and win. The pressure he applied to his staff is said to have driven the weaker members to the verge of insubordination. In Fredendall's time, at the request of officers kept to a late hour of the night in the corps command post, breakfast had been available till 8.30 a.m. This he took as a gross affront: in his eyes all good soldiers on active service, staff officers included, should 'stand to' before sunrise ready for the day's battle. In future, he laid down, no breakfast would be served after 6.30 a.m. Murmurs of resentment from some members of the staff, stung at this further reminder that they were the servants and not the masters of the front-line troops, reached Eisenhower. Accordingly on 15 March he looked in at Patton's headquarters. What he saw he liked: the staff were working with exemplary intensity and obvious sense of purpose. A new spirit animated every officer and soldier he saw that day.

On arrival at II Corps headquarters Patton had found Bradley in residence there in the vague role of Eisenhower's representative. This anomalous situation in his eyes violated the very first principles of command: no commander can operate with equanimity with a potential spy from a higher headquarters breathing down his neck. He was quick to say so to Eisenhower. Bradley must be under his command or quit the headquarters. Eisenhower saw the point and promptly appointed Bradley Deputy Corps Commander and Patton acting Lieutenant-General. With startling promptitude his aides produced the appropriate insignia. Thus for a time two of the most outstanding generals of World War Two came to work together. The situation intrigued Alexander who in his biography described them as:

Two completely contrasted military characters; the one impatient of inaction, the other unwilling to commit himself to active operations unless he could clearly see their purpose. On one of my visits to the American headquarters, I was fascinated to hear this characteristic exchange:
Patton: 'Why are we sitting down doing nothing? We must do something.'
Bradley: 'Wait a minute George! What do you propose we do?'
Patton: 'Anything rather than just sit on our backsides.'

Both were good soldiers. Patton was a thruster, prepared to take any risks; Bradley, as I have indicated, was more cautious. Patton should have lived during the Napoleonic Wars—he would have been a splendid Marshal under Napoleon.

Harmon thought so too: 'There was an electric quality about him which communicated itself to masses of men.' Alexander realised that he was burning with desire to fall upon the enemy; nevertheless he had every intention, for the immediate future at any rate, of keeping him on a tight rein. He felt strongly his responsibility to Eisenhower to ensure that II Corps did not become involved in another disaster; nothing in the performance of Patton's subordinate commanders to date indicated that they had the tactical skill and experience to take on the Afrika Korps with their almost uncanny ability to spot tactical error and rapidly punish it. At all costs there must be no further misunderstandings between the British and the Americans. The Americans must succeed and their success must be proclaimed to the housetops in the British and American Press. In his mind and indeed in that of Churchill and his circle there lurked the fear that their great ally might lose interest in the war in Europe in favour of the operations against Japan. For the moment therefore he allotted Patton a subsidiary role in the battle for which he now issued orders: the main effort against the Mareth Line would be entrusted to Montgomery and the Eighth Army.

In brief the Eighth Army was to smash the immensely strong defensive position at Mareth and break out through the Gabes Gap into the coastal plain. Patton was to support Montgomery by drawing away enemy reserves from his front. In more detail his task was to re-capture the Thelepte airfields and thrust on Gafsa to establish a forward maintenance centre there from which the Eighth Army could in due course draw supplies to maintain the momentum of its advance. Alexander emphasised to Patton that he must be on his guard against the vicious counter-attacks the enemy would certainly launch against him when his flanks and rear were threatened. In no circumstances was he to thrust forward in strength beyond the Eastern Dorsale.

Inevitably tight control like this, however justified at the time, placed a great strain on the patience of Patton and his officers. He didn't like the restrictions and he liked still less the British system of command. His mind reeled back to his days with Pershing in the First War and his persistent refusal to allow American troops to serve under Allied generals. His determination to strike a smashing blow and win a spectacular victory which would wipe out the reverse of Kasserine was manifest. Here Bradley's great tact and commonsense came to the rescue. Working in close cooperation with McCreery, Alexander's Chief of Staff, he ensured that orders from the Army Group in no way offended American susceptibilities or Patton's self-esteem. By D-Day 17 March Patton had come to see what was essentially an Army Group battle in terms of Second Bull Run with himself in the role of Stonewall Jackson descending as it were from the Manassas Gap into the enemy vitals and fighting another equally bloody and victorious battle on some Stony Ridge, somewhere in the plain of Tunis. Montgomery had to be rather improbably cast for the part of Longstreet but he would have to do. Alexander anyhow had some of the virtues and charm of Robert E. Lee. In the event he would modify Patton's directive no less than six times to meet Montgomery's rapidly changing needs.

Now II Corps consisted of the 1st, 9th and 34th Infantry Divisions, the 1st Armored Division and the 13th Field Artillery Brigade. On 17 March in heavy rain, three days ahead of Montgomery, Patton opened the battle. After an approach march of 45 miles during the night, the 1st Infantry Division carried Gafsa with little trouble apart from mines. Next day 1st Ranger Battalion pushed on to El Guettar whither the enemy had withdrawn. The rain was incessant; the streams were full to overflowing; cross-country travel was impossible for wheeled vehicles. It was not therefore until 20 March that Ward with the 1st Armored Division was able to start the thrust Patton had ordered towards Station de Sened which fell without great difficulty on 21 March.

Meanwhile blasted in by a very heavy and vicious bombardment of the type the Royal Artillery had now raised almost to the level of a fine art, Montgomery's attack with the XXX Corps had opened up near the coast. It found the terrain very difficult and the going hard. Montgomery therefore decided to switch his main effort to the western flank using the New Zealand Corps and the X Corps in a wide sweep with air support on an unprecedented scale. This operation he called 'Supercharge'. As it would take several days to get going he suggested to Alexander that Patton should help by thrusting towards the sea to cut the enemy's main artery along the road from Gabes to Sfax—a task known to be very much after Patton's own heart. Alexander however, still anxious not to expose the Americans to undue risk, watered down the concept in his orders to Patton to the capture of the pass in the Eastern Dorsale east of Maknassy and the despatch of a raiding party of light armoured vehicles to beat up the enemy airfields ten miles to the east. Patton jumped at the chance. The weather was appalling. On 22 March nonetheless 1st Armored Division took Maknassy. A quick attack now might perhaps have carried the pass as well. Instead Ward chose to stage a deliberate attack, fully coordinated and after full reconnaissance. When it eventually went in, it was too late. *Kampfgruppe* Lang from Fifth Panzer Army had arrived.

Meanwhile Patton had pushed the 1st Infantry Division on the Gabes road to east of El Guettar. As Alexander had expected, on 23 March the 10th Panzer Division, eager to repeat its triumph at Kasserine, descended in full force upon them. It was a Homeric battle. In the early morning the huge hollow square of tanks and self-propelled guns interspersed with carrier-borne infantry carried all before it. Two field artillery battalions and some of the infantry were over-run. Then the tide of battle turned. The rest of the American artillery and the tank destroyers of 601st and 899th Tank Destroyer Battalions stood fast and fought back. Soon the 10th Panzer Division faltered, then reeled back leaving 30 burning tanks upon the field. Later in the afternoon they returned to the attack only to be once more blasted off the field. The 1st Infantry Division had stepped off on the right foot: they would never look back. This would be only the first of their many battle honours.

East of Maknassy, however, 1st Armored Division in its attack had got nowhere. Late on 24 March, Patton, returning from the front of the 1st Infantry Division, was furious to find that Ward's tanks had thrown their tracks on the rocky ground and that their infantry had stalled. With all the emphasis he could command he told Ward to lead the attack in person next morning. Ward did so but regrettably the fire had gone out of 1st Armored Division. By noon 24 March he had to suspend operations at Maknassy: the initiative had passed to the enemy.

Although it seemed to Patton and his soldiers that they had so far at most only achieved partial success, they were in fact doing, and doing very satisfactorily, exactly what Alexander wanted them to do—drawing towards themselves 10th Panzer Division and other troops just at the very moment when 80 miles to the south Montgomery was on the point of launching the decisive sweep with massive air support towards El Hamma which would compel the enemy to abandon the Mareth Line. The vital need now was to continue to keep 10th Panzer Division away from Montgomery. On 26 March therefore, as Montgomery's great sweep got under way, Alexander ordered Patton to suspend operations on the Maknassy front and attack with the 1st and 9th Infantry Divisions and the 1st Armored Division from El Guettar towards Gabes. At the same time 34th Division was to seize the gap at Fonduk in the Eastern Dorsale to enable the British 6th Armoured Division to break out into the coastal plain. His orders went into far greater detail than Patton thought necessary. Nevertheless he concealed his exasperation and faithfully obeyed.

The 10th Panzer Division and its supporting troops were posted in a position of great strength: to give way would mean the collapse of the whole Axis front. Their resistance therefore to the attack by the 1st and 9th Infantry Divisions was obstinate and highly skilled. The 9th Division paid the penalty of inexperience and got nowhere. By 30 March Patton had to suspend its operations for reorganisation. In their place he committed Task Force 'Benson' from 1st Armored Division to a further attempt to break out on the Gabes road. The fighting continued for three days to no avail. In fact the Axis defences were immensely strong; there are grounds too for believing that the constant changes of plan ordered by 18th Army Group added to their difficulties. By 1 April they were exhausted.

Meanwhile Alexander in the hope of breaking out at Fonduk with the British IX Corps under Crocker had placed the 34th Division under his command. It was to prove an unhappy partnership. Crocker was a man of few words and what he sometimes said was cold and cutting. His own soldiers understood him: the 34th Division whom he treated as if they were British soldiers did not. Eisenhower certainly thought Crocker's handling of the affair indifferent. After failure on the part of 34th Division to get its objectives Crocker had had to commit 6th Armoured Division in their place. It eventually broke out but only after heavy losses and too late to cut off the enemy withdrawing after Montgomery's bloody victory at Wadi Akarit before II Corps and Eighth Army to the Enfidaville position. There were mistakes, misunderstandings and lack of tact on both sides the repercussions of which reached United States where the public had quite wrongly been encouraged by the Press to expect an American drive to the sea cutting off the Axis armies. This had not happened: nevertheless on 11 April First and Eighth Armies linked up at Kairouan and the Axis forces completed their withdrawal to the last corner of Tunisia for the final round of the campaign. There must now be a pause to enable the Allies to regroup before the *coup de grâce* could be delivered.

It had been a period of intense strain and frustration for everyone and particularly Patton. Not only had he had to launch many raw troops into their first battle and ensure their triumph over the inevitable shock but he had had an even harder task—to restore the confidence of those, particularly in 1st Armored Division, who had experienced humiliating defeat. As Montgomery was wont to remark: once a unit has stepped off on the wrong foot, it is hard to get it back into step again. Only too often it continues clueless like a man who has missed a vital turning in bad weather on a motorway.

For Patton it had meant constant presence in the forward area at some personal risk, persuading, cajoling and indeed where necessary almost kicking officers and men into battle. His action on 7 April when the Germans were pulling out was characteristic. Task Force 'Benson', reduced to one battalion of tanks, one tank destroyer company and one company of armoured infantry stopped at a minefield. Thereupon, after hounding Benson on the air, he impulsively drove forward and led the way through it. He then continued southeastward ahead of his troops until he reached the 70th kilometre milestone from Gabes. Then reluctantly turning back he told him 'to keep going for a fight or bath'. Task Force 'Benson' rolled eastward as never before. Later, when CCA of this division under Brigadier-General McQuillan struck another minefield strewn with anti-personnel mines and showed reluctance to advance, he sacked its commander on the spot and sent him to the rear. 1st Armored Division in fact had temporarily shot its bolt: on top of its heavy losses in February it had sustained 1,500 further casualties since 17 March. Convinced now that only a fresh commander could revive its sagging morale, Patton took the extreme step of relieving Ward of his command and replacing him with Harmon. It was to prove an inspired decision. Ward was an unlucky man and no army can afford unlucky generals: to employ him further was a risk Patton could no longer take.

Inevitably as the protracted operations dragged on tempers grew short. When on 1 April Patton in his situation report complained with every justification that the Axis air force had bombed his forward troops all the morning, virtually undisturbed by the USAF and the RAF, he got a sarcastic and supercilious reply from Coningham, the commander of the Tactical Air Force casting a reflection on the courage and efficiency of his men. Patton, through Eisenhower, indignantly demanded an apology, and eventually, but not until after considerable trouble, got one which he considered adequate. The incident drew Tedder and Spaatz in person to Gafsa on 3 April to pour oil on the stormy waters: fortunately four Focke-Wulf 190s chose that very moment to bomb the place. The force of the explosions brought down the ceiling of the room in which they met Patton and jammed the door so tightly that they could not get out. Spaatz turned to Patton and said: 'Now how in hell did you manage to stage that?' 'I'm damned if I know,' shrieked Patton above the din, 'but if I could find those sonsa bitches who flew those planes, I'd mail them each a medal.' A characteristically generous letter from Patton to Coningham closed the incident:

My dear Coningham,
    Please accept on the part of myself and the officers and men of II Corps our most sincere appreciation of your more than generous signal. Personally, while I regret the misunderstanding for which I was partly responsible, I cannot but take comfort and satisfaction from the fact that it gave me an opportunity of becoming better acquainted with you, because to me you exemplify in their most perfect form all the characteristics of the fighting gentleman.

Within less than a month he had revitalised a baffled and be-wildered II Corps and done all that Alexander asked him to do—to maintain a constant threat to the enemy's line of communications and, by attacking, attract towards himself a formidable part of the forces opposing Montgomery. In the event he had drawn off the equivalent of two divisions, including the redoubtable 10th Panzer Division whose presence at the time of the great sweep by Freyberg and Horrocks might gravely have embarrassed Montgomery and caused the British further losses which they could ill spare. Whether he could at any stage have done more with the means at his disposal, had he been allowed by Alexander, is doubtful. What is certain is that Alexander never intended to let him fight a major battle in the coastal plain. It is clear that at this time he had not fully grasped the potential of the American soldier or realised the effect on public opinion in United States of his policy with regard to II Corps. If he had he would almost certainly not have maintained so tight a hold over Patton's operations and kept him so long in leading strings.

It was at this time on a visit to Alexander's headquarters that Patton discovered that II Corps was to be allotted only a very minor part in the final battle now obviously imminent. American prestige alone demanded that their troops should play a part commensurate with their contribution to the victory which was now virtually certain. Alexander politely declined to change his plan. On logistic grounds he was on a firm footing: to move 30,000 vehicles and 110,000 men to the north across the restricted British lines of communication in the midst of a wholesale regrouping presented the staffs with a problem of the utmost complexity. Patton therefore despatched Bradley to protest to Eisenhower who was quick to see the point. As a result Eisenhower explained to Alexander that American public opinion was a force to be reckoned with and must be considered. The people of United States had expected Patton, admittedly with little justification, to push through to the sea and cut off Rommel and he had not done so. The corps must now be given a worthy part with all its divisions in the last battle of the campaign whatever the logistic objections. He went on to emphasise the danger to the alliance if the Americans were not allowed their fair share in the final triumph to which, quite apart from the vast quantities of equipment including Sherman tanks as well as ammunition and food, they had supplied to the British, the efforts of their troops had contributed. Alexander saw the light.

When he had assumed command of II Corps on 6 March Patton had clearly understood that his stay would be brief and that he would soon have to return to Morocco to continue with the planning of 'Husky', the Sicilian invasion. It was for this very reason that Eisenhower had posted Bradley to him as Deputy Commander: the handover could therefore be accomplished with the utmost ease. It was indeed high time Patton got back to join his planning staff at Rabat. The landing in Sicily was scheduled for 10 June a bare seven weeks ahead and not even the provisional outline plan had so far been agreed between the many staffs involved not only in North-West Africa but also in London, Washington and Cairo. The situation was not merely urgent: it was alarming.

On his way back Patton spent the night of 16 April with Eisenhower at his house in Algiers. At breakfast next morning there arrived a message from Marshall saying: 'You have done a fine job and have justified our confidence in you.' That was all he wanted and that was all that mattered. He was happy to allow Bradley to collect the laurels which his own efforts in revitalising II Corps in the short space of less than a month had made possible. He was out for bigger game. The prospect of a landing in Sicily with all its classical associations had captured his imagination: he would too be commanding not a mere corps but an army.

6

Sicilian Summer

To command a division and to command an Army are as different as chalk and cheese—they require quite different qualities, though the greater will, of course, include the less.

Wellington, quoted in The Croker Papers

Much of the popular literature and even some of the more ponderous official and academic histories written in the past 20 years give the impression of incessant bickering and divergence of view between the Americans and the British. In fact the reverse is the truth: in few alliances in recorded history, thanks to a great extent to Roosevelt, Churchill and Eisenhower, was cooperation between two allies more sincere and effective. Nevertheless at this time both armies had much to learn of each other's virtues, prejudices and limitations. It is doubtful whether many Americans realised how the British had to pinch and scrape the bottom of the manpower barrel to keep their armies in the field; how they had had to bring their women into their war effort to a greater extent than the Russians and Germans; how their soldiers' wives and children had to subsist, often under air bombardment, on a weekly meat ration less than that provided for a GI for a day and the effect this had on their approach to battle. The British on their part, because they shared a language of common origin, only too often assumed that American reactions in all circumstances would be the same as their own and that the curt, deliberately understated and forthright expressions they used amongst themselves were appropriate when dealing with allies whose values and vocabulary were very different. Above all, from Alexander downwards, they never realised the immense influence of the American Press and the need at all times to consider public opinion

in the United States and the real power which its people wield. After
Pearl Harbor it had been touch and go when operations in North-
West Europe, the only theatre in which the Army could play the
predominant part, had been given priority over the Pacific: there
were still forces not unconnected with the United States Navy working for a reversal of the policy. It was vital therefore to the Army
that it should be given a prominent and at least equal share in the
battles and the glory that lay ahead. Fame to a considerable extent
in their eyes consisted of what was said on the Radio or written
in the headlines of the Press. So far it seemed to them that the
world had been told only too often that Montgomery and the Eighth
Army alone, apart of course from Rommel and the Afrika Korps,
knew anything about the Art of War. In the American Army, as
in the British, there were many generals and would-be generals
eager, and rightly eager, to display their talents in battle—no army
has ever suffered from a shortage in this respect. Some lacked battle
experience; all realised the pressing need for it and for their troops.
Their impatience to blood their soldiers can be understood. The
lodestar of Patton's life in particular had always been the dream
that he would one day command a great army which winning spectacular victory after victory by surprise and speed would enshrine
for ever the glory of American arms and his own name. Now, in
the largest combined operation in history, it seemed to be on the
verge of realisation and in the romantic setting of Sicily, the step-
ping stone between Africa and Europe where Hannibal, Scipio and
Belisarius once had trod.

The island itself presented the invaders with problems of great
complexity demanding the reconciliation of the needs of the three
services. Combined Operations as understood later were still in their
infancy. No one knew to what extent forces could be maintained
over beaches by the DUKWs, LSTs, LCMs and LCIs. Early possession
of the major ports therefore loomed large as an essential consideration. The largest was Messina: this was out of fighter range and
known to be strongly defended. The west-coast ports of Palermo,
Trapani and Marsala, also out of fighter range, could maintain about
half the force; Catania, Augusta and Syracuse could supply the other
half. The small ports on the south coast would be of some use. If

the operations were to get anywhere the invaders must have the use of the 30 airfields on the island with all speed. These fell into three groups: the Gerbini group in the Plain of Catania, the Castelvetrano group south-west of Palermo and the Ponte Olivo and Comiso group near the south-coast ports. Inland Sicily is rugged, with mountains rising in Mount Etna in the north-east corner to 10,000 feet. Good roads ran along the east and northern coasts: elsewhere they varied from bad to indifferent. The north-east corner thus offers every advantage to a defending army—secure flanks, restricted approaches, difficult terrain and superb observation for artillery. Malaria was endemic. The Allied navies had to convoy 45th US Division from United States, the Canadians from the United Kingdom, most of the Americans from along the coast from Bizerta to Algiers and the British from various ports between Sfax in Tunis and Syria and deliver them ashore in the teeth of opposition from land, air and sea en route and on arrival. The mere problem therefore of bringing the invading forces to the island and establishing them ashore presented the Allied commanders and staffs with many options and unprecedented difficulties. Whether or not, absorbed in the immediate problems of getting ashore, they gave adequate thought to what they would do thereafter would soon be seen.

Study of the photographs of the generals of World War Two gives the impression that each nation imposed its own pattern on their faces. The Italians appear to be about to burst into the 'Soldiers Chorus' from *Faust* at any moment. The Germans have been unkindly described as looking like frosty-faced bank managers who have taken to crime. The Russians look like over-promoted prison governors. The British seem to be trying to copy Haig who in the immortal words of one of his admirers was 'neither unduly elated by success nor depressed by failure'. Most of the Americans are correctly dressed, uniformly tight-lipped and have an air of instant readiness for a personal rough and tumble with the enemy. In most theatres of war each general seems to have come out of his own national box. This generalisation however is not applicable to the Italian Campaign. Seen as a clash of highly original and brightly contrasted personalities it has human interest outshining the other scenarios of World War Two.

Guzzoni, the Italian commander in Sicily, despite his 66 years, was active and professionally competent and looked the part. Eisenhower's opposite number, Kesselring, Supreme Commander in the Mediterranean, was a soldier who at 40 had become an airman and a commander capable of handling with considerable skill and imagination air and ground forces in cooperation. He was one of the few German commanders with the courage to stand up to Hitler when ordered to take a course of action he considered to be strategically unsound: in the poisonous atmosphere of German–Italian relations he managed to survive with a measure of dignity. With regard to the military value of the Italians or their integrity he had no illusions. Guzzoni's German Adviser, von Senger und Etterlin, a cavalryman and Bavarian aristocrat, had fought with great success as commander of a Panzer corps in Russia. An ex-Rhodes Scholar and an Oxford graduate, socially at home in British higher society and a Benedictine lay brother, he was in odd company amongst the Nazis. Baade, the commander of the Messina Straits which controlled the ferry service and the 70 anti-aircraft batteries protecting them, was highly efficient and, as will be seen, successful. Hube, the commander of XIV Panzer Corps, was a better commander of armoured forces than the Allies had so far produced. He would soon show his talent for handling infantry as well.

Eisenhower was fortunate in the commanders of both his naval and air forces: Cunningham and Hewitt thoroughly understood each other; between Tedder and Spaatz there was professional respect and solidarity transcending mere national interests. The prestige of Alexander with his long battle experience and record of victory in Africa was high in both British and American eyes. He trusted Eisenhower completely; Eisenhower had equal confidence in him. Despite however the fine performance of II Corps in the final operations in Tunisia it is doubtful whether Alexander's confidence extended to American troops. Beneath him he had two armies, the Eighth under Montgomery and the Seventh under Patton, both startling personalities, equally strong-willed, equally ambitious, equally publicity-seeking and equally unorthodox when judged in the light of the traditional standards of their respective armies. Montgomery, sharp as a ferret and about as lovable according to his enemies, would brook no opposition. In argument he was verbally incisive and utterly ruthless: if he had taken up law he would have been one of the great prosecuting counsels of his country. He not only said in words of unmistakable clarity what he conceived to be the truth, however unpalatable it might be, he also rubbed it in and underlined it as well. Within his own army his influence reached down to every individual soldier. According to his chaplain he honestly believed he had been chosen by God to defeat the Germans: it was the Divine Will therefore that all who stood in his way should be swept aside or brutally ignored. In the Desert Alexander had been happy to let him have his head; now however he must accept his position as a member of a team on an equal footing with Patton. A clash between the two was therefore inevitable; on the manner in which Alexander handled it the ultimate issue would, to a considerable extent, depend.

Eisenhower's planning team for Husky had been established in *École Militaire* at Algiers since February. They were not alone: there were other planning staffs in places as far apart as Norfolk House, London, Cairo and Rabat. They were staffs only: all the commanders concerned were more than fully occupied fighting the battle in Tunisia which did not end until Arnim finally surrendered on 13 May. Altogether the planning staffs considered seven possible plans. The sailors wanted a dispersed landing; the airmen insisted on the neutralisation of the three groups of airfields on the island; the logistic experts wanted ports—no one knew to what extent the force once landed could be maintained over beaches. With the end of operations in Africa and loss of direct contact, intelligence would be harder to get; few expected that when their homeland was invaded the Italians would prefer to live rather than die for it. Over all hung the deadline of July when reasonably calm weather could be expected: August would be too late in the year. When Patton moved his own planning staff to Mostaganem on 26 April, the seventh version of the plan had been reached. This envisaged a British landing in the south-east corner of the island astride the Pachino peninsula, attracting the Axis armour towards itself, and an American landing a few days later about Palermo. This interesting anticipation of the concept behind Montgomery's own plan for the

Normandy battle gave the Americans their own line of supply and liberty to develop operations on their own front untrammelled by British restrictions. Little is to be gained from narrating the inter-Allied and inter-service bickering which now ensued. Tedder insisted that control of the Ponte Olivo group of airfields must be secured at the outset: this made a landing on either side of Gela imperative. Montgomery maintained that severe opposition must be expected; the Allies at all costs must not fall into the error of dispersion of force. The British and American task forces must therefore attack side by side in the south-east corner. This meant that Patton inevitably would lose the measure of independence on which he had set his heart and get the more difficult landing into the bargain. Swept off their feet by Montgomery's arguments, Eisenhower and Alexander gave way: Seventh Army would land at Gela concurrently with the British. When Alexander personally conveyed this decision to Patton, militarily sound though uninspired as it was, like a good soldier and loyal ally he took the blow on the chin. Montgomery had scored another victory but the price in American resentment would be great. Alanbrooke ominously recorded in his diary at this time:

> Montgomery arrived last night and I had a long talk with him until the Prime Minister sent for him. He requires a lot of education to make him see the whole situation and the war as a whole outside the Eighth Army orbit. A difficult mixture to handle, brilliant commander in action and trainer of men, but liable to commit untold errors, due to lack of tact, lack of appreciation of other people's outlook. It is most distressing that the Americans do not like him and it will always be a difficult matter to have him fighting in close proximity to them. He wants guiding and watching continually and I do not think Alex is sufficiently strong and rough with him.

In the final plan the Eighth Army was to land on a 30-mile front with two corps, the XIII Corps (Dempsey) just south of Syracuse and the XXX Corps (Leese) astride the Pachino peninsula to ensure the early capture of the airfield there. Patton planned to land the Seventh Army on a 70-mile front in three simultaneous seaborne assaults, two on the east flank by Bradley's corps with 45th Division at

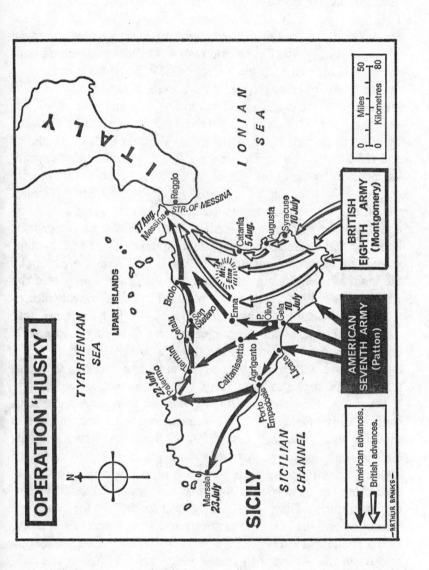

OPERATION 'HUSKY'

SICILY

ITALY

Reggio

STR. OF MESSINA

Messina
17 Aug.

Catania
5 Aug.

Augusta

Syracuse
10 July

Mt.
Etna

Enna

Brolo

San
Stefano

Cefalù

Termini

Palermo
22 July

Calanissetta

Agrigento

Porto
Empedocle

Gela
10 July

P.
Olivo

Licata

Marsala
23 July

IONIAN
SEA

TYRRHENIAN
SEA

LIPARI ISLANDS

SICILIAN
CHANNEL

N

BRITISH
EIGHTH
ARMY
(Montgomery)

AMERICAN
SEVENTH ARMY
(Patton)

American advances.
British advances.

Miles
0   50
Kilometres
0   80

—ARTHUR BANKS—

Scoglitti and 1st Division, on Patton's insistence, at Gela. The 36th
Division which had no battle experience had been originally cast
for this role. On the left the 3rd Division, directly under command
of Seventh Army, was due to come ashore at Licata. All these troops
were war-hardened with the exception of 45th Division which had
the reputation of being the best trained in the United States. In floating reserve Patton had 2nd Armored Division and part of 9th Division. Both the British and American landings were to be preceded
by airborne assaults by the British 1st Airborne Division in gliders
and the 82nd Airborne Division parachuting. Plans for the estab-
lishment of the initial bridgehead by all three services were precise
and clear: how the campaign would be developed once the armies
were firmly ashore and how the island would finally be reduced Alexander did not specify in his orders. There are strong reasons for
believing that lacking confidence in the Americans, and under Montgomery's influence, he intended that the Eighth Army should make
the main effort driving ahead along the east coast 'to capture the
whole island' with Seventh Army relegated to the minor role of protecting the British left flank. Alexander may well have hoped that
events would spare him the unpleasantness of having to over-rule
Patton or make Montgomery toe the line. If this is true, and it is
highly probable, then his attitude was more like that of a diplomat
than that of a strong commander: it would be rewarded accordingly.

When Guzzoni arrived at Etna to take over command of the Sixth
Italian Army in May he found it, even by Italian standards, in a
shocking state. Although about 200,000 men were drawing rations
and pay only four divisions were relatively mobile: the rest were
low-grade coast-defence units consisting of men who had either succeeded in evading service in Africa or were manifestly unfit for active operations. They were poorly trained and badly equipped.
Except around the major ports the coast defences were perfunctory.
One corps headquarters presided over the destinies of these unhappy
soldiers in the western half of the island and another in the east.
The state of the *Regia Aeronautica*, the Italian Air Force was, if
possible, worse whilst the main Italian battle fleet was many miles
away at La Spezia where its personnel had every intention of keeping

out of harm's way. How low Italian morale had sunk no one in Eisenhower's forces seems to have realised.

With the Germans however it was far otherwise. In Sicily under Guzzoni's command and detached from XIV Panzer Corps on the mainland were 15th Panzer Grenadier Division under Rodt and the Hermann Goering Division under Conrath. They numbered about 30,000 all told and included a Tiger tank company of seventeen tanks (Mark VI) and about 90 Mark III and Mark IV tanks. Morale was high. Guzzoni, with considerable perspicacity anticipating a double-headed invasion as originally planned by the Allies, sited 15th Panzer Grenadier Division ready to pounce on any invasion at the west end of the island and the Hermann Goering Division, divided into two combat teams, the stronger at Caltanisetta about 20 miles inland from Gela and the other called Battle Group 'Schmaltz' ready to intervene in the Catania plain. Guzzoni's one hope of success lay in rapid counter-attack by these German divisions and the Livorno Division and their speedy reinforcement from XIV Panzer Corps from the mainland.

The vast scale of the Allied enterprise is not easy to convey. Mountbatten, watching the convoys as they passed on their way to the rendezvous south of Malta, described it as a sight unique in his experience in 27 years at sea: 'It was like the Spithead Review multiplied by twenty. There were just forests of masts in every direction, as far as the eye could see. It was a most imposing and inspiring sight, and all the troops and sailors had their tails so obviously vertical that when you went anywhere near them they broke into cheers.' Altogether seven and a half divisions in 2,760 ships and major landing craft were afloat including the *Monrovia,* Hewitt's flagship, carrying Patton and his army headquarters—reassuring evidence that Tedder and Spaatz had already won the battle in the air and Cunningham and Hewitt at sea.

All however was not plain sailing for although 9 July had started as a hot day without a ripple on the water by 3 p.m. it was blowing Force 4; three hours later it was more like Force 7. Almost all the troops in the smaller craft were sick. As the Eighth Army came under the lee of the land, conditions for them improved but the Americans had no such shelter and had to disembark soaked to the

skin and in the full misery of sea-sickness. The high winds too had
widely scattered the airborne landings: in the British sector only
about a dozen out of 134 gliders reached their objective and many,
released too soon, were lost at sea. 82nd Airborne Division was
scattered over the whole south-eastern corner of Sicily and by dawn
only about 200 men had been able to reach their main objective,
the high ground of Piano Lupo. Uncertain of their whereabouts but
undeterred the rest, in small parties, roamed through the rear areas
of the coast-defence units, cutting communications and generally
causing despondency and alarm amongst the Italian defenders.

Eighth Army got ashore with comparative ease; such opposition
as there was from coastal batteries and field artillery was quickly
silenced by naval gunfire. US 45th Division was an hour late owing
to the gale and high seas but the rest were on time. First ashore
were the assault elements of 3rd Division at Licata followed rapidly
after first light by the rest of the division. By 06.30 hours guns and
tanks were coming ashore. At Gela, as the 1st Division, led by a
special force of Rangers called Force X, approached the shore, a
loud explosion signalled the destruction of the pier. The coast-
defence guns opened up to be quickly silenced by devastatingly accurate fire from the destroyer *Shubrick* and the cruiser *Savannah*.
The Rangers touched down and dashed inland in the early dawn
into the town, firing their bazookas as they advanced. The rest of
the division now swarmed ashore unchecked on to their first objectives. Meanwhile on the east flank 45th Division had got ashore
at Scoglitti. Thus to Patton on the *Monrovia* at 10.00 hours all
seemed to be going well: 3rd Division held Licata and eight miles
of coast line and was advancing inland virtually unchecked. At Gela,
1st Division held the vital road junction at Piano Lupo and the town
and airfield of Gela. The 45th Division, despite some confusion on
the beaches, was five miles inland and pressing on. From the British
front Montgomery reported only light opposition and operations
proceeding according to plan.

Meanwhile Guzzoni in his headquarters at Enna, notwithstanding
his shattered communications and the general confusion, had been
quick to diagnose the situation and reach a decision. He had little
news from Montgomery's flank and what there was was bad:

Schmaltz would have to deal with that on his own for the time being. It was clear however that no Allied landing was coming in the west: the greatest danger was the Americans at Gela. He therefore ordered 15th Panzer Grenadier Division to start moving towards Enna, thus creating for himself a reserve conveniently placed at the strategic centre of the island and at the same time ordered the Livorno Division plus two mobile groups and the Hermann Goering Division to stage a coordinated attack with all speed against the Americans at Gela. These orders never reached Conrath: the Italians in consequence attacked in the late morning with infantry and about 20 tanks. They did not survive for long: the 16th RCT using bazookas as their artillery had still to come ashore and navy guns soon drove the survivors back to the foothills north of the town. The counterattack by the Hermann Goering Division, accompanied by heavy shelling of the beaches and air attacks on the massed shipping off the shore, came in at about 2 p.m. It was a muddled affair and, despite the courage of the Germans, abortive. A second attempt about an hour later including Tiger tanks also failed and the Germans pulled back badly mauled. Confused fighting on the Gela plain and in the Acate valley continued till nightfall with the Germans still in possession of the Ponte Olivo airfield.

The immediate American need was to get their own tanks ashore. Anticipating an all-out German effort on the morrow Patton had during the afternoon upset the planned disembarkation schedules by ordering 2nd Armored Division and 18th RCT to start coming ashore. They continued to do so throughout the night. He had good reason for anxiety for Guzzoni in fact had ordered a thrust on Gela at first light on the morrow by the Hermann Goering Division from the east in three columns and another by the Livorno Division, also in three columns from the north-west. Patton, firmly resolved to go ashore personally next morning, faced with confidence what he knew would be the decisive day.

Duly at 9 a.m. in company with Gay, Stiller and some soldiers Patton embarked from the *Monrovia* in the Admiral's barge. He reached the beach about an hour later to be most effectively photographed coming ashore by the movie cameramen. Fire from enemy 88s added to the drama of the scene. For some time he waited on

the sand for his scout car to be de-waterproofed; he then set off
into Gela en route for the headquarters of the 1st Division about
three miles to the east on the coastal road. Whilst passing through
the town he caught sight of the flag showing the headquarters of
Colonel Darby and the Rangers and promptly decided to look in
before going on. It was fortunate he did so: if he had continued
along the road he would have collided with seven German tanks.
The Rangers in fact had been cut off from the 1st Division by the
Hermann Goering Division about a thousand yards from the eastern
edge of the town. All battles are chaotic: this one was even more
chaotic than most. During the night the news of the fall of Syracuse
to the British had reached Guzzoni: he had therefore modified his
orders to the Livorno and Hermann Goering Divisions. After driving
the Americans back to the beaches they were to swing east against
the British. Their attack had got going soon after 6 a.m. and was
now in full swing. Patton had thus arrived in the nick of time to
watch from an observation post a hundred yards behind the front
line the fighting in the streets of Gela between the Rangers, using
a captured battery of German 77s and their bazookas, and the Italians. Heavy shellfire rocked the town: two Hurricanes added to the
din by dropping their bombs on the Americans. Ten tanks, having
driven along the coast road all the way from Licata, joined in the
fray. Altogether the *Savannah*'s guns fired over 500 six-inch shells
in support of the Rangers. By 11 a.m. the Italians had had enough:
the Livorno Division ceased to be an effective unit and its remnant
withdrew from the town. Patton could now turn his attention to
the 1st Division on the right. Before leaving his observation post
he said to Captain Lyle the company commander on the spot: 'Kill
every one of the Goddam bastards.' No one was left in doubt as to
his purpose in coming to Sicily.

The Gela plain outside the town was an inferno of bursting shells.
Here Conrath had committed the major part of his division in a
desperate attempt to reach the beaches. They never got there nor
had the 1st Division any thought of allowing them to do so or of
re-embarkation. The 16th Infantry stood like a rock at Piano Lupo
three miles inland. The 32nd Field Artillery Battalion, coming
ashore in DUKWs, went straight into action and engaged the German

tanks over open sights; shore parties joined in the fighting. Tanks of 2nd Armored Division struggled off the soft sand of the beaches to enter the fray. In the teeth of their fire and that of the 1st Division, pounded by the shells of the Navy, the Germans faltered and then turned back leaving behind them a third of their tanks knocked out or burning on the plain. The crisis had passed when at about 3 p.m. Patton managed to get through to Allen the divisional commander. Further to the east the paratroops under Gavin on Biazzo Ridge still fought on against Conrath's infantry with magnificent courage. The beach-head never again however was to be in danger. By the evening almost all the floating reserve was ashore and warships stood ready to give full support on call if required. Patton therefore decided that the situation no longer called for his presence. Before leaving Allen however he reminded him that he still had not taken his D-Day objective—Ponte Olivo airfield four miles inland—and that this must be done with all speed. Whilst waiting on the beach for a boat to take him back to the *Monrovia* he passed the time by teaching some soldiers when and where, and how if ever, to dig fox-holes; two Hurricanes for the second time that day added liveliness to the lecture. He would often have time to speculate in the future as to which side some of the Allied airmen thought they were on. A Liberty ship loaded with ammunition and in flames added interest to the return trip to the *Monrovia*. Later, when thanking Cunningham for the fire support provided by the monitor, HMS *Abercrombie,* with her 15-inch guns, he summed up his personal adventures for the day. 'Admiral,' he said, 'I was no longer in command of an Army, but merely a reconnaissance unit.' He himself recorded that it had been the first day in the campaign on which he had earned his pay. He had certainly by his presence conveyed to the many who saw him in the midst of the fighting that if they could not get forward, they must, if necessary die where they stood and that it was better to face the enemy than Patton in a rage.

Early that morning he had decided to strengthen the Gela front by dropping 504 Combat Team consisting of two parachute battalions on the Gela airfield at about 23.30 hours that night: they were to follow the same route as the previous night. He had been assured that the naval anti-aircraft gunners would be warned to withhold their fire. Further, before going ashore, he had warned all his own units and particularly anti-aircraft gunners of the intended drop. Regrettably, through no fault of Patton and his staff, when the columns of aircraft came in every ship opened up against them: the parachutists when dropped were scattered over an area of 60 miles. All that could be assembled next morning in the landing zone was a scratch company and a few light howitzers. At best it was an expensive experiment.

The 12th was a day of steady progress: by the evening the Seventh Army held the airfields of Comiso, Biscari and Ponte Olivo and were approaching the final objectives prescribed for the bridgehead. Eighth Army on their right had captured Augusta and was about to continue the advance into the Catania plain: their left had reached Palazzolo. The first phase of the campaign was thus nearing its end. Late on the afternoon of 12 July Patton moved his headquarters ashore and opened up his command post 'in a very handsome mansion, abandoned by its owner in a hurry' on the outskirts of Gela. All was going well. Seventh Army should soon reach the Yellow Line, the final limit of the bridgehead about 20 miles inland. Alexander's orders allotted Route 124 from Vizzininito Caltagirone to Patton. He impatiently awaited further orders.

The solution of tactical problems on small-scale sketch maps, 28 years after the event, with knowledge of the situation on both sides denied at the time to the actual participants, is deceptively easy. Nevertheless a glance at the map of Sicily should be sufficient to convince anyone that possession of the road net around Enna is the key to an advance on to Messina round the western end of Mount Etna. Seventh Army was far more conveniently placed to carry out a thrust in this direction than Eighth Army which in any case had the east-coast route to Messina at its disposal. This in fact was what both Patton and Bradley expected Alexander would order them to do.

On the morning of 13 July Alexander arrived in person at Patton's headquarters. Patton pressed for permission to take Agrigento on his west flank to ease his logistic problems; Alexander restrained him stressing that for the moment his main task must be to protect Montgomery's left flank. He then departed to call on Montgomery.

Eisenhower and Mountbatten arrived later. According to Butcher, Eisenhower complained of the inadequacy of the progress reports Patton was sending to his headquarters. When he left Butcher noted an air of tension between the two. Meanwhile Montgomery's xxx Corps was racing for the same objective as Bradley—Route 124. Montgomery in fact, without consulting Alexander or discussion with Patton, had taken upon himself to make a left hook in Seventh Army's territory with xxx Corps along Route 124 towards Calta-girone, Enna and Leonforte. That evening a directive from Alex-ander confirmed the move of the boundary between the two armies in Montgomery's favour. Understandably Patton and Bradley were indignant at this brusque relegation to a secondary role: they felt, with justice, that the decision cast a reflection on their own ability and the battle-worthiness of their troops. Patton however, out of a sense of loyalty to Alexander, did not dispute the order. If he had done so he would at least have made clear the depth of American resentment. As a result the 45th Division had to be pulled back and passed round the rear of 1st Division—a tedious and time-wasting process calculated to exasperate all concerned. It was only on this day that Hitler authorised the reinforcement of the island with the remainder of xiv Panzer Corps and 1st Parachute Division and decided to hold the Allies, for the time being, on the line San Stefano–Mount Etna–Catania. It is thus hard to avoid the conclu-sion that at this crucial moment Patton's tactical instinct was right and Alexander's wrong and that if he had now given Patton the task of seizing the vital road net, instead of Montgomery, the cam-paign in Sicily could have been shortened by weeks. The xxx Corps employed on the east coast to strengthen the thrust there might also have helped to get a quicker decision. In the event Montgomery's right hook at Catania struck more resistance than expected and his left hook on Enna temporarily bogged down.

On 16 July a further directive from Alexander confirmed Messina as Montgomery's objective and once more relegated Patton to the invidious task of protecting his left flank and rear which in any case were in no danger. In the hope perhaps of softening the blow, he was allowed to seize Agrigento and Porto Empedocle. 'Montgomery was to get the first prize, Messina,' says the American official history.

'The Americans were to be denied even the consolation prize, Palermo.' This is fair comment. There is no doubt that in British circles the extent of American resentment even now was not appreciated. Stung to the quick, Patton on 17 July flew to protest in person to Alexander at his headquarters at La Marsa, Tunisia. When he pressed for his Army to be allowed to attack all-out Alexander at last grasped the depth of American feeling and politely agreed to his demand to drive on Palermo. Henceforward, in Montgomery's own words, 'His Army Commanders developed their own ideas of how to proceed and then "informed" higher authority.' He let the battle fight itself. He had underrated Patton, underrated the American soldier and failed to dominate Montgomery. It is hard to say this of so magnificent a man: the fact that he had lost his Chief of Staff McCreery and not yet gained Harding in his place provides some excuse.

Released at last from his straight jacket, Patton exuberantly launched his all-out drive on Palermo. To this end he had created a provisional corps under Keyes: the 82nd and 3rd Divisions would thrust forward to Palermo from south and south-east; 2nd Armored Division would follow in their wake at first, ready for the final blow at the city. Meanwhile Bradley's corps with 45th Division on its west flank would advance north to cut the coast road keeping in step with Montgomery's left flank. The city duly surrendered on 22 July and Patton entered it in triumph with the 2nd Armored Division to take up his quarters in the congenial and splendid setting of the Royal Palace. Alexander signalled congratulations on his great achievement. Judged as a demonstration of tactical skill, good staff work and initiative the drive on Palermo had been a brilliantly executed manoeuvre. In four days with the infantry riding on the tanks, in torrid heat and in the face of some opposition, the corps had covered 100 miles at a cost of only 300 casualties and captured 53,000 prisoners. On 23 July 45th Division of Bradley's corps struck the north coast just east of Termini Imerese: the island was cut in half. The American Press were jubilant: at last their Army, given a free hand, had shown what it could do. Seventh Army got a deepwater port capable of handling ships coming direct from the United States. Sicilian soldiers were sent home; the rest of the prisoners realised the dream of a lifetime—a free passage to the USA. Sad to relate this spectacular manoeuvre, judged strategically, was a waste of time—time which Hube with the four divisions of XIV Panzer Corps utilised with great skill to exploit the excellent defensive facilities of the Etna position, hold off Montgomery and plan the slow withdrawal from the island which Kesselring had now ordered. Mussolini had fallen on 27 July and the Germans needed time to regain their grip on the fluid military and political situation in Italy.

Having thus by his uninspired handling of both Seventh and Eighth Armies lost what would in fact be his last chance to encircle and destroy the German garrison, Alexander had condemned both Patton and Montgomery to a slow slogging match against what has been justly described as a Torres Vedras-type position in which the Germans to a considerable extent were able to call the tune. There was little scope for manoeuvre at Montgomery's and Patton's level. The renewed offensive with II US Corps on the left, XXX British Corps in the centre and XIII Corps on the right at Catania got going at the beginning of August. Both the Americans and British made steady, undramatic and costly progress against skilled and bitter opposition. 1st Division's battle at Troina was particularly grim. In Seventh Army, 45th and 1st US Divisions at first were in the lead, later to be relieved by the 3rd and 9th Divisions. To ease Bradley's task Patton staged three amphibious hooks or 'end runs'. There were only sufficient landing craft to lift a single battalion group. The first two were abortive; the third at Brolo on 11 August, at heavy cost, only just failed to trap a considerable number of Germans.

In one respect the Americans amazed the British. Like Wellington there was no matter in which Montgomery took less interest than dress and the minutiae of the barrack square. In light and casual clothes they fought in comparative comfort: it was even said that the Eighth Army looked like a vast gipsy camp on the move or a tribal migration. Patton however insisted on the wearing of thick regulation shirts and pants, leggings and helmets in the midsummer Sicilian sun. He himself, roaring along in clouds of dust, made it a personal matter to see that the regulations were obeyed. Every day he ranged the front, his own vehicle gaily decked with bright insignia and oversize stars and in company with an impressive entourage. All, irrespective of rank, felt the lash of his tongue: often angry, in his determination to infect every man with his own offensive spirit he sometimes seemed cruel and ruthless. To some of his critics it seemed that he tried, in a vernacular of his own, to rival in spirit Frederick the Great who in a moment of anger in battle exclaimed to his faltering soldiers, 'Dogs! Will you live for ever?' To use his own words his claim to be 'the best damn ass-kicker in the whole US Army' will never be disputed. Some of the weaker brethren as they trudged through the dust longing for Mother and Home were offended: there was hostile criticism in other quarters too. According to Bradley, Patton in Sicily was not the idol of his men he later became with the Third Army in Europe. The fact however is undeniable that when in the early morning of 17 August the last German left Sicily, he had created an army in his own image —battle-hardened, professionally skilled, aggressive, bursting with initiative, a wry sense of humour and generosity which endeared them to the British; and second to none in its will to win.

At 10 a.m. on this day he arrived in a cloud of dust at the crest of the ridge overlooking Messina. 'What the hell are you all standing around for?' he exclaimed. Then taking his place at the head of his cavalcade he roared down into the city to the accompaniment of artillery fire from the mainland. He had beaten the British by a short head. Just after he had accepted the city's surrender in a large park a British column clanked in. The Sicilian Campaign was over.

Strategically the Allies in 38 days had achieved the aims on which they were agreed. At sea the control of the Mediterranean had at last been won. Whatever the ungrateful Stalin might say, German divisions and air forces had been attracted away from his front. Politically, the defeat of the Italian garrison defending the island had precipitated the fall of Mussolini and the eventual exit of Italy from the war. The assault landing had demonstrated that with modern equipment an attack in the face of opposition on a fortified enemy coast was a feasible operation. A start, ill-starred though it had been, had been made in the development of airborne forces and close support of armies from the air. They had however taken far longer than they need have done and in the process XIV Panzer Corps had got away intact with practically all its equipment. For this partial failure Patton bore no responsibility.

With the commanders who were to carry out the landing fully engaged with the last stages of the battle in Tunis until mid-May, effective planning had started late: up to this time much of it had been in inexperienced hands. As a result there were shortcomings on the logistic side. Even then vital decisions had to be made by commanders situated many hundreds of miles away from each other. Alexander's own headquarters remained in Tunis until the last weeks of July before moving to the island. To the very end Tedder attempted to control the air forces from North Africa. Cunningham's headquarters was at Malta and Eisenhower's in Algiers. Rapidly agreed upon mutual decisions were thus not possible. As a result no joint plan was ever drawn up to bring the German evacuation to a standstill. Each of the three services did what they thought fit, independently of each other. In particular, the air operations were never from start to finish fully coordinated with the Navy and the Army: in consequence their efforts to help the Army had often been slapdash and erratic. Cunningham was convinced that much greater use of sea power could have been made had he been asked. From the moment when on 13 July Alexander allowed Montgomery to change his original plan and adopt a two-pronged attack on either side of Etna and to filch Route 124 from Patton the campaign was condemned to take its ponderous course. Montgomery in fact was a stronger personality than Alexander—clearer in thought, more incisive in speech, more ruthless and unscrupulous in execution and more venomous in argument. Only one man could ever shut him up. This was Alanbrooke and he was not there.

The fighting soldiers themselves—the XIV Panzer Corps, the Eighth Army and the Seventh Army—emerged from the operations with equal distinction. Judged as a display of professional ability, Hube's defence of the Etna Line and the subsequent withdrawal across the straits was a tactical masterpiece. Eighth Army sustained a reputation already made; Seventh Army showed the world what the American soldier could do when well led. This was the real military tragedy of the war: that soldiers with so many military virtues in common should have been called to fight each other.

Seventh Army, over 200,000 strong, was now a formation second to none in the Allied armies with an identity of its own. Its losses at 7,402 had been comparatively light (Eighth Army's were 11,843). In the actual landing it had taken practically the full weight of the counter-attacks and within 72 hours established a strong bridgehead. Deprived of its hopes of thrusting forthwith on Messina it had, at lightning speed, switched to Palermo, cut the island in half and then turning east, fighting every foot of the way in mountainous country, reached Messina before the Eighth Army. The names of Gela, Scoglitti, Vittoria, Agrigento, Biazza Ridge, San Fratello, Troina, Randazzo and Brolo would be for ever reminders of the fortitude and skill of the American infantry ably supported by the artillery. The rugged country had denied the 2nd Armored Division the chance of large-scale armoured action but its three days' sweep to Palermo had been a fine achievement. The engineers, signals and services had ably seconded the efforts of the assault arms. Many of the inefficient had been eliminated and at all levels the real leaders both in command and on the staffs were at least beginning to emerge. Morale was high. Patton in fact had put the stamp of his own aggressive, exuberant personality and will to win on almost every man in his army. That at times his methods had seemed out of date to some was deemed to be of little consequence: fighting soldiers expect their generals to win their battles; if they can do that they will excuse them almost anything. Like shareholders in a company so long as they get a high dividend they are happy to let the chairman have a free hand. Rampant in the forward area, conspicuous in his smart uniform, with his ivory-handled pistols, gigantic stars and theatrical entourage, he had made himself the idol of the press photographers and the popular Press both in the United States and Great Britain. Stories of his earthy wit circulating throughout the Allied armies gained in the telling. Now the glamorous commander of a victorious army, his standing as America's best fighting general seemed unassailable, and his claim to the highest command in her supreme effort in North-West Europe beyond dispute. How fragile the bubble reputation sought in the cannon's mouth can be would soon be seen.

7

Regrettable Incident

The evil that men do lives after them,
The good is oft interred with their bones

Julius Caesar

Like Churchill the flame of life and emotions in Patton burned with greater intensity than in normal men. Both had an eighteenth-century aristocratic spontaneity and lack of reticence: it was this which made them what they were. With the fall of Messina on 17 August had come the inevitable anti-climax: that night he recorded in his diary: 'Well: I feel let down. The reaction from intense mental and physical activity to a status of inertia is very difficult.

'I got a second DSC yesterday and ended a war. I feel that the Lord has been most generous. If I had to fight the campaign over again, I would make no change in anything I did. . . .' In fact, although he did not yet realise it, he had committed what at best could be described as a gross error of judgement which would come near to wrecking his career and which by casting a slur on his reputation, result in strategic opportunities both in Italy and France—which had they been exploited by him might have ended the war in Europe in 1944—being missed by leaders lacking his grand tactical brilliance and ability to inspire the American soldier to supreme effort.

In the heat and dust of a Sicilian summer he had come up against a human problem he did not fully understand in an evacuation hospital and found the wrong solution. Without realising the seriousness of the offence he had exposed himself to scandal and censure by blatantly losing his temper in public and personally assaulting soldiers he deemed guilty of cowardice. Judged today in the light of experience concerning the nature of fear and battle neurosis gained on all fronts by the British and Americans in World War Two and since, his offence seems heinous.

By the end of the war the medical authorities of both countries were generally agreed that in comparison with the First War men had 'been less scared of being afraid'. In the Eighth Army of the casualties evacuated from Sicily to North Africa about 11 per cent were cases of 'battle neurosis': in the Seventh Army the proportion seems to have been about the same. They ranged from the deliberate shirker happy to exchange the dangers of the front line for a sentence in jail to the genuine victim of what was popularly described as 'shell-shock' or 'bomb happiness'. Broadly speaking it seems that the basis of fear is awareness of danger. In itself this is healthy, for a man who is aware of danger automatically takes steps to provide against it. It is only when fear dominates the mind that it becomes unhealthy. All men are nicely balanced between courage and cowardice and any man is liable to break down when the strain becomes sufficiently great. The well-trained, well-disciplined and well-led soldier who has self respect is likely to control his fear better than the subnormal or psychologically unbalanced man who is likely to crash quickly. When the former class begin to show signs of battle strain a brief respite with the chance to catch up arrears of sleep will often suffice to restore efficiency although some may need longer rest: the dullards and the born neurotics are a liability and should be removed as likely to infect others. Much of the art of command in battle at close grips with the enemy consists in the ability to spot signs of battle strain in time. The subject is complex and generalisations concerning it are dangerous but it can be said that the better the medical advice available to commanders and the better they use it the more likely is the collective fighting spirit of a force to be maintained and justice done to the individual. These were not Patton's views.

He was a child of the First War and his prejudices were those of his generation of American and British soldiers: no man, he thought, should ever break down, or indeed be allowed to break down in battle. In his eyes courage and cowardice were alternative choices open to every man no matter what his emotional stress; furthermore he believed that every man had the power to choose between the two. To show cowardice in the face of the enemy in his eyes was the ultimate dishonour: anything done therefore to save a man from this humiliation was justifiable and indeed humane. He also believed:

> The greatest weapon against the so-called 'battle fatigue' is ridicule. If soldiers would realise that a large proportion of men allegedly suffering from battle fatigue are really using an easy way out, they would be less sympathetic. Any man who says he has battle fatigue is avoiding danger and forcing those who have more hardihood than himself the obligation of meeting it. If soldiers would make fun of those who begin to show battle fatigue, they would prevent its spread, and also save the man who allows himself to malinger by this means from an after life of humiliation and regret.

Strange as it may seem to a later generation, many of the older officers of the British and American armies and the tougher elements of the rank and file held not greatly dissimilar views at this time.

Nothing more vividly illustrates the wide sentimental gulf which separates the European from the North American than their attitude to casualties in battle and the award of the Purple Heart, except perhaps the American emphasis on the disposal of the visible remains of the fallen. Patton at heart was a humane and generous man: he hated hospitals and he had to force himself to face men minus legs and arms or blinded or disfigured. Few commanders however took what he considered to be his duty more seriously or spent more time touring the wards than he did, 'for he found in the bandaged wounds of soldiers the recognisable badge of courage he respected most'. These were the men he could understand. He joked with them, talked to them and pinned on their Purple Hearts. In each ward he would deliver a rousing collective speech. On one occasion he decorated an unconscious man wearing an oxygen mask who was near death, knelt down beside him, pinned the medal on the pillow, whispered in the man's ear and then stood up to attention. There wasn't a dry eye in the house. Nelson in his day in similar circumstances behaved much in the same way. Patton's wisdom can be questioned but not his sincerity: the emotional burden of this routine on a man approaching 60 in the heat and strain of the last days of the Sicilian Campaign must have been great.

It will be recollected that on 25 July Alexander had at last decided to give the Americans the chance of fighting on an equal footing with the British and timed the renewed offensive for 1 August. Patton accordingly had ordered Bradley's Corps to thrust eastwards from the San Stefano–Nicosia road on two axes, the Coastal Highway No. 113 and the parallel inland route No. 120 from Nicosia to Randazzo. It was to be 'a sustained relentless drive until the enemy is decisively defeated'. Put bluntly not only must Hube and XIV Panzer Corps be destroyed but Seventh Army must get to Messina before the British.

Ideally in Allied operations the interests of the whole should override all other considerations whether national or individual: nations should rise above the level of a football supporters' club. In World War Two, so far as international rivalry was concerned, they seldom did. In Patton's case four factors now raised the need for an all-out drive to the level of obsession. Firstly there was patriotism: whatever the cost the American Army must win; it must be shown to be the best and bravest in the world. This was also the will of his masters the people of United States as expressed on the Radio and in the Press. As Napoleon had done, it was his duty to feed the sovereign people on victory. Thirdly, there were those who had served in the First War who said that the troops now fighting in Sicily, although better trained, had less zest for battle than their forebears. They must therefore be given the stimulus which comes with success. Finally there was the element of professional rivalry with Montgomery. Both were masters of the histrionic side of their profession, markedly different in style but not in intention. It had been flippantly said that the Montgomery act owed a lot to the camp meeting; that of Patton to early twentieth-century melodrama. The rivalries and sensitivities of the stage are well known; within armies they can become equally unbalanced. The image of Patton must be exalted and that of Montgomery cut down to size. Thus possessed, Patton plunged into the new offensive.

On 3 August on the Randazzo road opposite Troina all was not going well with the 1st Division. The 15th Panzer Grenadier Division, fighting with all the skill of experience gained in fighting the British since early 1941, was exploiting terrain which inevitably canalised the American advance on to ridges and up valleys devoid of cover and in full view of the German artillery observers on the heights. Cooperation with the air arm was not working well: there had been far too many incidents of American airmen bombing their own troops; they had even bombed the headquarters of the British corps on their right. There was a disquieting proportion of men with no visible signs of wounds in the ever-increasing flow of men being evacuated to the rear. With a fighting record behind it longer than that of any other American division, it had developed characteristics of its own and was in grave danger of becoming a private army contemptuous of others, temperamental, a law unto itself and infected to some extent with self-pity. The troops were tired; what was worse, its commander Allen and its deputy commander, Roosevelt, both brave and original men, were at loggerheads and each had his own following in the division. Possibly realisation that they were due for relief by the 9th Division may have affected their will to go all out. Frustrated by the deadlock, Patton ranged the front daily. Realisation of the cost in human life and suffering bore heavily upon him. The sight of a man with the top of his head blown off and about to die had done nothing to raise his own morale.

On 3 August whilst in the 1st Division's area at Nicosia he and Lucas, who had been sent by Eisenhower to report on the operations, chose to look in at the receiving tent of the 15th Evacuation Hospital. The usual routine began—kindly commendation, display of sympathy, pinning on of Purple Heart. He then came upon a private from Company L, 26th Infantry, who had just arrived provisionally diagnosed as 'psychoneurosis anxiety state—moderate severe'. When asked by Patton what was wrong with him, the man answered: 'I guess I can't take it.' According to Lucas 'Anyone who knows him can realise what that would do to George.' He burst into rage and cursing the man slapped him across the face with his gloves. After the war Lucas wrote that at the time he could see nothing serious about the incident. Patton finished the inspection of the hospital and then went on his way to tour the front line. That night he sent out a memorandum to his senior commanders:

> It has come to my attention that a very small number of soldiers are going to the hospital on the pretext that they are nervously incapable of combat. Such men are cowards, and bring discredit on the Army and disgrace to their comrades who (sic) they heartlessly leave to endure the danger of a battle while they themselves use the hospital as a means of escaping.
>
> You will take measures to see that such cases are not sent to the hospital, but are dealt with in their units.
>
> Those who are not willing to fight will be tried by Court-Martial for Cowardice in the face of the enemy.

On return to North Africa Lucas did not consider the incident sufficiently important to merit mention to Eisenhower. Patton too does not seem to have been worried by it, merely recording in his own diary: 'I gave him the devil, slapped his face with my gloves and kicked him out of the hospital. . . . One sometimes slaps a baby to bring it to.' On 9 August the man's illness was finally diagnosed as chronic dysentery and malaria which had reached almost epidemic proportions in Seventh Army. The number of American soldiers evacuated to North Africa from Sicily with these diseases exceeded those wounded by 1,500—numbers which reflect little credit on those responsible for planning the medical aspect of the campaign.

When the Germans on the morning of 6 August abandoned the ruins of Troina with the precision of a peacetime exercise and in their own time, Patton had to face the fact that so far it had been Hube and not he who was calling the tune. Ill-based and tactless comments on the BBC giving the impression that the Americans were gorging themselves on grapes and bathing in the sea whilst the Eighth Army bore the burden and the heat of the day added to his exasperation. Allen and the 1st Division he felt had let him down: at all costs Truscott and the 3rd Division on the northern axis must strike a decisive blow. He had not come to Sicily to give the Germans a chance to stage a classic example of an expertly executed withdrawal. In this black mood he moved his command post to an olive grove on the coast within range of the German artillery.

Unfortunately, on the coastal axis, commanding ridge after commanding ridge gave the Germans tactical advantages at least as great as those they had exploited with such skill at Troina. Truscott chose to make his major effort round the inland flank supported by improvised animal transport: inevitably progress was tedious and slow. He had however one option denied to Allen: he could exploit the open flank on the sea and this Patton insisted he must do.

It is a startling reflection on the foresight of the planners at Supreme Headquarters that all that could be provided for Patton for an amphibious landing designed to cut the coastal road in the enemy's rear were sufficient landing craft to lift a single reinforced infantry battalion and no more. On 8 August after exasperating delays, Bernard's battalion group was at long last landed at Sant Agata —too late to cut off 29th Panzer Grenadier Division withdrawing according to schedule to the Naso ridge. Patton therefore ordered another similar end-run to land at Brolo on the morning of 10 August: his luck was out. A German aircraft the evening before sank one of the LSTs earmarked to lift the force; reluctantly he agreed to the postponement of the operation for 24 hours. On the morning of 10 August, firmly convinced that any further postponement would result in another fiasco and well knowing that Bradley and Truscott would protest that the landing would be premature and that Bernard's battalion would be destroyed before 3rd Division could link up with it at Brolo, he sent out orders for the operation to be carried out that very night. That very morning too Bradley, with Patton's approval, was due to carry out the painful duty of formally relieving Allen and Roosevelt of their commands—a blow which every professional soldier regards as only one stage better than sentence of death. With these anxieties on his mind he set out for Bradley's CP.

On his way to the front about 1.30 p.m. his eye lit on the signs of 93rd Evacuation Hospital: on the spur of the moment he ordered his driver to drive in. In justice to all concerned what followed is best told in the stark narrative form of the American official history:

(He) dropped in unexpectedly at the 93rd Evacuation Hospital (Colonel D. E. Currier) where he was met by Major Charles B. Etter, the hospital's receiving officer and taken to the receiving tent, where fifteen patients had just arrived from the front. Patton started down the line of cots, asking each man where he had been hurt and how, and commending each. The fourth man Patton reached was a soldier of Battery C, 17th Field Artillery Regiment, who had been previously diagnosed at a clearing station as suffering from a severe case of shell shock. He was huddled on his bunk and shivering. Patton stopped in front of the bed and, as was his way, asked the soldier what the trouble was. The man replied: 'It's my nerves' and began to sob. Patton, instantly furious, roared 'What did you say?' The man again replied: 'I can hear the shells come over but I can't hear them burst.'

Patton turned impatiently to Major Etter and asked 'What's this man talking about? What's wrong with him if anything?' Etter reached for the soldier's chart but before the doctor could answer Patton's questions, Patton began to rave and rant; 'Your nerves, Hell, you are just a goddamned coward, you yellow son of a bitch.' At this point, Colonel Currier and two other medical officers entered the receiving tent in time to hear Patton yell at the man: 'You're a disgrace to the Army and you're going back to the front to fight, although that's too good for you. You ought to be lined up against a wall and shot. In fact, I ought to shoot you myself right now, goddam you.' With this Patton reached for his pistol, pulled it from its holster and waved it in the soldier's face. Then as the man sat quivering on his cot, Patton struck him sharply across the face with his free hand and continued to shout imprecations. Spotting Colonel Currier, Patton shouted: 'I want you to get this man out of here right away. I won't have these other brave boys seeing such a bastard babied.'

Reholstering his pistol, Patton started to leave the tent, but turned suddenly and saw that the soldier was openly crying. Rushing back to him, Patton again hit the man, this time with such force that the helmet liner he had been wearing was knocked off and rolled outside the tent. This was enough for Colonel Currier who placed himself between Patton and the soldier. Patton turned and strode out of the tent. As he left the hospital, Patton said to Colonel Currier: 'I meant what I said about getting that coward out of here. I won't have these cowardly bastards hanging around our hospitals. We'll probably have to shoot them sometime anyway, or we'll raise a breed of morons.'

He then left the hospital area, still fuming 'about the cowardice of people who claimed they were suffering from psychoneuroses' and exclaiming that 'they should not be allowed in the same hospital with the brave wounded men'. Later, the 93rd Evacuation Hospital's psychiatrist confirmed the preliminary diagnosis.

Soon afterwards Patton arrived at Bradley's CP. 'Sorry to be late, Bradley,' he said casually, 'I stopped off at a hospital on the way up. There were a couple of malingerers there. I slapped one of them to make him mad and put some fight back in him.' Nothing in Patton's bearing indicated that he regarded the incident as important. What really mattered to the two generals was the Brolo operation timed for that very night with Patton determined, cost what it might, to have his way and Bradley, fearing a costly failure, hoping for its postponement at the eleventh hour. In the event Bernard's force came very near to rolling up the whole northern sector of the German defensive position. Postponement for another day would certainly have resulted in another fiasco. It had been an expensive but entirely justifiable operation. Patton had grasped what was going on on the other side of the hill far better than Bradley and Truscott.

Two days later Bradley was sitting in his trailer when Keen, his Chief of Staff, entered accompanied by the Corps Surgeon and handed him a typewritten sheet. It was a full report by Colonel Currier on the incident at 93 Evacuation Hospital. Startled by the contents Bradley asked Keen whether anyone else had seen it. On being told no he ordered Keen to lock it up in the safe and keep his mouth shut. He was in a very awkward dilemma. Obviously, according to the regulations of both the American and British armies, it was his duty to report the matter to Patton's superior officer—in this case Eisenhower thus by-passing Alexander the Army Group Commander who as an Englishman had no legal standing in a disciplinary matter of this sort. Bradley chose instead to be loyal to Patton and do nothing: some will regard his attitude as reprehensible but it makes him all the more likeable as a man. Probably most American and British officers in similar circumstances would have acted as he did: 'Dog does not eat dog.' Alexander, when he heard of the incident, wisely chose to treat it as essentially an American affair concerning which it would be bad manners and indeed improper for him to express an opinion let alone act.

Within an army on service it is almost impossible to conceal scandal of this sort. In a day or two it was common knowledge throughout the island that Patton had assaulted a soldier in hospital. Newsmen carried the story back to North Africa. By 16 August Eisenhower himself had a detailed report in his hands prepared by his Surgeon-General's office of both incidents. Thus at the very moment when his armies were about to enter Messina in triumph, when the Italian armed forces were known to be on the brink of surrender and when a further combined operation on the grand scale at Salerno was imminent, he had to deal with an apparently gross breach of discipline on the part of his country's most famous fighting general. He took the only possible course open to him: sat down and in his own hand wrote a letter calling upon Patton to give his reasons in writing for acting as he apparently had done (proverbially, in military circles it is well known that reasons in writing are only demanded when it is well known that there are none). The wording was forthright and unequivocal. 'I am well aware of the necessity for hardness and toughness on the battlefield. . . . I clearly understand that firm and drastic measures are at all times necessary in order to secure desired objectives. But this does not excuse brutality, abuse of the sick, nor exhibition of uncontrollable temper in front of subordinates.' Whilst appreciating the immense value of his services in the Sicilian Campaign, he went on to say that if most of the allegations against him were true, he would have to consider whether to give him the sack or not and concluded by ordering him to make amends, if any of the allegations against him were true, by apology or otherwise to the individuals concerned. Finally he made it clear that he would not 'tolerate conduct as described in the report by anyone, no matter how high his rank'. Eisenhower then assembled the press representatives, told them the whole sorry story so far as he knew it and the action he had taken, adding that he was sending Lucas, his special assistant to Sicily to talk to Patton and two other representatives to sense the reactions of the enlisted men of Seventh Army to the incident. To their eternal credit in view of the delicate military situation and the violent impact the story was likely to have on the people of the United States, they voluntarily agreed to hush the matter up. Eisenhower applied neither indirect pressure nor direct censorship to them: they acted as free agents realising that nothing could have raised German morale more at this crucial moment than the knowledge that Patton, 'the best ground-gainer in the American Army', had been sacked.

After lunch on 20 August Blesse, Eisenhower's Chief Surgeon, handed Eisenhower's letter to Patton in his headquarters in the Royal Palace at Palermo. That night he entered in his diary 'Evidently I acted precipitately and on insufficient knowledge. My motive was correct because one cannot permit skulking to exist. It is just like a communicable disease. I admit freely that my method was wrong and I shall make amends for that. I regret the incident as I hate to make Ike mad when it is my earnest desire to please him.' Lucas had arrived that evening and spoken to him in a 'kindly but very firm tone'. According to Lucas's diary he seemed 'chastened' and agreeable to 'everything I suggested including never doing such things again'.

Eisenhower had insisted that he should make a public apology. Accordingly all the doctors, nurses and enlisted men of the 93rd Evacuation Hospital who had been involved in the incident were summoned to Patton's headquarters in the Royal Palace at Palermo. Punctually at 11 a.m., after attending church in the Royal Chapel, Patton appeared on parade and expressed his regrets for his impulsive action. Whilst they stood at attention he went on to tell them the story of a friend of his who in a fit of depression had committed suicide in World War One. He felt that 'if someone had been rough with him and slapped some sense into him his life might have been saved'. The parade was then dismissed. Later Patton toured the divisions of his army and delivered an address to each. His notes for these speeches include a further apology:

In my dealings with you I have been guilty on too many occasions, perhaps, of criticising and loud talking. I am sorry for this and wish to assure you that when I criticise and censure I am wholly impersonal. I do it because I know that if you are permitted to drive head-and-tail, to fail to take cover, to fail to keep the roads clear, you are exposing yourself to needless death and wounds. For every man I have criticised in this army, I have probably stopped, talked to and complimented a thousand, but people are more prone to remember ill-usage than to recall compliments; therefore I want you officers to explain to the other soldiers, who think perhaps that I am too hard, my motives and to express to them my sincere regret.

When early in September at a public appearance to thank Norman H. Davis, Chairman of the American Red Cross for all they were doing for the troops, the august penitent stood up on the platform and said: 'I thought I'd stand here and let you fellows see if I am as big a son of a bitch as you think I am,' he was cheered to the echo. The sentiments of the majority of his audience on the subject of malingering probably differed very little from his own: in its own self-interest a group of soldiers in battle tend to regard the man who cannot take it as a liability they cannot tolerate and to expel him of their own accord with what can be described, according to taste, as either pity or contempt—both ultimately amount to the same thing. Although to the Seventh Army, as they sweated in their woollen shirts complete with neckties and rolled down sleeves in the torrid heat, he was never the idol he would be to the Third Army, he had nevertheless inspired them with respect tinged with an element of awe. On John P. Marquand, no mean judge of character, meeting him now for the first time, his impact was instant and profound:

He was taller and much more impressive than I thought he would be. In fact he did not need pearl-handled pistols to frame his personality. I remember thinking that his hands were unusually artistic and sensitive for those of a combat General. One always knows instinctively and at once whether or not a man has exceptional talents, and there was no doubt General Patton was head and shoulders above any sort of mediocrity.

Patton's formal reply to Eisenhower's official letter of 16 August demanding an explanation for his behaviour, reached him on 29 August. In it he claimed that he had had no intention of 'being either harsh or cruel' in his treatment of the two soldiers. His sole purpose had been 'to try and realise in them, a just appreciation of their obligation as men and soldiers'. He again referred to the friend of his in the First War who had broken down in similar circumstances and who, later, after years of anguish in consequence, committed suicide stating that 'Both my friend and the medical men with whom I discussed his case assured me that had he been soundly checked at the time of his first misbehaviour he would have been restored to a normal state.' He concluded by saying that the recollection of this incident had caused him to 'inaptly' try 'the remedies suggested' and 'after each incident I stated to officers with me that I felt I had probably saved an immortal soul'.

Unconvincing though this attempt to justify his actions may seem there is no doubt that it represented beliefs sincerely felt: nonetheless his frank admission of the allegations placed Eisenhower in a most embarrassing position. There was no officer in the theatre of adequate rank to try a lieutenant-general by court martial: Patton would either have to be reduced to his permanent rank or be sent back to the United States for trial. Nothing better illustrates his capacity for great affairs than the manner in which he handled the case. Patton's behaviour judged by normal standards whether civil or military had been cruel and unjust. He had acted on impulse, lost his self-control and struck a sick man. In giving his decision Eisenhower rose to his full stature as Supreme Commander in an alliance: rightly he took the view that the interests of the alliance overrode all other considerations. Patton had shown himself to be 'the best ground-gainer developed so far by the Allies'. It could be said of him as Lincoln said when he picked Grant 'This man fights.' Of the immediately available American generals Bradley was only just beginning to find his feet, Mark Clark's performance at Salerno had been unconvincing, Truscott was learning his job and Lucas had never commanded in battle. He decided to keep Patton. Summoning the press representatives he told them of his decision, stated frankly what the facts were and gave them his reasons for retaining him in command of the Seventh Army. The case so far as he was concerned was closed: it had however been a very close thing for Patton.

Inevitably sooner or later the story was bound to leak out in the United States. In November, Drew Pearson on the radio told all: the repercussions even judged by American standards of moral indignation were startling. Eisenhower however refused to alter his decision to retain Patton. As early as 24 August in a letter to Marshall he had made it clear that, although in his opinion Patton had fought a fine campaign in Sicily, he had nonetheless displayed faults of character of which both he and the Chief of Staff were already aware: 'Impulsive bawling out of subordinates extending even to personal abuse.' He added:

> I have had to take most drastic steps, and if he is not cured now, there is no hope for him. Personally I believe that he is cured not only because of his great personal loyalty to you and me but because fundamentally he is so avid of recognition as a great military commander that he will ruthlessly repress any habit of his own that would tend to jeopardise it. Aside from just this one thing he has qualities which we cannot afford to lose unless he ruins himself. So he can be classed as an Army Commander that you can use with certainty that the troops will not be stopped by ordinary obstacles.

Patton in fact so far as Eisenhower was concerned had reached his ceiling. He would later confirm this view in a future message to Marshall: 'In no event will I ever advance Patton beyond Army Command.' There would soon be vacancies in North-West Europe for commanders of army groups: so far as Eisenhower was concerned Patton would not be one of them. Henceforth the American yardstick for the highest commands in Europe would be conscientious mediocrity rather than tactical brilliance marred by temperamental outbursts. The tortoise rather than the hare would be backed to win the race. Furthermore, when later in the autumn the British were exerting every pressure to restore the momentum of the operations in Italy, the authorities in Washington would not consider the substitution of Patton for Mark Clark in command of the Fifth Army. Speculation with regard to the course operations might have taken had this been done is a dangerous but tempting exercise. It can however be safely said that if Patton had held command he would not have been content to slog his way up Italy like 'a bug up a trouser leg' to use Churchill's own words or to suffer Lucas to squat in the bridgehead at Anzio for five days before moving forward. Patton and Alexander understood and admired each other: together with Harding as Alexander's Chief of Staff they might well have gone fast and far and even made 'Anvil'—the ponderous blow in the air in the south of France in August 1944—even more obviously a distraction and waste of effort. It is indeed ironic to reflect that an outburst of temper on the part of a general in late middle age on a torrid afternoon in the heat of action should have helped to set in motion a chain of events which may well have helped to prolong World War Two in Europe by an unnecessary six months.

This at least is clear. Commanders, except in case of flagrant irregularities on the part of the medical authorities, should not be expected regularly to visit the wounded in hospitals. If they are sensitive men the sight of the grim results of their orders must inevitably weaken their resolve to carry through their grim duty to the end. All experience confirms the fact too that the last man a soldier suffering from shock and wounds wants to see is his army commander. The hospital is the province of the doctor and the chaplain not the general. Some of the casualties in every battle will inevitably be psychiatric and intermingled with them will almost always be a proportion of shirkers and malingerers. How they are dealt with will depend on the circumstances at the time. This however is certain: whatever action is taken should be based on the best available medical advice. As for Patton, he had at the very moment when his star was in the ascendant come very near to relegation to that limbo from which those who step into their shoes ensure they seldom if ever return: another indiscretion and even the combined influence of Eisenhower, Marshall and his old friend Stimson, the Secretary for War, might well not suffice to rescue him from the fury of the 'Sovereign People'.

8

Birth of an Army

Give thy thoughts no tongue, nor any
Unproportioned thought his act

Hamlet

In the blackout of 27 January 1944 the special train provided by
the British for Lieutenant-General John C. H. Lee, the commander
of the US Communications Zone, had rumbled northwards. On
board, although few so far knew it, was Patton en route to meet
the advanced party of the Third Army, which under his leadership
would soon take its place in company with the great armies of history: Hannibal's, Cromwell's Ironsides, the armies of Marlborough
and Wellington, Napoleon's Grande Armée, the Armies of Italy,
of Egypt and the Rhine, Lee's Army of Northern Virginia, the British Eighth Army of the Western Desert and the rest. In the sickly
half-light of the dawn of 28 January the train rolled into the shabby
railway station of Greenock. Outside a bitter wind swept the dirty
waters of the Clyde, the drab assembly of ships lying at anchor and
the ugly muddle of dockland buildings black with age-old industrial
grime. The *Queen Mary,* delayed by rough weather, was late. All
day Patton had to kill time inspecting depots and a hospital and
registering charm to the impressive party of British admirals, generals and air marshals who had come to welcome him. Not until
nightfall was he able to greet, amongst the confusion of a transit
shed and all the bustle of disembarkation of the thousands of other
soldiers also destined for 'Overlord', Colonel Edward T. Williams,
12 officers and 23 enlisted men of the Advanced Echelon of his
new army. This was neither the time nor the setting for an oration
or the staging of an historic event. All Patton could do was bid

them welcome, break the news that he was their new commanding general and tell them that a special train was waiting to take them within the hour to their new command post in and around the little town of Knutsford in Cheshire. In the dim bluish light of their blacked-out railway carriages they were ordered to say nothing or write anything about their new commanding general. The truth dawned on some of them slowly: it would be under the glamorous Patton and not the imperturbable Hodges that the Third Army would go to war.

Until now for two and a half years it had been little more than a training organisation with its headquarters at Fort Sam Houston, Texas, and its units scattered over a wide area extending from Mississippi to Arizona and from Arkansas to the borders of Mexico. Those who trained in its main manoeuvre area centred on Leesville in Louisiana never forgot it, offering as it did every tactical facility for strenuous combat training and almost every known physical discomfort. Third Army had already proved itself to be a hard and efficient school. Krueger, its first commander, although over 60, had been a brilliant trainer with a flair for vivid and penetrating critiques staged in large movie theatres. Hodges had taken over from him in 1943 when he left to join MacArthur in the Pacific. Reserved, unassuming and less brilliant in exposition than Krueger he would later in the war distinguish himself as the commander of the First Army. The event however would soon show that it had been one of the War Department's most inspired decisions of the whole war when they replaced him with Patton in January 1944.

Military organisations change with ever-increasing frequency. If therefore justice is to be done to the memory of Patton and his operations are to be understood then the composition of an American army in World War Two must be explained. The total number of men in an army varied from 100,000 to 300,000 depending on the number of corps and divisions assigned to it. It had to be able to live, to move rapidly and to fight and therefore it had to include everything and everybody needed to enable it to do just that. In fact to be found within it were almost all the necessities of life normally available in a great city.

The army headquarters consisted of a headquarters company and the specialist troops necessary to enable it to function. Under it were usually three or four corps headquarters organised on similar lines but on a smaller scale. Within the corps were infantry and armoured divisions and many supporting troops such as artillery, engineers, anti-aircraft artillery, tank destroyers and chemical warfare units to make up the teams for the fighting.

The army included military police to enforce law and order and to control traffic; medical units to care for the sick and wounded; the Quartermaster Corps to handle general supplies such as petrol, food and clothing; the Transportation Corps to carry the supplies; signal units to provide communications and engineers to perform almost any civilian task plus providing and fighting with specialised equipments as well. Regard for ensuring the minimum possible suffering to the civil population, both Allied and enemy, necessitated the provision in addition of civil affairs detachments. Practically all units were self-contained for transport and cooking.

Each army had its own shoulder patch: Third Army's had its origin in the First World War when it had held the American Zone of the Army of Occupation on the Rhine—hence the white A on a blue background, circled by a red O, standing for 'Army of Occupation'. Its code name, Patton's own characteristic choice, was 'Lucky': he had every intention that it should be and with good reason. 'Lucky Forward' thus became the code designation of his battle command post (CP). Others in the US Army were more pretentious: SHAEF—'Liberty'—with its appeal to democracy; Bradley's Twelfth Army Group—'Eagle'—United States over all; First Army—'Master'—with its suggestion of grim determination.

Third Army headquarters like the other armies was divided into two groups, five general staff sections, G1 (personnel), G2 (intelligence), G3 (operations), G4 (supply), and G5 (civil affairs), and 18 special staff sections controlling the various arms and services. Altogether the officially approved strength was approximately 450 officers and 1,000 enlisted men. Patton, unlike other army commanders, would never permit this strength to be exceeded, holding the view that it was unfair to deprive lower units of men needed for actual fighting and that further additions would mean loss of mobility.

Patton did not go to Greenock a second time to meet the rest of his headquarters when they arrived soon afterwards on the *Ile de France*. For the senior general staff officers, with one exception, a shock was waiting. On landing they were informed that Patton had replaced them with veterans who had served under him in Africa and Sicily. Practically all the new section chiefs were cavalrymen: some came from his old division, 2nd Armored. Below this level he made no changes. As he once said to Eisenhower, 'I don't need a brilliant staff, I want a loyal one.' This is what he got—an unobtrusive, highly efficient, thoroughly loyal staff which gave him its absolute allegiance and which he, in his turn trusted, rewarded and backed up to the hilt. The civil population around Knutsford, like all the British connoisseurs in matters of military deportment, dress, discipline and drill, were quick to realise that the new arrivals differed from some of the run-of-the-mill American soldiers they had so far seen. Well-cut riding breeches and boots were common attire. All, rain or shine, wore neckties. All were meticulously shaven. Hair was cut short. Saluting was punctilious and smart. All were polite in public. Many erroneously assumed with characteristic British snobbery that they came from a higher social level than the rest of the American Army. They made many friends. What they told the British about their commanding general had immediate effect: this man was a fighter and a war winner. Local civilian morale, tried to the utmost by rationing, almost every imaginable type of restriction and the black-out lasting 12 hours and more of the day, rose.

No commander ever dominated his command more effectively than Patton. He and his Chief of Staff both knew to a nicety where they stood. Third Army was fortunate: Brigadier-General Hugh J. Gaffey, a staff officer of genius and a tank expert, held the appointment until the early autumn of 1944 when he departed to command 4th Armored Division and eventually a corps. He would be succeeded by Brigadier-General Hobart R. Gay an old cavalry friend of many years standing who had been with Patton ever since Morocco. Both were equally competent in the exercise of their intricate craft; both were in the mind of their master: they would be asked to do what lesser men would think impossible and achieve it.

Of the General Staff, all the section chiefs and most of the other officers were, with few exceptions, regulars with long cavalry and armoured service. All were able men; unquestionably the most outstanding was Colonel Oscar W. Koch of G2, 'the "spark plug" of Third Army'. It is quite untrue that when confronted by a new situation Patton acted on hunches, inspired guesswork or the impulse of the moment. Always he had available in Koch's War Room the estimates of the situation of what was probably, in the field of intelligence, the most penetrating brain in the American Army. This scholarly, self-effacing and incredibly industrious man was to prove himself to be the most brilliant and original member of Patton's command team. Colonel Walter J. Muller had a different temperament: he was all that any commander could desire to look after his supplies and inevitably therefore the bane of SHAEF and the friend of the fighting troops. Some said he was the ablest quartermaster since Moses; others were not so flattering. At any rate he got the goods and he satisfied Patton who was quite happy to let him get on with his job without interference or indeed undue curiosity as to the means he employed. Patton insisted on one officer from each section visiting the fighting troops every day. There thus grew up a bond of understanding and feeling of solidarity throughout Third Army unequalled elsewhere.

Like Pershing and Wellington, Patton maintained his distance from the main body of his staff and lived apart with his command group. Closest to him, apart from his Chief of Staff, was his Chief Medical Officer, Colonel Charles B. Odom, an eminent New Orleans doctor and authority on vascular surgery whose flair for organisation and the forward and skilled treatment and evacuation of the wounded would play a not inconsiderable part in the maintenance of the troops' morale and the mitigation of suffering. Equally close to him personally was Lt-Colonel Charles R. Codman, a First War pilot with the *Croix de Guerre,* a rich and widely travelled man thoroughly at home in high social circles both in Europe and the United States, as fluent in French as in English, versatile, gallant and sophisticated. He loved France including her wines, cookery and wit. His gaiety, resource and sound sense would do much to mitigate the strain on his commander of the never-ending impact of new contacts and situations. Then there was his 'fighting aide', Major Alexander L. Stiller, a Texas cowboy and old friend of the First War and as good a pistol shot as his master. Wherever Patton went Stiller went too. He could thus enjoy in his relaxed moments the conversation of mature men of his own generation in sharp contrast to those other commanders who allowed themselves when off duty to be exposed to the artless prattle of youthful aides. Close too was his orderly, Sergeant Meeks, a Negro cavalryman of resource and courage, reminiscent of Napoleon's giant Mameluk bodyguard Rustam and responsible for his impressive wardrobe. Finally there was Mess Sergeant Phue P. Lee, an American-born Chinese, in his own opinion and that of his master, the best cook in the whole US Army. Patton enjoyed good food and like Mangin believed that men who have to fight do so all the better from being well fed. Fried potatoes for breakfast before the battle of Waterloo may well explain Napoleon's poor performance on that day. With a master of the culinary art in the shape of Lee, Patton was unlikely to be exposed to gastronomic risks.

At Peover Hall, a black-and-white timbered manor house in the traditional Cheshire style, where he lived in considerable comfort, he delighted in entertaining the many distinguished visitors who descended upon him. Later when winter came in Germany he would usually take over the best available country residence in the neighbourhood. Normally however, in the field, like Montgomery, he lived and worked in two truck-trailers. A converted Ordnance truck entered by steps from the rear provided his living quarters. This accommodated a built-in bed, a small wash stand, a bath, a desk with side drawers, electric light and two telephones: one with a green receiver providing a direct line to Bradley and Eisenhower and fitted with a scrambling device; the other for conversations with his own commanders. He never spoke to them on the air. The other trailer contained his office and was fitted with a desk, map boards and telephones. A mobile generator provided the necessary current.

A unique feature of Patton's headquarters was the War Room, first set up by Koch at Peover and later unquestionably the most comprehensive and spectacular in the American, British and Canadian Armies. The main feature, on a 1/250,000 scale, was a map showing the situation on the whole Western Front down to divisions both Allied and German. This was flanked by two others, one covering the Eastern Front and the other the Third Army's Zone. The latter on a 1/100,000 scale, showed the dispositions of units, including those of the enemy, down to battalion level. All maps were set up on dismountable boards. Many other maps, models, charts, graphs, orders of battle, all prepared by his G2 section or under its supervision, were on display. The terrain models, improvised by Koch's staff, were remarkably vivid and accurate. When Patton entered the War Room for the daily briefing, the first thing he looked at was the chart showing the casualty situation of the Third Army and that of the enemy, by the day, and the campaign. Whether it was accommodated in two huge store tents or in buildings, this installation never failed to provide him with the most accurate form at a glance. In the last few months of war it would reach an amazing degree of elaboration. Within its walls many of the decisive conferences and order groups of the war would be held. The staff, only one of whom was a regular soldier, included some of the most highly qualified and gifted men in the army. Conducted tours of the War Room by parties of soldiers out of the line for a rest became a feature of Third Army routine. Those lucky enough to be selected already believed themselves to be the members of the best army in Europe; a visit to the War Room further strengthened their faith in the supreme efficiency of their commander and his staff, a faith they were not slow to transmit to others, sometimes with advantages.

The daily briefings were of two kinds—a special briefing at 7 a.m. attended only by the Chief of Staff, heads of sections and General Weyland of XIX Tactical Air Command, and the general briefing of all sections of the staff at 8 a.m. The former were of an informal character in open-forum style, culminating in decisions by Patton which ensured that all were thinking alike.

From the very moment he took over, Third Army felt the crack of the whip. His experience in Tunisia and Sicily had, if possible, confirmed his conviction that the need for discipline overrode all other considerations. They were quick to learn that in his eyes there was only one sort of discipline—perfect discipline, and the outward evidence of it as shown in neat dress, personal cleanliness and shaving whenever possible even in the heat of battle. The officer who could not assert himself in the maintenance of his high standards by example and voice stood condemned in his eyes. 'The primary purpose of discipline', he proclaimed to the house tops, 'is to produce alertness. A man who is so lethargic that he fails to salute will fall an easy victim to the enemy.' When troops were not in action he insisted on their carrying out all the formal ceremonies—guard mounting, reveille routine, formal retreat under arms and the rest as a means of inculcating and sustaining that alertness in battle without which victories cannot be won.

Nevertheless he was no kill-joy. By no means a total abstainer himself he showed none of the enthusiasm displayed by other American armies for enforcing teetotalism. Indeed the day was not far distant when his army would enjoy one of the greatest collective bonanzas of all time made possible by the capture of gigantic quantities of liquid supplies stamped in German 'Reserved for the Armed Forces'. Neither did he treat his soldiers as if they were children by placing towns and villages unnecessarily 'off limits'. He was neither a nit-picker nor a prude. When a matter was under consideration he was receptive to comment and suggestions from his subordinates. Once however he had reached a decision and issued an order he was adamant. Furthermore he never attempted to emasculate his subordinates by commanding too far down and thus lowering their personal prestige and depriving them of their legitimate initiative. All the Third Army thus, from the very early days in England, knew exactly the limits of their individual authority and responsibility. They not only had found a mascot but a master as well.

At Peover, thanks to his efficient staff and clear doctrine of command, Patton managed to maintain daily contact with his troops without becoming unduly involved in detail and to get time to think and plan. He even managed to work in study of Wellington's campaigns and of Freeman's *History of the Norman Conquest*—all six volumes of it including the index. It was at this time that the eminent British military critic, Liddell Hart, in the course of a two months' tour of the American forces in United Kingdom, called on him at Peover Hall. He was immediately impressed by Patton's dynamic qualities and sense of drive and grip surpassing anything he had

seen elsewhere in the American Army. Patton told him that he had
spent a long vacation studying Sherman's campaigns on the ground
in Georgia and the Carolinas with the aid of his book. Together
they discussed the possibility of operations in the spirit of Sherman's
—movement stripped of impediments to quicken the pace, cutting
loose from communications if necessary and swerving past opposition as the Germans had done in 1940.

It was not until a fortnight after his arrival in England that he
learned in precise terms the part his army was destined to play in
Overlord. Montgomery, the Commander of the Land Forces for the
actual landing in Normandy, had arrived in England on 2 January;
Eisenhower followed a fortnight later. At this time the invasion plan
prepared by Morgan and his staff envisaged an initial assault with
three divisions and two airborne brigades to be followed up by three
other corps leapfrogging forward through the divisions already
ashore. With his experience of the landings in Sicily and with an
eye to the manner in which he proposed to develop the battle once
established on shore, Montgomery, with Eisenhower's approval, radically altered the original plan. First he insisted that the initial assault
should be made with larger forces—which meant extending the front
from 25 to 50 miles—and that the flooded areas on the western flank,
blocking access to Cherbourg, should be secured by airborne landings. He required that the build-up should be accelerated, swept
aside any proposals for leapfrogging troops as likely to cause confusion and allotted each corps its own beach area so that it could
get on with its operations unhindered. By 11 February his plan was
sufficiently far advanced for him to reveal it to his army commanders
—Dempsey, Second British Army, Crerar First Canadian Army,
Bradley First American Army and Patton.

The meeting took place in the ironic setting of the headmaster's
study of his old school, St Paul's at Hammersmith, an institution
which, academically speaking, he had not adorned in his youth. All
went well. What Montgomery had to say, as usual, was incisive and
clear as daylight. Patton liked the fundamental simplicity of the plan
to establish the bridgehead with the First American Army on the
right and the Second British Army on the left; he liked too the

emphasis on the need for speed and violence. Although according to de Guingand, Montgomery's Chief of Staff, apparently somewhat disappointed to learn that his own army was not to be let loose in the opening stages, he brightened up when he heard that his task would be to overrun the Brittany peninsula and exploit the breakout by Bradley's army. The meeting broke up in high spirits, Patton could return with a light heart and a clear mind to his headquarters to train his army for a role for which the event would prove that both he and his troops were, above all others, supremely well qualified. He was lucky indeed to be spared all the tedium, intricacies and frustrations which would be the lot of Bradley and Dempsey.

Not the least brilliant feature of Overlord was the deception plan known as 'Fortitude'. The plot, around which all operations connected with it were built, was based on the fiction that the campaign would open with an attack on Southern Norway launched from Scottish ports but that the main attack would come in the Pas de Calais by an army of twelve rising to 50 divisions. Any allies landing elsewhere would be merely a diversion. In the days before D-Day therefore, twice as many air missions were flown over the Pas de Calais as over Normandy, twice as many bombs were dropped north of Le Havre as west of it and the major bomber attacks were concentrated on the railways to the north and east of the Seine. A dummy operational headquarters was set up at Dover. Bogus camps, dummy landing craft, 'hards' and new roads and railway sidings were constructed in various parts of south-east England. To heighten the deception, 'build-up' divisions and much of Third Army were stationed in or near this area before D-Day. Extensive and plausible wireless traffic sustained the deception in this region. Inspired suggestions were skilfully circulated through press and diplomatic channels including those in Dublin where the German Embassy functioned without interruption throughout the war. Hitler and his intelligence experts swallowed the bait, 'hook, float, line and sinker'. With characteristic Teutonic logic they reasoned that the Allied main effort must inevitably come in the Pas de Calais, involving as it would the shortest sea passage and the possibility of virtually complete fighter cover from the airfields in Kent, Sussex and Essex.

The Dieppe Raid in 1942, they assumed, had been a rehearsal. Furthermore to land in the Pas de Calais meant taking the shortest route to the Ruhr, the strategic heart of Western Germany. As a result they stationed the bulk of their field divisions north of the Seine and would in due course for six weeks after the landing refuse to switch them south. So far in the war only one American general had impressed them by his performance. The Allied Press had spared no effort either to laud him to the skies or, figuratively speaking, drag him through the mud. His movements on his tour of the Mediterranean in Corsica, Italy, Egypt had been widely publicised. Now he was known to be in England. Obviously Hitler and his experts reasoned the main Allied effort would be American and obviously too under Patton. With an appreciation of his qualities greater than that of some of his own countrymen they promoted him to command 'Armee Gruppe Patton'. To this delusion, which would in due course be their undoing, Patton himself on 25 April in the little country town of Knutsford, when the deadly hush preceding D-Day was almost palpable, now proceeded on the spur of the moment to make his own entirely unanticipated, unauthorised and typically individual contribution.

None of the belligerents in World War Two made greater use of its women power than the British. Not least amongst their women's organisations, which enabled them to make a contribution to the ultimate Allied victory quite out of proportion to their numbers, was the Women's Voluntary Service (wvs). These mature women in their dark green utilitarian uniform were formidable; with that ruthless and tenacious maintenance of their aim in which their sex, when really roused, so often outclasses the middle-aged male, they had taken on their shoulders almost every form of welfare in its widest sense from the care of bombed-out families, and of the aged and infirm and the comforting of lonely soldiers to the mass production of rhubarb jam with the minimum of sugar and the popularisation, on behalf of the Ministry of Food, of a meatless concoction, known as Woolton pie, of bacon rinds, carrots, potatoes, onions and flour which lay like cement upon the chest. All their lives they had believed in doing good; now unlimited outlets had opened before them. Inevitably their eyes fell upon Patton's soldiers in the camps at Peover and Toft. Obviously these men longed for home and maternal sympathy; the need must be supplied; they must have their own home from home. By 25 April, the Welcome Club at Knutsford was ready for its formal opening.

The essence of successful voluntary effort is that all concerned should be given the maximum possible publicity and congratulation. The more exalted the dignitary called upon to declare a voluntary institution open, the greater the glory and social distinction attaching to the organisers. Normally the wvs of Knutsford would probably have had to make the best of the bumbling comments of some aged colonel in the Home Guard or local functionary groping for his aspirates, duly reported in the local Press after editing to ensure no helper's name was left out or platitude unrecorded. The ecstasy therefore of these good ladies can therefore be well imagined at having in their midst a real American general over six feet high with four stars, magnificently apparelled, the very embodiment of Sir Galahad in twentieth-century trappings, and apparently available to perform the opening ceremony. The club to be opened had been created by local voluntary effort for the benefit of his own soldiers; apart from gratitude, his innate kindness of heart and sense of chivalry, made a flat refusal impossible. He compromised, declining the honour of actually declaring the place open on the grounds that he did not wish to be 'too prominent', but agreed to look in at the proceedings informally—and this was his undoing. On arrival 15 minutes late at the ceremony he found to his embarrassment a number of press photographers waiting for him. He protested but was assured that they would release no picture in which he appeared and that no reporters were present.

Within the hall there were only about 60 people, mostly women. Duly the regional administrator of the wvs made a little speech and declared the club open. Mrs Constantine Smith, the local chairwoman, then asked him to say a few words. It would have been churlish to refuse. He did however insist that what he said must not be reported in the Press. Mrs Smith made this quite clear when introducing him. A man far less sensitive than Patton would have found it impossible to resist the warm surge of adoration from the audience. There are various versions of what he actually said.

Speaking impromptu of the need for understanding between the British and Americans he made the jocular remark that 'Since it seems to be the destiny of America, Great Britain and Russia to rule the world, the better we know each other, the better off we will be.' These at any rate are the words quoted in Eisenhower's report of 29 April to Marshall on the incident. Some newspapers next day in their account omitted any reference to Russia. Despite the assurance given to Patton that he would not be reported, Press reaction in the United States was immediate, volcanic and acid, mainly on the grounds that he had failed to mention Russia. The *Washington Post* was particularly hostile. Proponents of all shades of opinion girded their loins for the attack. Some Republicans construed his remarks as a general's intrusion into the political sphere on the side of Roosevelt's administration. He was denounced as 'an ally of the State Department'. Left-wingers accused him of insulting the Soviet Union. For Eisenhower, carrying on his shoulders the colossal burden of the preparations for the Normandy Invasion now reaching their climax, the pressure from Washington for an explanation must have been almost the last straw. Only a fortnight before, after having to waste a great deal of time concerning remarks made by Patton the previous year in an address to 45th Division concerning the need for the thorough elimination of the enemy and now rehashed with advantages at a court martial, he had firmly told Patton that he talked too much. So intense now was the furore in United States that it practically ruled out any hope of Senatorial approval for the permanent promotion of a long list of officers including Patton himself and Bedell Smith. There were those who vociferously demanded that he should be sacked: for days Eisenhower and Marshall debated his future by cable. Finally on 29 April, Eisenhower summoned him to London and delivered a formal admonition. It cut him to the core. In his diary he recorded:

May 1, 1944.
I feel like death, but I am not out yet. If they will let me fight, I will; but if not, I will resign so as to be able to talk, and then I will tell the truth, and possibly do my country more good. All the way home, 5 hours, I recited poetry to myself.

If you can make a heap of all your winnings
And risk it on one turn of pitch and toss,
And lose, and start again at your beginnings
And never breathe a word about your loss.
I dared extreme occasion,
Nor ever one betrayed.

My final thought on the matter is that I am destined to achieve some great thing—what I don't know, but this last incident was so trivial in its nature, but so terrible in its effect, that it is not the result of an accident but the work of God. His will be done.

For Eisenhower too, to have to reprimand the friend of a lifetime, older than himself, five years senior in the Army and with far greater battle experience, had been painful in the extreme. He had now risen to his full stature and informed Marshall that 'Patton's offence was not so serious as the newspapers would lead one to believe'. Secretary of War Stimson too had once more intervened with Marshall on his behalf. Marshall therefore had wisely left Eisenhower to decide whether Patton should be relieved or not. His decision to retain him in command of Third Army would be not the least of his great services to his country. Nevertheless his disapproval of his indiscretion was officially recorded. The formal letter read:

'I am once more taking responsibility of retaining you in command in spite of damaging repercussions from a personal indiscretion. I do this solely because of my faith in you as a battle leader and from no other motive.' Their personal relations were never quite the same again: so far as Patton was concerned the memory of the incident rankled to the end.

To posterity it seems incredible that so trivial a matter should have loomed so large at the tensest time of the war, the last days before D-Day when the security curtain had descended on the vast forces assembling for the great assault on Europe. No incident could better illustrate the immense difficulties which democracies, and particularly democracies in alliance, face in time of war. The lesson so far as generals in future are concerned may well be that when asked to speak in public at unveiling and similar functions at which the Press are present, they should follow the precedent of the legendary Commander-in-Chief, Aldershot Command, who having once in all innocence stirred up a hornets' nest, thereafter when called upon to speak at opening ceremonies confined himself to the formula 'It is my pleasant duty to declare this . . . (institute, prayer room, bath house or what-not) open. This I now do.' He would then sit down.

On the wider issue concerning statements by generals on any subject with the slightest political smell the action taken by the *Manchester Evening News* of the day following Patton's speech at Knutsford also provided guidance for posterity. The editor tactfully ignored whatever Patton had said at Knutsford and published a photograph instead on the following day with the caption: 'General ("Blood and Guts") Patton proudly presents Willie, his ex-RAF pet bull terrier, who has flown over Germany, after he had spoken at the opening of a "Warm Welcome Club" for Americans and Allied Soldiers in an English village.' He thus said all that needed to be said in the minimum number of words. He combined two newsworthy items, caused no offence and raised no issue likely to handicap the soldiers, embarrass his political masters, or strain the alliance. On this occasion at least there was truth in the proverb: 'What Lancashire thinks today, the world will think tomorrow.'

9

Within the Bridgehead

But now I am cabin'd, cribb'd, confin'd,
Bound in to saucy doubts and fears
Macbeth

It was an unforthcoming general whom Liddell Hart once more interviewed at Peover Hall on 19 June. Fourteen days had gone by since D-Day; the British were still stalled outside Caen and the Americans had not yet taken Cherbourg. The worst storm for 40 years was raging in the Channel. The repercussions of the slapping incident in Sicily and the official reprimand for his indiscretion at Knutsford obviously still rankled in his mind. Liddell Hart found him ill at ease and understandably irritated when the shortcomings of his army in the matter of security were gratuitously mentioned. In their conversation he frequently reiterated such phrases as 'You mustn't quote me', 'This is off the record', 'You haven't seen me'. Tedious though this became to Liddell Hart it is surprising that he was able to place on record as much as he did. He was told that there were 13 divisions in Third Army and that its artillery could put down more explosive in a day than the whole Allied bomber force of whose accuracy he had a poor opinion. To prove his point he produced a photograph of the Seine bridges which showed that, despite the claims of the airmen, they were still intact. Generally he thought that the devastation created by area bombing was out of all proportion to its military value. He agreed that the immediate problem of the British before Caen and the Americans, now becoming increasingly aware of the difficulties created by the *bocage,* placed the burden for the time being on the infantry. He personally however was still thinking of armoured tactics—when the time was ripe—embracing wide sweeps and deep penetration on the lines of von Rundstedt's great breakout at Sedan in 1940. He thought the Sherman was the best tank in the Allied armies and that the British Cromwells and Churchills were much inferior—an opinion their unfortunate users at that very moment would have heartily endorsed. He went on to say that in his experience the Intelligence Branch always tended to overestimate the enemy's strength and the difficulties of a situation. At a recent conference at his own headquarters he recalled with relish that he had said: 'G2 of the Third Army is the best in the whole United States Army' but had then added, 'It is always 50 per cent wrong.' The 'Q' side too he thought was likewise always too conservative in its estimates of what was feasible. He had found in Africa that it was possible to do three times better with regard to the number of troops moved and supplied than they considered possible. Nevertheless he expressed a high opinion of the organisation of Montgomery's staff at Headquarters 21 Army Group.

The record made at the time gives the impression in the light of later knowledge that Patton was playing a part for Liddell Hart's benefit—the part assigned to him in 'Fortitude' for he said that 'he would have preferred the invasion to be made in the Pas de Calais instead of Normandy as it was nearer the objective.' He quoted Drake, as compared with Rodney, as evidence of the value of a seaborne stroke close to one's objective. He did not add that the longer the Germans shared this opinion the longer they would keep the infantry divisions of their field army in the Pas de Calais, well away from where he personally was destined to erupt in due course; a leakage of information giving his alleged views of the advantages of a further Allied landing near Dieppe might well help to sustain their delusion.

With regard to the actual operations in Normandy he remarked 'that the American forces had penetrated much deeper than the British at every stage and that round Caen the British had failed to gain any of their objectives, whilst the Americans were overrunning the Cherbourg Peninsula.' He also said that there were more German divisions facing the Americans than the British. This was untrue. In fact, as Liddell Hart was not slow to point out, the British at

Caen were containing four Panzer divisions and thus easing the way of the Americans to Cherbourg. It struck Liddell Hart as curious that he should express such slighting comparisons to anyone with whom he had quite a short acquaintance. Unfortunately inability to understand the difficulties of the British and their point of view was not confined to Patton. Indeed this lack of comprehension, combined with other factors, would in due course ensure that the war, which might have been satisfactorily ended in 1944, dragged on till 1945, to the ultimate advantage of no one except Stalin. It is therefore necessary to reiterate the two factors which profoundly influenced the British attitude to the war. Firstly there were the scars left by the ghastly losses of the First War, affecting all classes of society, especially those from which the majority of the leaders were drawn. Public opinion would not stand for another holocaust such as the Somme. Even Churchill just before D-Day had had nightmares of the sea red with blood. Secondly, with manpower resources less than a quarter of those of the US, they were endeavouring to sustain large forces in France, the Mediterranean and the Far East; their commanders had to pinch and scrape for every man and article of equipment. Now that D-Day had come Montgomery was commanding Britain's last army; a reverse with heavy casualties would be an irreparable disaster. It was realised that the war protracted to 1945 must inevitably mark national decline in the long term and loss of influence in the alliance.

The American attitude was quite different. Their armies had only become involved in the First War in the last few months. In terms of total manpower their casualties in comparison with those of the other belligerents had been trifling. Furthermore they knew themselves to be vastly superior to any other Western power, Allied or enemy, in numbers, wealth, industrial power and technology: their armies were backed by vast air forces and ever-expanding fleets. They profoundly believed that they had a great ideal faith in America to inspire their soldiers who, supported by overwhelming material might, must inevitably be victorious. Thus motivated it is not surprising that hardly any of Eisenhower's generals with the exception of Bradley ever fully grasped the subtlety of Montgomery's plan for the Battle of Normandy. As already explained it was so to stage and conduct operations on the front of the Second British Army on the eastern flank as to enable the American First Army to gain territory for an ultimate mass breakout by Patton in the west. To this end Montgomery was prepared to draw and hold the full weight of the Panzer divisions onto the British about Caen. He was not interested in capturing towns and villages for their own sake. This lack of comprehension even extended to Eisenhower himself who as late as 1948 could write in his book *Crusade in Europe* that as the battle progressed he became alarmed at the semi-static situation at Caen and later on the Falaise road. Maladroitly Montgomery in April had issued a map showing phase lines purporting to show anticipated progress to D plus 80. This in British eyes was merely a tentative estimate of possibilities for the benefit of the logistical planners. The Americans however in late June and July interpreted them as promises which had not been fulfilled. In these doubts Eisenhower was influenced by Morgan, author of the original 'Cossack' plan and no friend of Montgomery, and by Tedder, his British Deputy Commander who, sore at the delay in capturing Carpiquet airfield, and having served as a subaltern in the infantry in the First War, felt fully qualified to pontificate on the handling of armies. If 'Cobra', when it finally went in on 25 July, had been a failure Eisenhower might well have been unable to resist pressure from the United States and his own generals to relieve Montgomery of his command.

The truth is that the Americans did not take kindly to Montgomery's methods and their generals in addition disliked him personally as a man: in their eyes both patriotism and their own career interests dictated the urgent necessity for getting overall control of operations in American hands. That their attitude distorted the strategy of the campaign is arguable: that it worked against the interests of the alliance as a whole is certain. Patton, in particular, made no attempt to conceal his own dislike of Montgomery. This was unfortunate for both possessed—at any rate in the eyes of their own soldiers and their enemies, particularly von Rundstedt and Speidel—to a high degree qualities which raised them both head and shoulders above their contemporaries in the Allied armies.

Surprisingly the two had much in common. Both were athletic;

both played to win; both were equally contemptuous of convention; both had highly developed histrionic tendencies. Both were ardent Episcopalians; both were communicants; both avidly read the Bible including the blood-thirsty chapters of the Old Testament; both believed profoundly in the efficacy of prayer as an aid to victory. Their attitude to women was chivalrous; both on occasion could be generous to the humble and meek. Both captured the imagination of their own soldiers to whom Patton became 'Georgie' and Montgomery 'Monty'. Patton's popularity even spread to the ranks of the British Army. Both could address large bodies of troops and, looking them straight in the eyes, carry them off their feet. Admittedly their style was markedly different. Some of Patton's orations are said to have raised profanity to a fine art, notably that delivered in June in England which included the startling passage:

> I am not supposed to be commanding this Army—I am not even supposed to be in England. Let the first bastards to find out be the goddam Germans. Some day I want them to rise on their hind legs and howl: 'Jesus Christ, it's that goddam Third Army and that son of a bitch Patton again'. . . . There's one great thing that you men can say when it's all over and you're home once more. You can thank God that twenty years from now when you're sitting by the fireside with your grandson on your knee, and he asks you what you did in the war, you won't have to shift him to the other knee, cough and say, 'I shovelled crap in Louisiana.'

Montgomery, in more decorous language as befitted the son of a bishop, could play with the emotions of an audience of British troops like a fanatical ecclesiastic launching a crusade, convincing them that provided every man played his part, the Lord, Mighty in Battle would guarantee victory to his anointed Montgomery and his chosen people. When he scored a victory he would say, 'We must not fail to give praise and honour where it is due: this is the Lord's doing and it is marvellous in our eyes. . . . Therefore with faith in God and with enthusiasm for our cause and for the day of battle, let us continue the contest with stout hearts and determination to conquer.' Disconcerting as these sentiments may seem to later spoon-fed generations who have neither smelt powder nor known privation, the fact remains that the words of both Patton and Montgomery carried conviction at the time to every one of their front-line soldiers. Anyhow in this war intellectuals in the forefront of the battle were as rare as virgins in Montmartre. Both too were equally destitute of political sense or guile and equally convinced of their own infallibility. He who would hypnotise others must first hypnotise himself: both had succeeded in this process.

Traditionally in the United States there has always been popular bias for 'coming up the hard way' that is, rising by sheer merit and force of character, from the dregs of society. Ironically Patton could not claim this qualification: he even boasted of the fact that his Army pay meant little to him. Unlike Eisenhower he had moved from his earliest days in the most influential and exclusive circles of the Army and cut a figure amongst the rich. Montgomery, the product of the stone-cold bedrooms of a Protestant rectory, had no private means and came from an unfashionable regiment of the infantry-of-the-line. Narrow means and to some extent personal taste had precluded the type of social activity in which Patton had been able to advance his own interests. Patton was a cordial, overwhelmingly hospitable and convivial host. Montgomery might remember to offer his guests a cup of tea; on the other hand he might not. Finally both loved to bask in the warm glow of publicity. Neither realised that there are some things better left unsaid. In an age of great eccentrics both could claim a place in the front rank; both were God's gift to the world Press, bored stiff by tight-lipped and frozen-faced generals. Eisenhower thus was like an impresario with two stars in one play competing for popular acclaim; this would be not the least of his difficulties.

For Patton the seven weeks after D-Day were the most frustrating of the war. At times his staff found him irritable and despondent, a prey to the fear that the war might end suddenly before he could play his part. He was bitterly conscious of his age: he was 59 and the younger generations were knocking at the door. At long last on July 6 he took off in a C 47 from an airstrip near Salisbury. It was a clear morning; soon he was over the Channel. Seen from 10,000 feet the sea looked a dull grey-green. Then the white line of breakers along the coast of the Cotentin came in sight and what remained of Cherbourg. Next came the rack and ruin of Omaha beach—half-submerged ships, landing craft of all kinds at crazy angles, uprooted beach obstacles, shattered pill-boxes, huge dumps of supplies and columns of trucks moving inland through the dunes. On touching down, he and his party were met by an officer of Bradley's staff. So dense was the two-way traffic on the road from the beaches that, although Bradley's headquarters in a partially wooded field near Isigny was only a few miles inland, they took over an hour to get there. He spent the afternoon in conference with Bradley and Hodges and later with Collins of vii Corps. Next morning he attended the morning session with Bradley and his staff for which Montgomery and his Chief of Staff had driven over from Bayeux. Meanwhile Gay, his own Chief of Staff and an advance party, having crossed the Channel in LSTs from Southampton, had opened up Third Army headquarters unobtrusively in an overgrown apple orchard accessible only by a grassy lane in the *bocage* south-east of the little town of Bricquebec near the village of Nehou in the centre of the Cotentin peninsula and about ten miles behind First Army's front line. Weyland was quick to establish xix Tactical Air Command headquarters close by: he and Patton from now onwards would work hand in glove. From this concealed headquarters, his presence in the bridgehead still officially a close secret, he would sally forth in his jeep almost daily after the day's briefing, to visit the headquarters of viii and xv Corps and their divisions. A second jeep always followed partly for protection and partly in case of tyre trouble or breakdown. Both were fitted with machine-guns. He liked to drive fast at 50 to 60 miles an hour: when the aide responsible for navigation overshot a turning he never lost his temper.

In the seven-week ordeal of the First United States Army and the Second British Army, which would create the opportunity for him to break out on Bradley's west flank he played no part. For the First Army it was as tough an ordeal as any American army had to face in the Second World War. First there had been near disaster in the shambles of Omaha beach, then the exasperations of the advance to Cherbourg and finally the costly battles for attrition lasting three weeks in the hedgerows. St-Lô, scheduled to be taken on 11 June, did not finally fall until 18 July. Even then the road from Lessay to Périers was still in German hands, and St-Lô itself was under shell and mortar fire. The 17-day advance of seven miles west of Vire and a bare four miles east of it cost 40,000 American casualties, 90 per cent of whom were infantry. Montgomery's offensive 'Goodwood' starting on 18 July, spearheaded by three armoured divisions and supported by Bomber Command and US Eighth Air Force was halted three days later seven miles short of Falaise. Then the weather broke. Montgomery in fact had accomplished what he had set out to do. By 25 July when the skies cleared and Bradley was at last ready to strike his decisive blow, that is Cobra, the British Second Army was holding on its front six Panzer divisions, mustering 645 tanks and 92 infantry battalions, all deployed primarily to meet an expected British breakout towards Falaise. Two Panzer divisions only, with 190 tanks, faced the Americans. At long last the time was ripe for Bradley, supported by over 2,000 heavy, medium and fighter bombers of the Allied Expeditionary Air Force, to create the breach for Patton to exploit.

The slow progress of the First Army in the Cotentin in the first weeks of July inevitably compelled Eisenhower and his staff to consider the possibility of breaking the deadlock by means of an amphibious landing by Third Army in Brittany in the Morlaix area 100 miles west of the Cherbourg peninsula. The 28th US Division, which had been trained for this type of operation, had been held in reserve in case this should be necessary. Patton therefore almost immediately after landing in France was ordered to plan on these lines. He was quick to submit a proposal for a provisional corps of one armoured and two infantry divisions to be landed at Morlaix. They would then thrust east via Dinan and St-Hilaire, swing north and strike the Germans facing First Army in the rear. This done they would drive east once more in the general direction of Alençon and Argentan. Thereafter, depending on circumstances, they would head for either Évreux or Chartres in 'a great coup'; one of Patton's civilian biographers has claimed that if this plan had been adopted, First Army would have been spared much of the agony of the fighting in the hedgerows and the pace of the advance accelerated. It is hard to justify this assumption. Admiral Ramsay, the Allied Naval Commander, when the plan was referred to him was quick to point

out the fact that the coast defences were formidable, that the naviga-
tional hazards were complex and that the near proximity of the German U-boat bases would expose the fleets to unjustifiable risks.
When British and American admirals raise objections of this sort
all experience shows that to argue is a waste of time. How the problem of air support, difficult enough already in view of the limited
real estate owned by the Allies in the Cotentin, would have been
solved is a matter on which the official histories are unanimously
unenlightening.

When therefore on 11 July Bradley submitted his own Cobra plan
to Eisenhower he met with an enthusiastic response. In it Collins
the commander of VII Corps would exploit a massive air blow in
the centre of Bradley's front by creating a comparatively narrow
breach and then thrusting with his armour in mass towards
Coutances thus unhinging the German defences facing VIII Corps
on the coastal flank. This would be the prelude to a later drive to
the southern base of the Cotentin, the gateway into Brittany. Here
on a bluff 200 feet high stands Avranches, overlooking the Bay of
St-Michel. Five roads from the north and east converge here. The
little town lies between two rivers, the See and the Sélune which
flow westward to the Atlantic. Below Avranches all the roads converge into one main highway leading due south for five miles across
the Sélune near Pontaubault. This would soon become known as
the 'Avranches Gap'. Thereafter the roads fan out east, south and
west. Once clear of this bottleneck as Kluge, who had succeeded
von Rundstedt as C-in-C West, himself said 'the Americans would
be out of the wood' and able to do whatever they wanted. Through
this defile, when captured, Bradley therefore proposed to pour the
Third Army to clear the whole of the Brittany peninsula so as to
free the ports and develop a port complex in Quiberon Bay for the
logistic support of an American army eventually rising to a hundred
divisions. Having done this Patton would strike due east. He in fact
had been considering a plan on these lines ever since 13 May.

When planning, Patton personally always used a Michelin tourist
road map; as he said, it gave all that he wanted—'rail-roads, road
nets and rivers, all that you have to know about terrain in general'.
He left his staff to wrestle with the details on the larger-scale maps.

When away from his headquarters he always had with him a special map of the immediate area of operations, covered and waterproofed, about 10 by 20 inches in size to the scale of about 8 miles to the inch showing the most important towns and crossroads all marked with secret code identification numbers. By referring to these numbers he could tell his headquarters staff where he was and what he wanted done. His Chief of Staff, his signal officer and Colonel Koch had identical copies. Koch furthermore had a complete terrain model of Brittany. Patton anyhow was thoroughly familiar with the topography of the peninsula having reconnoitered it in 1912 and refreshed his mind, partly with the aid of Freeman's *Norman Conquest,* well knowing that wherever William the Conqueror had gone the going was bound to be good because he had obviously followed the watersheds. These routes, he reasoned, would be negotiable by his tanks in wet weather if the Germans, as was their invariable custom when withdrawing, resorted to demolitions on the maid roads.

All Patton's plans were conceived in the light of the cavalry tradition—quick decision, speed in execution, calculated audacity: better a good plan violently executed now than a perfect plan next week. As a matter of general policy he laid it down that in the coming operations the advance guards of every column when they struck opposition would surround and contain the enemy. Meanwhile another advance guard would continue the forward sweep until the next opposition was encountered. The process would then be repeated as in leap-frog. The enemy swept off his feet in this way would thus be given no time to mount a counter-stroke. This, in spirit, was the doctrine which had brought victory to the Germans in Poland, France and North Africa in the early years of the war.

How effectively he had now captured the imagination of his army is shown in a young officer's letter to his father, written about 25 July and quoted by Semmes:

The Third Army staff had been assembled by order on the lawn of a chateau. Suddenly the front doors were thrown open and a strange officer walked out and stood in a ray of sunlight, looking them over and at first saying nothing. Everyone stopped talking and looked at him and soon he began to speak, in a high and somewhat unpleasant voice. Their first impressions were of a powerful figure, immaculately and superbly uniformed, shining boots and insignia, looking every inch the soldier and leader. And before he had talked very long, they knew he was a soldier and a leader.

As the writer said 'I suppose the performance was carefully staged and that he came to hook us all, but I'll say he did it. As for me, he not only hooked but landed me, and I will go with him to the ends of the earth.'

The plan for the exploitation of Cobra which he now evolved had the hallmark of Patton at his brilliant best: he was not interested in opening ports to satisfy a crowd of chairbound logistic experts: he was out for the annihilation of Army Group B, and soon. As a curtain-raiser 4th Armored Division, thrusting forward from the Avranches Gap, would head straight for Rennes and Quiberon cutting the Brest peninsula near its base, isolating the Germans within it and preventing their reinforcement from the east and south. The 6th Armored Division would head for Brest via the central plateau, liberating in the process a vast area of France and driving the Germans into the ports to be dealt with by the infantry later. Finally a provisional unit called Task Force A was to secure the railway, which follows generally the line of the north shore, by seizing the bridges before the Germans could blow them up. This accomplished, Third Army would then drive eastwards through the German rear areas at lightning speed spreading death and destruction as it stormed forward. To them all he gave a free rein: at all costs they must press on beyond the point of exhaustion—a task temperamentally congenial not only to his men but to every true American.

To keep his own finger on the pulse of the battle he had directly under his own personal control Colonel M. Fitchett's 6th Cavalry Group. Popularly known as 'Patton's Household Cavalry', the task of this unit was to provide patrols with radio sets to range far and wide along the whole front and flanks and to send continuous situation reports direct to his own advanced command post. So efficient would they soon show themselves to be, like Montgomery's 'Phantom' which had a similar role, that he and his staff would often be better informed of a particular situation than the corps or division directly concerned. The knowledge that Patton knew as much and perhaps more of what they were up against would prove a powerful stimulant.

Bradley had intended to stage Cobra on the 24th. Owing to bad weather he cancelled the attack at the last moment, too late however to stop some 300 bombers from releasing their bombs: some fell amongst his own troops with tragic results.

At long last on the morrow at 11.00 hours the great air attack went in. This time it was on target. Panzer Lehr, twice the size of a normal Panzer division, the best equipped and a *corps d'élite* and the 13th and 15th Parachute Regiments were, in the words of Bayerlein, caught in 'a corridor of death' four miles wide and two miles deep. Trenches were buried; anti-tank gun positions were wiped out; dumps of petrol, ammunition and supplies were set on fire. At least half the Germans caught here were exterminated, killed, wounded, buried alive or driven insane. Tanks and guns were smashed to scrap; the roads were impassable. Half an hour later the fighter-bombers pounced on anything that still moved. When therefore the VII Corps advanced to the attack they were hampered more by the fantastic destruction caused by the bombers than by the remnants of the Germans on their immediate front. Collins, seeing that the German defences were now ruptured committed two mobile divisions next morning at first light. The first, advancing east of Marigny met little resistance and by the 27th had almost reached Tessy-sur-Vire; the other column thrusting towards Coutances still met with fierce resistance. Before them Bayerlein, his headquarters reduced to a bare 20 officers and men, struggled from an old farm house to collect the scattered remnants. American tanks closed in upon his little band of survivors. The building burst into flames. Last to leave it was Bayerlein himself. In the dusk he was seen walking down the road to the south. He was alone. His superb division had ceased to exist—the famous Panzer Lehr, the flower of the Panzer Corps, of which Guderian had said that very spring 'With this division alone you will throw the Anglo-Saxons back into the sea.'

The time had come for VIII Corps on the coast to go all out. The sooner they got to Avranches the sooner Patton would be able to let loose his own army. That evening therefore Bradley called him forward to act as his deputy on this front. The VIII Corps' staff, accustomed to the deliberate procedures of First Army, reeled under the shock. Henceforward their operations had the Patton touch. On the morrow two armoured divisions would lead the attack to the south. Hausser, in the hope of evading the blow, ordered the survivors facing VII and VIII Corps to break clear to the east instead of to the south. They thus ran head on into VII Corps' armour and were cut to bits. The way was open. Coutances fell on the 28th. Granville and Avranches on the 30th. Meanwhile Montgomery had launched the British Second Army, pivoting on Caumont, into the attack. On 1 August Third Army would become officially operational as part of a new army group—Bradley's 12th Army Group. Hodges would take over the First Army. Montgomery for the time being would continue to exercise general control over operations, although as the days went by his decisions would become more and more subject to American criticism and consent.

At this time Patton with VIII Corps forward at Avranches had in depth behind them XV and XX Corps straining at the leash. Behind them XII Corps headquarters was controlling the forward movement of the Third Army units still en route from the United Kingdom and the beaches. The seven-week struggle to the death neared its end. The possibility of a second Jena loomed up. After his victory Napoleon had let loose Murat with the great cavalry mass in an annihilating pursuit of the Prussian and Saxon armies. Now on this night of 31 July, Patton and the Third Army stood poised, fresh, eager and ready to deliver the final blow. The hour, the man and the men were matched.

10

War on the Michelin Map

Pour suivre la route choisie utilisez
La Carte Michelin au 1/100,000

Ever since D-Day the German front line had resembled the sea defences of a low-lying coast continually battered by high seas and
unprecedented storms, sometimes breached but always patched up
somehow or other and giving the impression of strength, flexible
and well-tempered like fine steel. Now suddenly in the sunshine and
dust of the first day of August all was changed: on the extreme
west flank at Avranches a vital dyke was down and the flood of
the Third Army with ever-increasing ferocity was roaring through.
The crisis of the Battle of Normandy had come: as hour succeeded
hour the situation on the whole front, especially that of the Third
Army, changed and changed again. A quarter of a century later
these days lose little of their tension with the lapse of time.

In the British Army one of the reasons for Montgomery's hold
on the morale of his soldiers was his insistence on all of them being,
to use his own words, 'kept in the picture'. As a result his commanders neglected no opportunity to show their men on the talc covering
their own personal maps where the enemy was and how the battle
was going. Montgomery himself, always on the move but never apparently in a hurry or worried, would often round up a group of
soldiers and on his own map point out to them where the Panzer
divisions were, what the Americans were doing and what he, Montgomery, had in mind. As a result he had tamped down the forbidden
question: 'Why, if we are fighting most of the Panzer divisions on
our front, are the Americans so slow in breaking out?' Now the
would-be strategists from platoon level upwards had their answer.

The query of the hour would henceforth be, although his presence in the theatre was supposed to be secret, 'Where is Georgie Patton now?' Saturated as they were, thanks to the movies, with the sentiments and mythology of Hollywood in the forties, they were quick to see in him another 'man of destiny'. Already in their pantheon they had one great eccentric hero; now they had an all-American one as well. Stories which lost nothing in the telling passed from mouth to mouth all the way from the Falaise road to the River Vire. To them with the emergence of Patton the war had suddenly acquired the dramatic quality of the second half of an international match with the home team on the verge of victory. Patton swinging right in one gigantic wheel would smite the German armies hip and thigh as Samson smote the Philistines and, cutting off their retreat, leave them only their eyes with which to weep. The Germans must pull out now or go under. As an appreciation of the situation shared by many of their seniors this solution had its merits. Unfortunately there was one factor of which they knew nothing and could at the time know nothing: the repercussions of the bomb planted by von Stauffenberg under the table at the conference presided over by Hitler in the 'Wolf's Lair' near Rastenburg in East Prussia on 20 July.

A few minutes before midnight on 31 July, when the men of the 4th Armored Division were snatching what sleep they could before breaking out from the bridgehead they had seized intact at Pontaubault, on the morrow, another conference assembled at the Führer's headquarters to consider Jodl's proposals that planning 'for a possible withdrawal from the coastal fronts' should start at once. Apart from Hitler, only Jodl, Warlimont his deputy, the ss representative and three minor staff officers were present. Hitler held the floor for a whole hour. Miraculously the verbatim record of the proceedings survived. In a formless monologue betraying his physical degeneration he admitted that inflammation of the ears precluded his travelling by air and that he could not stand upright for long without fits of giddiness. Sometimes too he found it difficult to walk straight. He then launched into a tirade directed against the senior officers of the Wehrmacht and especially the General Staff: not one, he said, was to be trusted. They and they alone were to blame for Germany's present plight. Rambling over the strategic situation on all fronts, he credited the British with the power to stage amphibious landings on every coast of Europe, no matter how remote—hence the need for keeping matters as they were. At long last coming to the end of this diatribe, he eventually got down to the real purpose of the meeting. He did not trust von Kluge, the C-in-C West; he therefore would henceforth personally direct the operations in France. Von Kluge must be told firstly that 'he must fight here in all circumstances, secondly that this battle is decisive, thirdly, that the idea of operating freely in the open is nonsense.' Having thus for all practical purposes hamstrung his C-in-C in France, Hitler proceeded to order the formation of a special staff at OKW to draw up plans in case a withdrawal should become necessary. The need he said would be to gain time. Therefore firstly all the French ports would be made into fortresses to be held to the last man and the last round and all installations would be destroyed. Secondly, when troops fell back on orders from OKW, all bridges, railway workshops and signal facilities in France must be blown up. The enemy must be presented with scorched earth as in 1917 when the Germans withdrew to the Hindenburg Line. Hitler then dismissed Warlimont with orders to go and tell von Kluge to 'keep his eyes riveted to the front and on the enemy without even looking backward'. Whatever had to be done in rear would be the responsibility of OKW and OKW alone.

The contrast between the lack of trust between Hitler and his generals is startling when compared with the unanimity and mutual loyalty of Eisenhower, Montgomery and Bradley at this time. Journalistic and literary capital has been made of the clashes of opinion and alleged interest between the British and the Americans in this campaign, giving sometimes the impression of unceasing bickering and misunderstanding. In fact the reverse is the truth, especially at this time. Bradley even went so far as to state that during the operations in Normandy, Montgomery exercised his Allied authority 'with wisdom, forbearance and restraint' and, whilst coordinating the movements of First United States Army and Second British Army, 'carefully avoided getting mixed up in US Command decisions, but instead granted us the latitude to operate as freely and as independently as we chose'. Within the British Army those of his contemporaries whom he considered unfit to fight under his command were wont to say 'that he commanded every platoon of the BLA'. In this criticism there was an element of truth. No one could get the smell of a battle better than he could. When an operation on any part of the British front showed the slightest sign of a hitch he would descend upon it like the wrath of God and ruthlessly put it right. No one realised better than he did that to act in this way with the Americans would neither be politically nor militarily possible. Inevitably too, when Bradley became an army group commander like himself on 1 August and Eisenhower took up residence in camp at Tournières on 7 August, his influence over American operations began to grow less and less. This loss of control to some extent explains the turn the tide of battle would take in the coming climacteric weeks.

The Avranches Gap itself presented the staffs and engineers of Third Army and VIII Corps with one of the most baffling and complex problems of the whole campaign. On the coastal flank of the Cotentin there were only two main routes to the south: both were choked with bomb and shell debris, dead animals and wrecked vehicles and strewn with mines. In places they were completely blocked by the rubble of bombed villages and towns. Luckily there was no shortage of bulldozers to clear the way forward, particularly in Avranches itself. The two main roads to the south converged at Coutances and again at Avranches. The worst bottleneck however was at Pontaubault. Through this chaos all transport for Brittany had to pass. The weather had turned hot and the traffic threw up dense clouds of dust. Against this defile the Germans directed the entire bomber force of *Luftflotte* 3. The amazingly rapid passage of two armoured divisions through this bottleneck in less than 24 hours gives some indication of the efficiency of Third Army staff work, of the anti-aircraft gunners and Allied fighters and of the units themselves. Patton and his subordinates, sometimes violating all the rules in the teeth of air bombardment by day and night, certainly imparted a drive to the two divisions never beaten in this campaign. One divisional commander wrote that he had 'spent most of his time as a traffic cop'. Patton himself was not averse to working off his own energies in this way. When held up in Avranches by 'a hopeless snarl of trucks' he leaped from his jeep and sprang into an abandoned umbrella-type police box in the centre of the square and for an hour and a half directed the traffic with verve and *élan*. The effect on the drivers is said to have been electric which is more than can be said of similar interventions by other commanders elsewhere in this theatre who only succeeded in making confusion more confounded when they personally took over the duties of a military policeman. Nevertheless, despite these checks, by mid-morning on 1 August 4th Armored Division was moving freely south of Pontaubault.

By this time Hitler's orders to hold the ports as fortresses, which in view of the Allied dominance of the air and the lack of mobility of the coast-defence divisions were not without some justification, had been transmitted with marked distaste by von Kluge to Hausser of the Seventh Army. Both saw that as a result some 200,000 troops would be isolated when some at least might have been sent back to prepare reserve positions in rear of the Army Group. Hausser, his hands already more than full in Normandy, passed the thankless task of defending Brittany to Farmbacher, the commander of xxv Corps and washed his hands of it. Two-thirds of the original divisions defending Brittany had already been sucked into the Normandy battle. What remained consisted of the 2nd Parachute Division and the 343rd Infantry Division about Brest, the weak 266th Division near Morlaix and the static 265th Division at Lorient, St-Nazaire and Nantes, supplemented by anti-aircraft batteries, coastal artillery units, anti-tank groups, engineers and navy and air force personnel. To reinforce them came the remnants of the 77th and 91st Divisions from Normandy. These Farmbacher despatched to strengthen the garrison of St-Malo and to defend Rennes. He himself, having issued orders to the fortress commanders that their primary task was to protect the submarine bases of St-Malo, Brest, Lorient and St-Nazaire and to fight on to the end, established himself at Lorient. Thereafter, owing to lack of communications, he was able to exercise little more than local control. All the Germans who could commandeer a motor vehicle lost no time in leaving the French in the interior of Brittany to their own devices and, faced with the alternative of being assassinated by the FFI or shot up by American tanks, scuttled like rabbits into the ports.

Rennes, the provincial capital, is a city of over 80,000 people, 60 miles from Avranches and a further 60 miles from the south coast at Quiberon. From it radiate no less than ten main roads. Wood, of 4th Armored Division, was ordered by Middleton, the commander of VIII Corps to take Rennes and no more. When Patton took control on 1 August he specified Quiberon 60 miles further on so as to seal the Brittany peninsula. Wood, also a cavalryman, naturally chose to obey him. By early evening his leading tanks had reached the outskirts of Rennes. Here they struck surprisingly strong resistance from a battle group of the 91st Division under a lt-colonel who had reached the city just before them. He was joined soon afterwards by two further battalions numbering 1,900 from Le Mans. All put up a vigorous defence and by nightfall the Americans had lost 11 tanks. During the night, Koenig, the 91st Division's commander, arrived with further troops and assumed command. Wood, short of petrol, ammunition and rations, decided that a deliberate attack more appropriate to infantry than to armour would be necessary to take the town. Middleton agreed and despatched the 13th Infantry from the 8th Division to Rennes for this purpose. Refuelled, Wood on his own initiative once more took off and in two great arcs outflanked the city and cut seven of the ten main highways converging on it. The place was thus virtually isolated.

6th Armored Division's breakout was equally dramatic. Early on 1 August Middleton had ordered Grow, another commander from the Patton stable, to thrust for Dinan that very afternoon. An hour or two later Patton himself arrived and putting his hand on Grow's shoulder said: 'Take Brest!' Grow asked whether there would be any intermediate objectives. Patton told him to by-pass resistance and added that he had a bet with Montgomery that he would be in Brest 'by Saturday night', that is 200 miles away in five days' time. This was enough for Grow. As a cavalryman he was delighted. 'That was,' he said, 'what we have spent years studying and training for.' Nevertheless he had no easy start. Six miles beyond Pontaubault an obstinate German detachment blocked the way at a defile until eliminated as night was closing in. Sunrise on the 2nd however found the division in the clear 'with no boundaries to worry about, no definite information, in fact nothing but a map of Brittany and the

knowledge that resistance was where you found it'. That day they
forged ahead until after a 35-mile advance they were checked by
strongly organised resistance on the outskirts of Dinan. Reconnaissance showed the place to be strongly fortified. That night Grow
held a conference with his staff who pointed out that it would take
the trains and the 79th Infantry Division days to catch up with them.
His Chief of Staff advised that henceforward the division should 'be
kept consolidated for security'—in other words pull up its tail and
await further support before proceeding. Grow to his astonished staff
announced that the advance would be resumed on the morrow.
Accordingly after a brush with the enemy at Mauron they thrust forward a further 30 miles. A peremptory order now arrived from Middleton directing them to concentrate, go back on their tracks and
take Dinan as a first step towards a full-scale Corps attack on St-
Malo. Grow immediately despatched a protest to Middleton but got
no change. Thus on the night of 3 August, Grow's leading troops,
disappointed and bitter, were at Loudéac stalled by higher authority
still a hundred miles short of Brest. Patton, the Army commander
and a cavalryman and Middleton, the VIII Corps commander and an
infantryman, were as the poles apart.

Next morning, when Grow and his staff at their headquarters in
a wheatfield were engrossed in planning the attack Middleton had
ordered on Dinan, Patton burst in unannounced and apparently in
a towering rage. 'What the hell are you doing here?' he demanded.
'I thought I told you to go to Brest.' Grow told him that he had
been halted on a written order from VIII Corps. This the Chief of
Staff now handed to Patton. It was a note from Middleton. Patton
read it; then folded it up and stuffed it in his breeches pocket. 'And
he was a good doughboy too!' he said quietly as if thinking aloud.
Then turning to Grow he said: 'I'll see Middleton. You go ahead
where I told you to go.' When time was the vital consideration Middleton had wasted a day: he had failed to realise that their only
hope of being able to seize Brest depended above all things on speed
—speed in exploiting the panic of the Germans before the defenders
of Brest could sort themselves out and consolidate. Patton was out
for bigger game than St-Malo which in any case was likely to be
wrecked as Cherbourg had been.

Left: Aged 7
Below left: At West Point 1909
Below right: Proud Father 1914

Right: Aide to Pershing in Mexico 1917
Far right: On Hukupu Hunter Trails 1938
Below: My War Face 1927
Below right: Fort Meyer 1920

Left: The Eveni
Before Leaving
Morocco
Below: Patton calls
the Sultan of Moro
at Rabat

In Tunisia

Left: Eisenhower pins the third gold star of a Lieutenant General on the Commander of US II Corps
Below left: At an informal lunch with King George VI, June 1943
Below right: Montgomery, Alexander and Patton with their Chiefs of Staff, July 25, 1943

Inspecting a task force for the Sicilian landing with
Alexander and Rear Admiral Kirk

The Overlord plan, with its emphasis on the need to get the Brittany ports to enable the advance towards the Seine to be sustained, had in fact become outdated. By 2 August it was evident to Eisenhower and Montgomery that the situation had taken a turn never anticipated by the planners. Firstly there was the rapidly widening gap between Avranches on the coast and the loose end of the German front; secondly, so many troops had been taken away to bolster up Hausser's crumbling Seventh Army that only sufficient remained in Brittany to hold the ports. One corps would therefore be adequate to clear and hold Brittany in cooperation with the FFI, estimated at 20,000, now springing to life. These were the unanimous conclusions of Montgomery, Bradley and Dempsey when they met on this day. The upshot was Bradley's second 'Letter of Instruction'. In it he ordered Hodges with the First Army to advance in the Vire–Mortain Zone and establish himself in the area Mayenne–Domfront prepared for action eastwards. Patton's previous orders were cancelled: he would now complete the clearance of the Brittany peninsula and secure its ports using 'only minimum force'. With the rest of his army he was to clear the country southwards to the Loire and be prepared for further action 'with strong armoured forces' towards the east and south-east—that is, in the open country south of the *bocage* in which First Army and Second British Army were still deeply involved. Here the Germans apparently had no reserves and the going for armour was good.

Resistance to Hodges' steady pressure towards Mortain from 11 Parachute Corps, LXXXIV Corps and XLVII Panzer Corps continued obstinate and bloody. Nevertheless, aided by the Second British Army's offensive east of Vire towards Condé-sur-Noireau, the First Army forced back the German left flank at Mortain. Between here and the Loire, a distance of 80 miles, yawned a great gap. Into it Patton had already set in motion the XV Corps to the line of the Mayenne river 35 miles to the south-east between Mayenne and Château Gontier and the XX Corps due south towards the Loire. Third Army's next bound would be Le Mans, 45 miles further east. What would be done thereafter Patton did not for the moment specify but he did tell Haislip, the commander of XV Corps, not to be surprised if he received in due course orders to move north-east or even due north. A glance at the Michelin map should convince anyone why he already had in mind the possibility of surrounding the Germans west of the Seine. If he got control of the road centre at Argentan and the British got Falaise then Fifth Panzer Army, Panzer Group Eberbach and the Seventh Army would be enveloped. As for Montgomery, the forecast he had made in April had now for all practical purposes been realised: the Americans had reached a position from which a wheel eastwards could begin. At the end of June he had ordered Bradley to make plans for 'a strong right wing in a wide sweep south of the *bocage* country to successive objectives Laval–Mayenne, Le Mans–Alençon'. This had now begun. In his directive of 4 August he said: 'Once a gap appears in the enemy front we must press into it and through it and beyond into the enemy's rear areas. Everyone must go all out all day and every day.' He was preaching to the converted: Eisenhower, Montgomery and Bradley were all of one mind and saying the same thing. Sound sense seemed to indicate that von Kluge, if he wished to survive and stage a come-back later, must pull out now or be crushed.

Brittany was thus at a single stroke reduced to the character of a secondary theatre. Nevertheless nothing can obscure the fact that 6th Armored Division's lightning advance to Brest was a remarkable achievement: they actually reached the outskirts on the evening of 6 August to find the place strongly held. An attempt to bluff the garrison into surrender failed. Grow in fact found the defences to be much stronger than he had anticipated and that forces stronger than he could muster would be needed to reduce the place. He therefore settled down in close observation to await the arrival of relief by infantry. Nevertheless his advance of over 200 miles in less than a week at a cost of only 130 killed and 400 wounded had been a brilliant achievement. Whether, if he had not been halted by Middleton for 24 hours when in full cry, he could have further exploited German disorganisation and bounced the defences of Brest will always be an open question. The old French fortifications were very strong and the 15,000 defenders included the 2nd Parachute Division under the redoubtable Ramcke. Admittedly Patton had lost his bet with Montgomery by a short head but 6th Armored Division at the very least had succeeded in penning a numerically greatly superior force in Brest with its back to the sea. Task Force A's clearing of the line of the railway and the north shore had been equally impressive. The 4th Armored Division with equal speed and dash now closed in on the Lorient and Nantes defences. Grow and Wood were cavalrymen after his own heart: he had every reason to be proud of them.

It would be an exaggeration to say that the reception of the Allies by the French had been cordial. It would have been tactless at this time to remark in the ruins of Vire 'Lafayette nous voici' or for the British in Caen to mention the *Entente Cordiale* of the days before 1914. It was otherwise in Brittany. Here the Resistance between 20,000 and 30,000 strong had been sustained ever since 1941 by the Free French, the British SAS and the RAF. With the appearance of the first American tank the FFI sprang to life to provide guides, give information, round up and write off German soldiers unfortunate enough to be caught away from their units, and cut off the hair of girls who had collaborated too enthusiastically with the Germans. From 3 August Patton managed to maintain a measure of control over their activities through Colonel Eon and his staff who were parachuted into Brittany on 4 August. Patton, almost alone amongst the Allied generals and statesmen could pronounce French names after the manner of the French and speak the language well. Time and the disasters of 1940 had in no way diminished his romantic love of France and all her traditions. In less than a week he had liberated a whole province: no organised German resistance remained in the interior. Such Germans as remained had been corralled in St-Malo, Lorient, St-Nazaire and Brest. That these major ports still remained in German hands now seemed to lack importance. He could well leave the tedious task of besieging them to others and turn his energies to the slaughter of bigger game.

To many, in both the opposing armies, able to offer an intelligent opinion on the general situation, it seemed self-evident on military grounds that the Germans if they were to avoid disaster, must break off the battle in Normandy, fall behind the Seine and evacuate the south of France. This course, von Kluge told Warlimont, Hitler's emissary, who arrived with the Führer's orders on 1 August, must be adopted. The Seventh Army and Panzer Group Eberbach could thus be saved for a massive counter-stroke in due course. Admittedly the Seine with its many twists and turns was not an ideal defensive line to hold, but behind it the Somme–Marne–Saône position, if occupied in time, was very strong and would at least enable the guided-missile sites to be retained and the sacred soil of Germany kept inviolate. Behind this there was a further strong defensive position along the Albert Canal and the Meuse in advance of the West Wall. There still remained, therefore, ample scope for protracted defence on French soil and the possibility of in due course turning the tables on the Allies. War industrial production to replace the losses in material was now in full spate despite the efforts of the Allied air forces and thanks to Speer. On these assumptions therefore Montgomery amplified his orders of 4 August by directing Bradley's Army Group to advance on a broad front and to 'arrange for the right flank to swing rapidly eastwards and then north-eastwards towards Paris'. A strong airborne force (including two British divisions) would be used ahead of the Americans to secure the Chartres area and prevent the enemy escaping between Orléans and Paris. He asked the Air Commander-in-Chief 'to divert the main air power to help the swing of the right flank and ensure that all enemy movements across the Seine between Paris and the sea, would be stopped as far as possible'. He thus, he thought, placed the ball at Bradley's and Patton's feet. They responded with lightning speed. By the evening of 6 August Hodges was heading for Domfront as a first step for a drive towards Alençon and Patton's xv Corps, now well in rear of von Kluge's armies, was only 20 miles short of Le Mans. They were thus, to Montgomery's unconcealed admiration and delight, already well on their way to outflanking the Germans west of the Seine.

That 200 miles now separated the 6th Armored Division at Brest from the xv Corps near Le Mans worried no one, least of all Patton who, as usual planning in his own mind two battles ahead, had for some time been thinking in terms of another Cannae with his xv Corps swinging north on Argentan when it reached Le Mans to meet the First Canadian Army striking due south from Falaise. It seemed self-evident, as Montgomery had so often said since D-Day, that in view of the Allies' almost complete command of the air the enemy was incapable of staging a counter-offensive. The longer he stayed where he was the worse it would be for him.

In these dramatic early August days with three corps all operating in different directions, more than a hundred miles apart, Patton still retained a measure of control. What is astonishing is his amazing ubiquity. Every night he had a fresh command post. By day he ranged his vast battlefield sometimes flying at low altitude in an L 5 up and down the fronts of his divisions, sometimes in his jeep; sometimes he would be seen marching in the ranks with the infantry occasionally darting out to haul an officer taking cover in a ditch on to the road or to upbraid another who had taped over the badges of rank, which he insisted should always be displayed on the helmet. Bombing and low-flying attack, often from Allied aircraft, he brushed off like water from a duck's back. With him it was never sufficient to give an order: always when humanly possible he would personally see that it was being carried out. His aide, Codman, who scarcely ever left his side at this time, describes him as 'pushing, pulling, exhorting, cajoling, raising merry hell' and 'having the time of his life'. Completely unconcerned for his own personal safety, at least on one occasion he drove right through a German division. Everywhere he went he preached his gospel: 'Don't worry about flanks'; 'Our Tactical Air will know before you do and will clobber it'; 'Go where you can as fast as you can.' He had 'an uncanny gift for sweeping men into doing things which they did not believe they were capable of doing, which they really did not want to do, which, in fact, they would not do unless exposed to the personality, the genius—call it what you will of this unique soldier who not only knows his extraordinary job but loves it'. Not surprisingly his army was now responding to his leadership with typical American aggression and capacity to generate and express enthusiasm in what has been described as 'the biggest rampage in the history of War'.

On the evening of 6 August to everyone in the Allied armies from the British 6th Airborne Division on the extreme north flank of the Allied line to Patton's xv Corps 100 miles to the south approaching Le Mans, all seemed to be going in Montgomery's own words 'according to plan'. Koch's big map at Third Army headquarters showed Crerar's First Canadian Army about to stage a massive blow with heavy bomber support on the Falaise road; Dempsey's Second British Army having seized the most dominating height in Normandy, Mont Pinçon, making for Conde and Argentan; Hodges First Army fighting its way grimly forward towards Domfront with a view to advancing later on Patton's left on Alençon and Patton's xv Corps hell bent for Le Mans. South of Avranches with their supply lines running through the 12-mile gap were no less than 12 divisions. That the Germans would recoil and strike at this jugular vein in the American logistic system and cut it occurred to few.

At 2 a.m. on the 7th the intelligence section duty officer woke up Koch: word had just been received from a 'usually reliable source' that a large-scale counter-attack against the First Army was imminent. Koch got up and groped his way in the black-out to the tent occupied by Colonel Maddocks of the operations staff. Although not doubting for one moment that First Army would hold firm, both felt that the news was serious enough to justify waking Gay, the Chief of Staff. At this very moment Third Army had one of its divisions, the 35th, moving through the gap: if it were halted and then moved east it would be in a position to add depth to the First Army's defences. With this recommendation the three proceeded to Patton's van and woke him up. After a few minutes' discussion he gave orders for it to be committed in support of vii Corps of First Army.

There probably had never been until this time a campaign in which both sides, partly as a result of bad radio discipline, bad map reading, ill-defined fronts, talkative prisoners and air reconnaissance, knew more of the location of their opponents on their immediate front. The prospect of realising the dream which had haunted the minds of great generals ever since Hannibal, the Cannae Manoeuvre of Double Envelopment, was there for all who had the imagination to see. Only a madman would dare to attempt to stage a counter-offensive without command of the air. Patton concluded that the attack was merely an attempt to conceal imminent withdrawal. He would be wrong with good reason and in good company—the whole Allied hierarchy in fact from Eisenhower down.

11

The Cannae Manoeuvre/ Anglo-American Version 1944

He either fears his fate too much
Or his deserts are small,
That puts it not unto the touch
To win or lose it all.

James Graham,
Marquis of Montrose

Exactly four days previously at one o'clock in the morning, von Kluge, faced by a crisis in the centre of his front in the Caumont sector where a British breakthrough appeared imminent and on his left flank where First Army was creating an ever-widening gap east of Avranches, had just decided to move II SS Panzer Corps from the Caen front to stabilise his centre between the Orne and the Vire when a bolt from the blue arrived from Hitler: he must concentrate all his armour on his left wing and regain contact with the coast at Avranches. Patton's army would thus be isolated and in due course destroyed: what would be done after that was less clear. According to Speidel, Chief of Staff of Army Group B, the arch-strategist then intended to roll up the whole of the Allied front from the west. Whatever von Kluge thought about this preposterous order he nonetheless immediately proceeded to implement it.

German headquarters staffs lived through many nightmare situations in World War Two: none can have been worse than the next four days. To move the 21st, 9th and 10th SS Panzer Divisions from the British Second Army Front would inevitably result in complete collapse: they must stay where they were. There was incessant telephoning between the headquarters involved: OKW, C-in-C West, Army Group B, Seventh Army and Panzer Group West—now in the process of splitting itself into Fifth Panzer Army and Panzer Group Eberbach. The move forward of infantry to replace the armour and their redeployment produced fantastic traffic congestion under continuous Allied air attack in ideal weather conditions. In consequence replacements and reinforcements failed to join their units: all moves were behind time. All von Kluge could produce for the thrust from Mortain to Avranches was four Panzer divisions, all under strength. According to his son, Lt-Colonel von Kluge, only 145 tanks were available, the average strength of an Allied armoured division: of these only about 80 seem to have crossed the start line. By 6 August it was only too apparent that Patton's forces unless stopped would soon reach Hausser's headquarters at Le Mans. It was now or never: whether the attacking divisions were complete or not the attack would have to go in on the night of 6/7 August. At the last moment, Hitler insisted on Eberbach commanding instead of Funck. Von Kluge, almost in despair told OKW on the telephone 'I am pressed for time and have no guarantee that the infantry will hold the position for long against the English and American attacks. I must therefore attack as soon as possible.' As a result when the attack went in soon after midnight on 6/7 August the four Panzer divisions were short of men and tanks, badly briefed and tired out. From the start the operation was doomed to failure. On the right 116th Panzer Division never left its assembly area; immediately south of the river See, where the Americans had only light forces, a column of 2nd Panzer Division managed to advance a few miles until decisively halted by 3rd US Armored Division. The US 30th Division between Mortain and St-Barthelemy faced the attack of 1st SS and 2nd SS Panzer Divisions with determination; both villages were over-run in the darkness and early morning mist but thereafter the enemy were firmly held. On Hill 317 immediately east of the village of Mortain 2/120 Infantry refused to budge an inch and gravely embarrassed the development of the German attack.

Until mid-day low cloud and mist precluded flying: then the skies suddenly cleared enabling the rocket-firing Typhoons of 83 Group RAF mercilessly to destroy the German tanks and vehicles strung out nose to tail in one vast traffic jam along the roads and byways whilst the American Mustangs dominated the skies above the battle-field. German anti-aircraft retaliation was feeble in the extreme. Pilots of the Typhoons returning from the front to re-arm reported a breakdown in German morale. Men were abandoning their tanks everywhere and seeking cover. According to the Chief of Staff of XLVII Panzer Corps 'the activity of the fighter-bombers was well nigh unendurable; the 1st SS Panzer Division have had no previous ex-perience of fighter-bomber attacks on this scale'. Never before had so many vehicles been caught at a standstill. What was equally im-pressive was the American retaliation on the ground: overwhelming and accurate artillery and anti-tank fire halted the attacking columns in their tracks; reinforcements moved up rapidly to meet the threat. By the end of the day Collins and VII Corps had five infantry and two armoured divisions barring the way forward. For several days fighting would continue on a bitter and costly scale: nevertheless the Germans from noon of the first day had lost the initiative for good.

The German attack in fact, so far as weight of explosive used and general violence, compared with Montgomery's blow on the Canadian front on the very same day, was a mere cough in a thun-derstorm. That night from 11 p.m. to about midnight 1,000 heavy bombers of Bomber Command dropped a belt of high explosive on the German positions astride the Falaise road. At midnight the 2nd Canadian and 51st Highland Divisions, each in bullet-proof vehicles, and supported by an armoured brigade, thrust forward into the dust and darkness carrying all before them. Simonds, the corps com-mander, intended, when daylight came, to pass through them the 4th Canadian and the Polish Armoured Divisions directed on Falaise. That night Montgomery bursting with confidence sent a tele-gram to Alanbrooke, the CIGS. In it he stated: 'Enemy attack in Mortain area has been well held by the Americans.' He added that 'he had no fear whatever for that part of the front and (am) proceeding with my offensive plans everywhere without change'. He followed this with a report on Patton's progress towards Le Mans and concluded 'If only the Germans will go on attacking at Mortain for a few more days it seems that they might not, repeat not, be able to get away.'

It will be recollected that up to this moment he had planned to make a wide enveloping movement with the southern American flank to the Seine about Paris and at the same time to drive the centre and northern sections of the Allied forces straight for the river. The German counter-stroke at Mortain now led him to decide, after discussion on the telephone with Bradley, 'to attempt concurrently a shorter envelopment with the object of bottling up the bulk of the German forces deployed between Falaise and Mortain' and thus annihilate them. Patton's XV Corps, sweeping all before it and now nearing Le Mans, was admirably placed to swing north towards the Canadian forces coming south towards Falaise and Argentan. It seemed that, if the Germans remained where they were for a few more days, and Patton and Crerar fought their way towards each other to meet somewhere between Falaise and Argentan, a German *débâcle* on a gigantic scale would be inevitable. He therefore requested 12th United States Army Group to swing its right flank due north to Alençon 'at full strength and with all speed'. At the same time he ordered First Canadian and Second British armies to converge on Falaise 'with all possible speed'. A great victory was clearly imminent: the issue now was whether it would be annihilating or whether some of the Germans would get away.

Study of the events of the next ten days as recorded in the British and American official histories and in Eisenhower's, Montgomery's and Bradley's own personal accounts is liable to leave the reader in doubt as to where ultimate responsibility for the decisions now taken ultimately lay. Neither of the official histories, both of which are outstanding achievements in this field and of indisputable integrity, highlights the fact that from Monday 7 August, the day of the Mortain counter-attack and the Canadian attack 'Totalize' on the Falaise road, Eisenhower was in residence in his personal camp called 'Shellburst' near Tournières and Maisons. Tedder, his so-called British Deputy Commander, claimed that this move from the United Kingdom was at his suggestion. Here in an area surrounded by hedgerows ten feet high, except on the east where the hedge had been trimmed to provide a view of an adjoining field where liaison aircraft could land, he had his own caravan, two caravans for WACs and a spare which could be used for office purposes. Aides and other staff were accommodated in tents close by. This advanced head-quarters was connected with Montgomery's and Bradley's head-quarters by telephone. The signal centre and the press camp were a quarter of a mile away. From here he could and did reach Mont-gomery's and Bradley's headquarters within the hour by car. Apart from 10 August when he flew to England for the day to inspect 82nd and 101st Airborne Divisions, he was based here for the next ten crucial days. No one in the broadest sense was better placed to know who was doing what, to whom, how and why on the whole front.

Eisenhower by his very physical presence in Normandy assumed direct responsibility for the decision, now to be taken—a responsi-bility incidentally which the American people expected him to exer-cise. Bradley in fact goes so far as to say that it was he who suggested to Montgomery in Eisenhower's presence on 8 August that First and Third US armies should now swing north towards Flers and Argentan—a course incidentally which practically every commander, staff officer and press correspondent in the Allied armies would, if asked, have been more than eager to suggest and which justified itself by its obviousness. There is no doubt whatever that the orders now given to Patton and Hodges had the unanimous approval of Eisenhower, Bradley and Montgomery. In precise terms Patton was ordered to turn XV Corps due north from Le Mans and advance 'on the axis Alençon–Sées to the line of the Army Group boundary'. This ran along the line Sées–Carrouges south of Argentan. On ar-rival here he was to be prepared for further action against the enemy flank and rear in the direction of Argentan. Further to strengthen his arm he was given the 2nd French Armoured Division which had just arrived in the theatre. Meanwhile Hodges on his left was ordered to thrust towards Flers. At this stage Bradley apparently envisaged XV Corps on arrival at the Carrouges–Sées line south of Argentan acting as the anvil to the hammer of 21st Army Group thrusting towards Argentan—a course unlikely to appeal to Patton's aggressive temperament. He for his part interpreted his orders to mean that the aim of the Allied armies was to surround and destroy the German armies west of the Seine wherever found and without restriction. He accordingly directed xv Corps on Alençon with the armoured divisions leading, 5th Armored Division on the right and 2nd French Armoured Division on the left. On arrival at the line Carrouges–Sées they were to be prepared to fight their way northwards on a relatively narrow front until they made contact with the First Canadian Army: the enemy would thus be completely encircled. Boundaries in Patton's eyes were never sacrosanct unless they suited him. To protect his left in the 20-mile gap which separated his army from the First Army he moved the newly arrived 80th Division into the Évron area.

The French Armoured Division commanded by Major-General Le Clerc had a distinguished fighting record in Africa and much was expected of it. Now equipped with American material its men, exalted by their return to their native soil and the rapturous welcome of their countrymen and -women, were like hounds straining at the leash to take their revenge on their hated enemy and to restore the tarnished honour of France. After landing on 30 July they had moved into the Le Mans area on the 9th where the corps engineers had already constructed bridges to enable them to operate beyond the Sarthe. Soon after dawn on 10 August all was ready for the advance. Little was known of the enemy ahead. In fact the defence of the Le Mans–Alençon axis was the responsibility of LXXXV Corps consisting of two weak divisions, part of 9th Panzer Division and remnants of Panzer Lehr and Seventh Army. Sharp tank skirmishes and harassing artillery fire rather than larger-scale operations characterised the operations on this day. Driving forward under the eye of Patton himself they made 15 miles in the day, half way to Alençon, and lost 36 tanks in the process. Next day the armour bypassed the Forêt de Perseigne on both sides leaving the infantry to mop it up. A succession of road blocks covered by concentrated artillery fire slowed down the pace but nonetheless by nightfall 5th Armored Division reached the Sarthe and got a crossing north-east of Alençon: 2nd French Armoured Division paused momentarily to reconnoitre four miles south of the city. Now, thoroughly alarmed at this threat to his rear, von Kluge at last got permission from OKW to suspend the Mortain operations and to move Panzer Group

Eberbach south-eastwards towards Alençon with a view to mounting a full-scale counter-stroke against the west flank of xv Corps. With this end in view Eberbach drove into the town during the afternoon to find everything in confusion and packed with administrative troops and others fleeing in panic before Patton's tanks. There were burning vehicles knocked out by Allied aircraft and tanks everywhere both in and outside the town. In the course of two days' fighting, xv Corps had reduced 9th Panzer Division to the equivalent of about a battalion of infantry, a battalion of artillery and perhaps a dozen tanks. All that could be produced to defend Sées was a bakery company. When night fell a French task force audaciously forced its way over the bridges of the Sarthe and entered the town.

With dawn of the 12th, 5th Armored Division crashed through Mamers and seized Sées. Haislip, sensing the chaos behind the enemy lines, had already proclaimed Argentan as the day's objective: 5th Armored Division was to swing to the north-west and take the place whilst 2nd French Armoured Division took Carrouges. The possibility of a link-up with the Canadians south of Falaise by the two armoured divisions, supported by the 79th and 90th Divisions holding a shoulder between Argentan and Alençon, and the complete encirclement of the Germans now loomed large on the horizon of both Haislip and Patton. Both in fact planned to act in the spirit of the directive issued by Montgomery, still nominally commanding the land forces, on this day 'to destroy the enemy's main forces where they were'. If however it appeared likely that they might escape, the Allied armies were to be ready to execute the fuller plan, that is the wider encirclement west of the Seine previously envisaged.

Commanders are wont to claim that operations on which they pride themselves proceeded according to plan. In real life operations seldom do: as Hannibal remarked 2,300 years ago, war is dogged by the elements of chance and unpredictable human error. Both were present on this vital twelfth day of August. Astride the axis of xv Corps' line of advance lay the Forêt d'Écouves five miles southwest of Argentan. Haislip's orders to Le Clerc clearly instructed him to pass west of this forest and emphasised the fact that the main highway from Alençon to Argentan was reserved for the use of 5th

Armored Division and for their use only. Le Clerc in his eagerness to get forward chose deliberately to ignore this restriction and to send one combat command east of the forest, one through the centre and one on the west. These three French combat commands in due course partially cleared the woods and successfully fought their way forward to within sight of Écouche, and their objective for the day—the Argentan–Carrouges line. Unfortunately in the process they completely blocked the road from Sées to Argentan and held up for six hours the petrol trucks needed by 5th Armored Division's tanks for their assault on Argentan. By the time their attack got going in the late afternoon the Germans had had time to organise a strong defence and the attack did not get very far. Launched six hours earlier it would have encountered little opposition. During the day however units of 116th Panzer Division of Panzer Group Eberbach had arrived from Mortain. The rest of the division arrived during the succeeding night, bolstering up the defence of their east flank with what remained of 331st Division. During the day the xv Corps had destroyed 100 tanks and taken 1,500 prisoners. Despite the check they had administered to 5th Armored Division the situation of Panzer Group Eberbach that night was, in actual fact, desperate. 116th Panzer Division had had to be committed on arrival in a defensive role; 1st ss and 2nd Panzer Divisions due to become available next day, the 13th, would have a hard struggle to survive let alone mount a full-scale attack. Their supply base at Alençon was in American hands. So complete was the Allied dominance of the air in excellent flying weather that supply and troop movement by day was for all practical purposes impossible. If the Canadians got Falaise and the Americans Argentan only 13 miles would separate them. The moment when the Germans on the Western Front would be completely encircled seemed very near. When night fell Haislip, undeterred by the check to 5th Armored Division, ordered Le Clerc to take Argentan on the morrow and 5th Armored Division to be ready south-east of the town to drive through the French and head all-out to meet the Canadians at Falaise. On telling Patton what he intended to do and asking for additional troops to block the roads north of Alençon, he got prompt and wholehearted approval in the early hours of the 13th. On reaching Falaise he was to continue 'to push on slowly until contact with our Allies was made'. According to Bradley it was on this night that Patton said to him jocularly on the telephone, 'Let me go on to Falaise and we'll drive the British into the sea for another Dunkirk.'

Le Clerc was off the mark with the dawn of the 13th. First he cleared the Forêt d'Écouves, then pushed on to Carrouges and Écouche and, as ordered, proceeded to build up a line to Argentan. One of his patrols actually got into the place but was soon flung out. 5th Armored Division's efforts however to break through ran into well concealed 88s on dominating ground north of Argentan and were momentarily stalled. 1st ss and 2nd Panzer Divisions had in fact somehow or other succeeded in breaking clear at Mortain and despite incessant air attack, traffic jams and lack of fuel got through. Nevertheless the situation of Panzer Group Eberbach on this day, the 13th, at Argentan was desperate in the extreme. Eberbach had to push his troops into action piecemeal: 1st ss Panzer Division arrived with only 30 tanks and minus its infantry; 2nd Panzer Division had only 25 tanks and was at half strength in men; 116th Panzer Division had 15 tanks; 9th Panzer Division had been for all practical purposes destroyed on the previous day. In all Eberbach had only 70 tanks; his men after six days' almost continuous exposure to artillery and air bombardment were tired: inevitably his defences at Argentan were paper thin. In sharp contrast, xv Corps could muster over 300 Shermans and 22 battalions of artillery and two infantry divisions, all with sky-high morale, fresh and under the experienced leadership of Patton, Haislip, Le Clerc and Oliver all spoiling for a fight and, added to all these advantages, complete command of the air. The Canadians admittedly, largely because their commanders of armour lacked experience and because their air support had so far been hamfisted, were temporarily halted. Nevertheless Montgomery had in hand another massive blow on the Falaise road called 'Tractable', once more supported by every available aircraft of Bomber Command, for the morrow. The British Second Army and First us Army were relentlessly pushing back the infantry and armour on their fronts despite the difficulties of the country. Sepp Dietrich, as tough a commander as any in the whole German Army, had already told OKW that the

Fifth Panzer Army was on the verge of collapse and that if they, what remained of Seventh Army and Panzer Group Eberbach were not given permission to withdraw without delay they would all be inevitably surrounded without hope of escape. The stage was set for a gigantic triumph in which Patton, Haislip, xv Corps and the Canadians would play the leading roles.

Then suddenly early in the afternoon xv Corps was halted in its tracks by a peremptory and unequivocal order from Bradley to Patton and transmitted by him to Haislip: all further movement northwards to meet the Canadians must stop. Any troops who might be in the vicinity of Argentan were to be pulled back; xv Corps was 'to concentrate for operations in another direction'. Patton protested but obeyed. He made no attempt however to conceal his resentment and to the day he died remained convinced that xv Corps 'could easily have entered Falaise and closed the gap'—an opinion which the Germans concerned were later unanimously to endorse and which subsequent research completely justifies. This decision of Bradley's to pull up Patton in full cry and thus stop him closing what by now had gained the name of the Falaise–Argentan Gap has been the subject of considerable controversy between highly qualified historians and others. It is therefore with due humility that a writer whose sole claim to comment rests on the fact that he was commanding an infantry brigade of Second Army at the time and that, when the gap was finally closed on 19 August, he managed to find the time whilst waiting to take his place in the advance to the Seine, to drive round what had been the xv Corps front at Argentan. His impression then was that if Patton had been given a free hand he would have closed the gap, probably on the 14th and that hardly any of the Germans would have got away. The country was not unsuitable for armoured tactics exploited by a master hand. Contrary to the popular view, most of the German casualties in armour seemed to have been the result of anti-tank and artillery fire rather than air action.

There is no doubt that the decision had the approval of Eisenhower. He was on the spot and had access to the same information as Bradley. According to Butcher's diary, Eisenhower dined at Bradley's headquarters the night the decision was reached not to

At the time of the breakout at Avranches

Below: On the road to Rheims, August 30, 1944
Right: The Liberator — Patton finds time in his headlong thrust across France to talk to children — Third week August 1944

"Radio th' ol' man we'll be late on account of a thousand-mile detour."

Over the Rhine, March 23, 1945

Boston, Mass., June 1945

George S. Patton Jr. General 02605.3D Army

proceed northwards of Argentan. In the end therefore, it is hard to evade the conclusion that responsibility for what happened was his, a responsibility which incidentally he afterwards neither emphasised nor evaded. He had in fact by his very presence in France tacitly taken over command of the land forces, the role still assumed by the British to be that of Montgomery until Eisenhower's main headquarters was established on the Continent. He was thus already playing two parts as he continued to do for the rest of the war—Supreme Commander and at the same time Commander of the Allied Land Forces. This is like a musician trying to play the first fiddle and conduct the orchestra at the same time.

It was rumoured soon afterwards that the air forces had dropped timed bombs behind the German lines and that if xv Corps had advanced they would have had to face the possibility of being blown up, 'hoist by their own petard'. Knowledge of this risk is alleged to have induced Bradley to hold them back. In fact the bombs in question were fused for a maximum of 12 hours' delay: this excuse can therefore be dismissed. The troops, both American and British, anyhow were already well-schooled to take a risk of this sort in their stride and to treat the prospect of being blown up by their own airmen as one of the facts of life.

Bradley later stated that if xv Corps had been allowed to go forward they might have collided head on with the British and Canadians and caused 'a calamitous battle between friends' which is a polite way of saying they might have shot each other. He would have done well not to make this excuse. Indeed he himself suggested later that a conspicuous feature or landmark might have been laid down as a junction point; alternatively, parallel axis of advance could have been prescribed for xv Corps and First Canadian Army thus cutting the German escape routes in two places instead of one. Incidentally both British and Americans would have had no difficulty in putting up agreed light signals: both had ample supplies of pyrotechnics. Every man in the British armies had, or should have had, a virulent yellow triangle of celanese to indicate his position to the air forces. The opportunity had not yet arisen for them to be given away as souvenirs to French girls only too eager to be liberated. Wireless security too was deplorably bad: in the bedlam on the air American and Canadian accents came over with an unmistakable clarity only equalled by those of the Scots, especially the Glaswegians, and of the Cockneys. The air in fact was a never-ending babble of Allied voices. No one could possibly have remained long in ignorance of the near approach of friends. Finally, in the British armies, divisional commanders and others, if still in doubt as to the whereabouts of their allies, could always get into one of the Auster aircraft of their attached AOP Flight and go up to look for themselves. There was no mistaking the white star conspicuously painted on all Allied tanks.

A further objection to allowing Allied forces to approach each other seems to have been that it would have made the allocation of artillery and air targets difficult. This is true but it is for the solution of this type of problem that staffs exist: it was not insoluble. In the highly fluid operations of the next few days the Allied artillery seem to have had little difficulty judging by the shambles in the Forêt de Gouffern, most of which was their handiwork.

Bradley in his book *A Soldier's Story* stated that he was reluctant to send American troops beyond Argentan because he preferred 'a solid shoulder at Argentan rather than a broken neck at Falaise'. Later he said that he had not doubted the ability of xv Corps to close the gap—what he doubted was their ability to keep it closed. Quite erroneously he seems to have believed that elements of 19 German divisions were already 'sluicing' (sic) through the gap and would literally in a gigantic ugly rush trample down the American line. Anybody with the forward troops, British or American, could have told him that it was not the Germans' hurry to depart but their reluctance to go which was at the root of all their trouble. There may well be some justification for the view that considerations of security justified to some extent the halting of xv Corps. There was no threat from the east but on their west flank there was an empty gap of about 25 miles between the 2nd French Armoured Division and the 1st Division of First Army at Mayenne. It is just conceivable that Eberbach might have exploited this as, in fact, OKW expected him to do. Bradley does not stress this: indeed it does seem improbable that Panzer Group Eberbach, having staged a costly fiasco at Mortain five days previously and been battered almost round the clock by the Allied air forces and artillery ever since, would have been allowed by Patton to pull off a spectacular *coup*. In retrospect it is astonishing that Bradley should have doubted Patton's ability to deal with a situation of this sort.

In one respect it must be admitted Bradley was technically within his rights in not going beyond Argentan by the fact that the boundary between his Army Group zone and 21 Army Group ran south of Argentan. Bradley never asked Montgomery's permission to cross it: neither did Montgomery forbid it. The two might have been taking part in a football match instead of a battle. This is all the more surprising in view of the fact that it was Bradley who had originally suggested the short hook to Argentan. Montgomery overestimated the ability of the Canadian commanders, with the exception of Simonds, making his main effort down the Falaise road, and expected them to get to Argentan first. He also underestimated the dynamic drive imparted by Patton and Haislip to xv Corps. Later Bradley stated that he and Patton doubted 'Monty's ability to close the gap at Argentan' and that they had 'waited impatiently' for permission to continue northward. They had apparently impotently watched the enemy escaping eastward through the gap, squeezed by the British Second Army like toothpaste out of a tube. He later wrote: 'If Monty's tactics mystified me, they dismayed Eisenhower even more. And . . . a shocked Third Army looked on helplessly as its quarry fled (while) Patton raged at Montgomery's blunder.' This ill accords with Patton's own statement in his book *War As I Knew It* that xv Corps 'could easily have entered Falaise and completely closed the gap . . . this halt was a great mistake, as I was certain that we could have entered Falaise and I was not certain that the British would'. With his two subordinates, Bradley and Montgomery standing on their dignity at this crucial moment, Eisenhower, who was on the spot, would have been fully justified in intervening. Indeed he thought so later, implying long after the event that the gap could have been closed and the Germans annihilated. The truth seems to be that consciousness of his own lack of experience of front-line fighting led him to accept advice rather than make his own decision. He never really got the feel of the battle. Most certainly his intelligence advisers failed to give him a sound assessment of the predicament of the Germans in the pocket.

Posterity, with its knowledge of the actual plight of the Germans at the time denied to Eisenhower, may justifiably conclude that the complete annihilation of the Germans could have been achieved and a decision reached which might well have enabled the war to be ended in 1944. Patton and Haislip, with the 2nd French Armoured Division, 5th Armored Division and the rest of xv Corps at grips with the battered rump of Panzer Group Eberbach, had it within their power to fight a decisive action at half-price in terms of American life. Argentan might have been as great a battle honour in the annals of the American Army as Second Manassas or Chancellorsville. The French would have been able to add another long-overdue victory to the impressive list on the Arc de Triomphe—also at a bargain price. As Le Clerc bitterly wrote to de Gaulle at the time 'I had the feeling that it was 1940 in reverse—complete enemy confusion, surprised columns etc. The climax on the French front at Argentan–Falaise could have been splendid. The high command decided otherwise: history will condemn them.' Eisenhower and Bradley might even have qualified for inclusion in the same class as Robert E. Lee. They had under their command, eager to take all risks, the most able leader of armoured forces the Allies ever produced in World War Two, at the height of his powers, a man who had devoted the whole of his life for an opportunity such as this, commanding troops whose morale was at its zenith and supported by overwhelming airpower. They failed to exploit his talents and in the process took the first of the steps which would ensure the unnecessary prolongation of the war to 1945.

12

The Wider Envelopment

Ahead for a hundred miles in the August sunlight towards Paris stretched the very heart of France and Europe, a many-coloured chequer board of gently rolling plains, cornfields and small woods— country over which Patton's tanks could romp almost without let or hindrance. In the chalk plateaux of Évreux, Dreux, Chartres and Châteaudun lay unlimited sites for the airfields which would be needed for the support of the armies when they reached the Seine. A magnificent road net traversed the whole area running generally north-east and east with ample laterals to north and south. The Loire guarded the right flank. Bradley now ordered Patton to leave Le Clerc's Second Armoured Division and the 90th Infantry Division to hold the position at Argentan and advance due east to a line running roughly north and south through Orléans, Chartres and Dreux. This move would bring them on a 60-mile front within striking distance of Paris and it was here that he proposed to halt for a while for logistic reasons. This was one of the great moments of Patton's life. With characteristic exuberance he declared at a conference on 14 August: 'As of today Third Army has advanced farther and faster than any Army in history.' It would now go farther still, xv Corps directed on Dreux, xx Corps on Chartres and xii Corps on Orléans. All on reaching this line were to be prepared to thrust forward north, north-east or due east according to the demands of the situation as they found it. When briefing Haislip he added 'If I say so myself, it is a hell of a good plan and wholly mine.'

A disarming feature of Bradley's character was his frankness in admitting his mistakes. Having let loose Patton to the east beyond recall, a decision incidentally which he had taken on his own without reference either to Eisenhower or Montgomery, he had second thoughts: should he instead have directed him north-east on Cham-

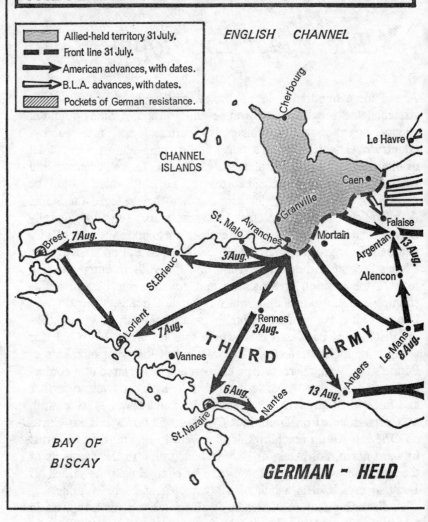

THE ALLIED ADVANCE DURING AUGUST

Allied-held territory 31 July.

Front line 31 July.

American advances, with dates.

B.L.A. advances, with dates.

Pockets of German resistance.

ENGLISH CHANNEL

Cherbourg

Le Havre

CHANNEL ISLANDS

Caen

St. Malo

Avranches

Granville

Falaise

Brest *7Aug.*

3Aug.

Mortain

Argentan *13Aug.*

St.Brieuc

Alencon

Lorient *7Aug.*

Rennes *3Aug.*

T H I R D

A R M Y

Le Mans *8Aug.*

Vannes

6Aug.

Nantes

13 Aug. Angers

St.Nazaire

BAY OF BISCAY

GERMAN - HELD

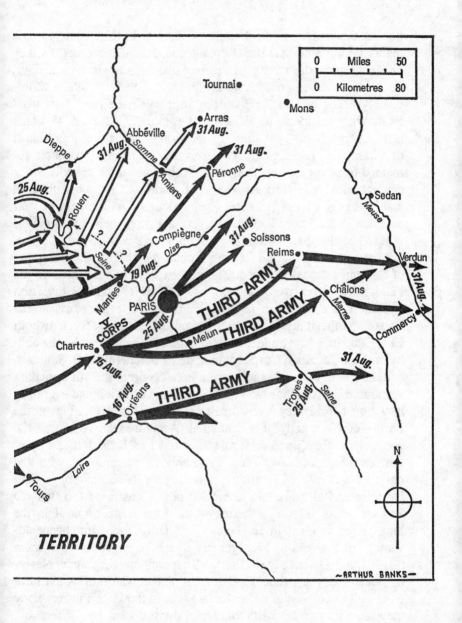

TERRITORY

~ARTHUR BANKS~

bois at the mouth of the Falaise pocket? If he had done so it is highly improbable that the Germans could have succeeded as they did in keeping the mouth of the bag open for a further six days; certainly far fewer would have escaped the Allied net. When Montgomery asked him for help on the 16th he ordered v Corps from First Army to intervene. When they eventually attacked 48 hours later Eberbach brought them to an abrupt halt three miles short of Chambois. The six-mile gap between Trun and Chambois remained open for another two days. 90th Division admittedly made contact with the Polish Armoured Division at Chambois on 19th and broke the ring of II Panzer Corps around Coudehard. For four days the Poles' losses had been severe and their heroism homeric: relieved earlier their sufferings would not have been so great. It was not until the 21st that all fighting around the ghastly charnel house of St-Lambert finally ceased. The last six days of the Battle of the Falaise Gap from the launching of 'Tractable' and the diversion of Patton to the east on the 14th constitute a tragic story, as the Canadian official historian admits, of misapplied brute force by both First Canadian Army and Bomber Command, redeemed by the ability of the II Canadian Corps commander, Lt-General H. G. Simonds, and the valour of the Canadians and Poles. Neither the 4th Canadian Armoured Division nor the Polish Armoured Division had ever been in action before they were thrust into the fiercest fighting of the Battle for Normandy. The Canadian Armoured Division was the youngest of the Canadian formations and had been denied opportunities for collective training. Inevitably its commander, who had only taken it over in February, was sacked; its shortcomings were by no means all traceable to him. It is fair comment too that the 2nd Canadian Infantry Division would have done better if in the long period it spent in England it had taken more intelligent advantage of the lessons Montgomery had been eager to teach them in 1941 and 1942, only to meet with supercilious resistance. Nevertheless it does seem that the Canadian official historian would have done well to emphasise more the fact that in the Fifth Panzer Army they were up against battle-hardened divisions led by officers and NCOs of outstanding quality and experience, fighting literally with their backs to the wall and prepared to pay the price of the terrible slaughter about St-Lambert where in the closing stages 'the dead lay so close as to be practically touching' and where the stench of decay was so strong that even the pilots of light aircraft from above could smell it. Bradley indeed had good reason for his misgivings after he had turned Patton away from his immediate prey at Argentan on the 13th, eight days before the final closure of the gap.

Meanwhile with few maps, practically no knowledge of the enemy situation ahead and without prior reconnaissance the XII Corps under Major-General Gilbert R. Cook, a First War veteran had plunged boldly forward on the 15th towards Orléans by the direct route and also via Châteaudun. Just before nightfall they swamped the anti-tank and anti-aircraft defences of the large airfield at Orléans and pressed on in the fading light to the outskirts of the city. Next morning whilst two armoured columns attacked from the north the 137th Infantry burst into the city from the west to receive a rapturous welcome from the inhabitants. Resistance was slight: wild rejoicing continued all day. That night the world learnt that the city of Joan of Arc, as the Press naturally hastened to call it, had fallen to Patton and the Third Army. The secret of his whereabouts was out at last; there is no truth however in the allegation that Eisenhower had withheld the announcement out of jealousy.

Patton's critics have asserted that at this time he failed to appreciate the possibility of German troops south of the Loire raiding his communications and those of 12th Army Group. Nothing could be farther from the truth. Weyland and XIX Tactical Air Command throughout dominated the line of the river both by day and night, engaging formed bodies of Germans wherever found. Artillery observation aircraft kept continuous observation over the Loir, a tributary of the Loire. To supplement this air surveillance 4th Armored Division swept the north bank of the river from Lorient to Orléans. These operations, combined with the activities of the FFI, now supplying Koch with a vast amount of information some of which was accurate, so shook the nerves of the Germans that they blew up all bridges as far east as Blois; thenceforward to Orléans 117th Engineer Group destroyed the rest. Patton's southern flank was thus reasonably secure.

Loyalty to his friends was one of Patton's endearing characteristics. When Orléans fell he found himself faced by a personal dilemma which moved him deeply. Cook, apart from being an old friend, was also a fine soldier and an audacious leader whom Patton could ill spare. He now had to go sick with a circulatory malady which was so severe that his retention in command of XII Corps could no longer be justified. To have to deprive him of his command at the very climax of his career shook Patton to the core, realising as he did the mortal blow he was delivering to an old friend. He did all he could to soften the blow telephoning Eisenhower direct and asking him as a personal favour to ensure he got the DSM he certainly deserved.

XX Corps' thrust to Chartres was equally speedy and dramatic. Originally directed on Dreux the 7th Armored Division had made 15 miles on 14 August before it was diverted in the afternoon to Chartres. In consequence the re-adjustment necessary during the following night resulted in some delay when the advance was resumed on the 15th. On reaching the outskirts of Chartres, CCB attacked with two forces: one entering the city from the north-west and the other from the south-west. In the fading light the latter column suddenly struck strong resistance. What had happened was this: First German Army, in whose area the city lay, had designated it as a rendezvous point for stragglers from the Normandy battle. These on arrival had been organised into battlegroups, a technique in which the Germans, partly as a result of experience in North Africa and Russia, excelled. Furthermore when CCB burst into the city the commander of the First Army in person, *General der Infanterie* Kurt von der Chevallerie, happened to be holding a conference there to decide how the 48th Division from Northern France and the 338th Division from the south, ordered there by Hitler, should be deployed on arrival. In face of this unexpected resistance the tanks recoiled in the gathering darkness. During the night 35th Division reached the south-western outskirts of the city into which further German reinforcements were now pouring. In consequence XX Corps next day was unable to secure more than a precarious hold over part of the built-up area. There was further indecisive fighting in the streets on the 17th and it was not until the 18th that all opposition could be crushed by a full-dress operation, by infantry and armour supported by the Corps artillery. Great care was taken to avoid doing undue damage to the ancient buildings by artillery fire and in particular to the historic cathedral. Over 2,000 prisoners were taken and a large German Air Force installation captured intact. xx Corps now stood within 50 miles of Paris.

Meanwhile on the northern flank xv Corps with 79th Division on the right directed on Nogent le-Roi, and 5th Armored Division on Dreux had advanced 60 miles from Argentan, brushing aside contemptuously a few lightly defended road blocks. By the morning of the 16th, 5th Division were over the Eure and encircling Dreux which the Germans were quick to abandon. Simultaneously 79th Division captured Nogent le-Roi almost unopposed and established a bridgehead over the Eure. Patton now had five bridges over the Eure and at Dreux stood within striking distance of Paris, now only 37 miles away. The immediate need however, as Eisenhower, Bradley, Patton and Montgomery clearly saw was not to liberate Paris but to complete the destruction of Army Group B. They therefore planned to pinch out the city rather than become involved in fighting in the streets not only with the Germans but amongst the French themselves. They faced too without enthusiasm the problem of having to divert 4,000 tons a day of supplies to feed the population, now erroneously believed to be on the verge of starvation: the longer it could be deferred the better. Patton's unprecedented advance in fact was placing an almost intolerable burden on the supply system. In under four weeks he had stretched the line of supply from St-Lô almost to the Seine. In Brittany he was conducting several sieges. Now his leading troops were 250 miles from Cherbourg. The railway to Le Mans was working but bombed bridges were hampering further progress: French rolling stock was short and decrepit as a result of the Allied bombing of engines and, in particular railway workshops, both before and since D-Day. Already four British truck companies had had to be borrowed to keep Patton on the move and a shortage of petrol was beginning to be felt. Until the third week of August air transport had been held in reserve for airborne operations in the Orléans Gap. Patton's progress however now enabled it to be released for logistic purposes: from now onwards a daily emergency airlift for Third Army would become a matter of routine and, incidentally, a subject of constant debate between his head-quarters' staff and Eisenhower's who seldom met to the satisfaction of either party. Despite the strain on his supply services Bradley on the 17th now ordered Patton to push forward xv Corps a further 25 miles from Dreux to the Seine, and to seize the communications centre of Mantes Gassicourt, cutting off in the process Germans attempting to escape to the south-east. Simultaneously he brought forward xix Corps to fill the gap vacated by xv Corps between Gace and Dreux.

William the Conqueror sacked and burnt Mantes in 1087. When 79th Division entered the place unopposed they found that it had been heavily bombed by the RAF and not improved in the process. The bridge over the Seine, which here is 800 feet wide, had been destroyed; machine-gun fire was coming from the northern bank. Patrols sent to within a few miles of the suburbs of Paris reported many small parties of Germans making for the capital but no large formed bodies.

The time had now come to round off the Battle of Normandy. Despite the disaster at Falaise, Model still retained a measure of control over the remnants of Seventh Army and Fifth Panzer Army, now combined under Sepp Dietrich and estimated at 75,000 men and 250 tanks, withdrawing to the crossings over the Seine between les Andelys and Rouen with the main concentration in the two big loops of the river, south and west of the city. They included troops from the Fifteenth Army who had not been involved in the Normandy battle west of Falaise and who were comparatively fresh. Accordingly Bradley, Montgomery and Dempsey met on the morning of the 19th to decide how their final encirclement was to be achieved. Immediately west of the Seine with its main axis parallel to it, is a superb road net ideally suited for a strong thrust by xv and xix Corps from the positions they had now reached, on to the concentration of Germans south and south-west of Rouen. Their advance here however would involve crossing the front of the Second British Army. Bradley tactfully offered to provide transport for the long 300-mile haul round the rear of the First Army and through the area of the Third Army. Montgomery, short of men as a result of two months' fighting and with little prospect of reinforcement and now planning for his next bound to the Somme and Antwerp, declined Bradley's kind offer without reluctance. The administrative inconvenience of American troops operating in the British sector would have to be accepted. Patton's troops would thus not be denied the opportunity of being in at the death. Accordingly 5th Armored Division of xv Corps was diverted northwards along the west bank of the Seine on to Louviers and xix Corps onto Elbeuf. That night, Patton, who had spent the day at Mantes, flew back in bad weather to get Bradley's approval for his plan to establish a bridgehead at Mantes four to six miles deep, and to build a bridge there for vehicles, tanks and heavy equipment. Bradley quickly gave permission not only for the crossing at Mantes but also for further crossings to be carried out with all speed east of Paris by xx Corps at Melun and Fontainebleau, and by xii Corps at Sens. Near Mantes, 79th Division had found a dam which provided a narrow footway across the river. That night in torrential rain, hanging on to each other in single file the 313th Infantry made their way across unmolested. Other troops got over with light equipment in assault boats. By the afternoon a light bridge had been constructed and by nightfall the greater part of 79th Division was over the Seine. Next day they flushed out the command post of Army Group B five miles down stream at la Roche Guyon and chased away the German division which had been moving into the area. By the 23rd a Bailey bridge capable of taking all classes of traffic was open.

5th Armored Division given the objective of Louviers by Patton, were off with the dawn on the 20th. It was to take them five days, fighting a succession of battlegroups, to cover the 20 miles to Louviers. The country favoured the defence and the Germans fought well. At Louviers they made contact with the Canadians and then withdrew to the south. xix Corps simultaneously, on their left, fought their way forward to Elbeuf. Here they struck stubborn resistance. A fully coordinated attack by 28th Division had therefore to be mounted on 25 August to take the place before handing it over to the Canadians. Their task completed, they then withdrew to their own zone, leaving behind them a clear run for the Second British Army to close up with the Seine about Vernon and les Andelys.

Although during these last days of August the Germans had succeeded in getting some thousands of vehicles across the Seine this American drive did in fact deprive them of half the ferries they had been using. In consequence the two big loops made by the river south and south-west of Rouen became packed with troops and transport waiting to cross under the hammer of the RAF and the Canadian artillery. Carnage similar to that in the Falaise gap soon developed. Nonetheless five further days of desperate fighting lay ahead before the killing ceased. In the tangled mass of some 4,000 burnt out and smashed vehicles on the south bank there were at least 150 tanks. Speidel, still Chief of Staff of Army Group B, and ironically to be Commander-in-Chief of the *Bundeswehr* in happier days, thought that a great opportunity finally to seal off the survivors of his Army Group was missed here. In his opinion Patton's 5th Armored Division should have thrust along the excellent roads on the north bank of the Seine instead of the south and sealed off the exits from Rouen on the far side of the river. Liddell Hart thought so too. Had they done so, Speidel was convinced, the morale and efficiency of 5th Armored Division being at its zenith, all that remained of Army Group B would have been eliminated. As it was, between 20,000 and 50,000 escaped to fight again another day, notably at Arnhem. Patton expressed no recorded opinion on this matter which lay in Bradley's province not his. In any case his eyes were now turned elsewhere to the dazzling prospects offered by the Seine crossings south of Paris and the great roads leading from there to the heart of Germany.

On the 21st he had let loose XII Corps, now under Eddy, for a further great bound forward. CCA of 4th Armored Division in the lead gathered speed as it advanced, bypassed resistance at Montargis and raced for Sens. Here they surprised German officers on leave in dress uniform, captured the city and, by dawn next day had a bridgehead over the Yonne. German resistance in Montargis caved in to attack by 35th Division several days later. On the 25th, 4th Armored Division lunged forward a further 40 miles towards Troyes and, deploying on the outskirts in desert formation with tanks approximately 100 yards apart, roared into the town.

XX Corps progress on their left to seize bridgeheads over the Seine between Melun and Montereau was equally fast and overwhelming. Despite strong opposition at the Essone river the 5th Division made 40 miles on the 21st; pressing on next day in the face of increasing resistance about Fontainebleau, they reached the Seine at Montereau on the 23rd and got a crossing. On their left 7th Armored Division made equally spectacular progress towards Melun. Thus by the 25th, Third Army had four bridgeheads over the upper Seine south of Paris between Melun and Troyes, and had handed over the bridgehead at Mantes to First Army. So great had the speed, dash and efficiency of Patton's army been that they had literally swept large numbers of bewildered Germans off their feet.

In the heady atmosphere of the Liberation nothing seemed impossible to them. Evacuation figures for battle exhaustion or self-inflicted wounds had sunk almost to zero. There is no better stimulant to high morale than success and this was success on a gigantic scale. For the French the foul smell of German occupation vanished with the arrival of the first American tank. The people, normally ebullient, abandoned all restraint, pressing wine and fruit upon the conquerors and garlanding the tanks with flowers. The sun shone and the fruit was ripe. All and more that the Germans had taken by force was freely offered and eagerly taken. In every town and village as it was liberated the *tricolore* of the Republic appeared like magic along with hastily improvised versions of the Stars and Stripes. Everyone came out into the streets and never seemed to tire of waving as the troops went by. The children shouted themselves hoarse sometimes demanding 'Cigarettes pour papa'; mothers held up their babies to see the soldiers. The old men of the First War proudly displaying their medals pressed forward to shake their liberators' hands. The mayors of every village and town, resplendent in their big *tricolore* sashes, proudly awaited the chance to pay their respects to the American commanders as they passed through. Of the deeply felt gratitude to the Americans of the mass of the French people there was ample evidence; so far as the peasants and workers were concerned it was without reservations: their liberation raised no problems which could not easily be solved.

This unfortunately could not be said of Paris and its citizens, from whom reports were now filtering through the lines of imminent starvation. In some quarters it was alleged that the city would need a daily lift of supplies equivalent to half that of 12th Army Group. With the battle still raging around the crossings at Rouen, Eisenhower and Bradley were hoping to defer the relief of the city still longer. On one point they were both firm: Patton must not become involved, firstly because he and his troops must concentrate all their thoughts and energy on the continuation of the pursuit and secondly because they remembered what had happened in Morocco, when he had been allowed a far too free hand in the political field. Some of his French friends too were far from *persona grata* with Roosevelt and Churchill. Neither Eisenhower nor Bradley looked forward to becoming involved in the political witches' brew in the French capital and the real danger of fighting in the streets between the Communist, Pétainist and Gaullist factions. Events in Paris however forced their hands.

On the evening of 22 August a small Citroen carrying five rather seedy looking civilians had driven into the American lines at Neauples-le-Vieux. No one took much notice of it at first until one of the party, a British agent, managed to persuade the local unit that they had a message for General Eisenhower. Duly escorted to the rear they reached Corps headquarters about midnight. Here a suspicious duty officer took his time to satisfy himself that they were sufficiently important to justify onward despatch to Patton's headquarters near Chartres. They were in fact a deputation from Paris consisting of Nordling, the Swedish Consul's brother, a British agent, Jean Laurent a former cabinet secretary to de Gaulle, and a German officer in civilian clothes representing von Choltitz, the Military Governor of Paris. Brought before Patton about 8 a.m. they informed him that they had come to arrange a suspension of hostilities. He at once raised the telephone and told Bradley. Convinced that all they wanted was 'to save Paris and probably save the Germans' and still irritated because he had been officially told that the liberation of Paris was no concern of his, Patton then contemptuously despatched the party in light aircraft to Bradley's headquarters at Laval.

The actual liberation of Paris forms but a very small part of the saga of Patton and the Third Army. The myth however that the city was liberated by the spontaneous uprising of the Resistance and the people of Paris and the lone efforts of Le Clerc's 2nd Armoured Division, which has been fostered by interested parties since World War Two, in justice to Bradley's Army Group needs to be dispelled. The truth is that without the support of Gerow and the v Corps and the connivance of von Choltitz, the German Military Governor, Paris might well have been the scene of large-scale bloodshed in the streets and irreparable damage to historic monuments. De Gaulle was not the unanimous choice of the French people.

As Patton's tanks thrust forward towards the Seine, de Gaulle, now in France as head of the provisional government recognised by United States and Great Britain, had begun to apply pressure on Eisenhower to sanction the forward move of Le Clerc's division from Argentan to lead the entry of the Allies into the capital. He even had the effrontery to hint that if Eisenhower did not consent he himself would order Le Clerc forward on his own. Where Le Clerc would have got his supplies and petrol from is unknown. He certainly tried Eisenhower's forbearance and urbanity to the limit. Nevertheless Eisenhower with great magnanimity on 22 August gave permission for the move of the division as part of v Corps towards Paris. Accordingly v Corps with Le Clerc's division on the left and 4th Infantry Division on the right duly forced its way through the ring of German troops on the periphery on 24 August. It was no walkover; German resistance although sporadic was at times determined. It is certain that without the help of 4th Infantry Division Le Clerc's division would have suffered more severely than they did. They might even have become involved in fighting with the large Communist element in the Resistance forces with disastrous results. Regrettably some of the toughest men in the FFI were Communists and had as little use for de Gaulle as they had for Pétain and Laval.

In retrospect de Gaulle's attitude to his major ally to whom, along with the British, he owed almost everything was discourteous and high-handed. He personally appeared in Paris on the afternoon of 25 August, after spending the previous night in the President's bedroom in the Château de Rambouillet between Marshal Pétain's sheets, uninvited and unannounced. Le Clerc treated Barton, the commander of 4th Infantry Division with rudeness only equalled by that of Koenig in his dealings with Gerow the Commander of

v Corps. Whether de Gaulle liked it or not, Gerow was the representative of the Supreme Allied Commander in the city. Regrettably
behind the scenes of jubilation in the streets there was much friction
and misunderstanding between v Corps, de Gaulle and his myrmidons. To add to Gerow's embarrassments, Brigadier-General Pleas
B. Rogers and the Communications Zone advance party descended
almost immediately on the city and proceeded to requisition all the
best hotels for the veritable army of military bureaucrats and their
hangers-on soon to arrive in their train. From the very moment of
entry Koenig, appointed Military Governor by de Gaulle without
even mentioning the fact to Gerow, had started to issue orders on
all civil matters. There was regrettably much plain speaking. To
cap the lot, when Eisenhower very politely asked Montgomery to
join him in making a formal call on the 26th on de Gaulle in Paris,
other duties prevented him from accepting the invitation. Reluctance
to take part in a ceremony in which he would not be playing the
leading role had nothing to do with Montgomery's refusal. For the
moment the British, mindful of the resentment they had incurred
when they stood alone in 1940 in sinking the French Fleet because
they could not trust Pétain and Laval, were happy to allow their
major ally to carry what Churchill from bitter experience had called
the Cross of Lorraine.

In fact de Gaulle behaved at this time with a lack of grace bor-
dering on arrogance. Although the population of Paris looked well-
nourished he at once demanded and got from Eisenhower 1,500 tons
of supplies of food, medicines and petrol, to be delivered per day
including 500 tons by airlift at the expense of military needs. He
also pressed for vast quantities of arms, equipment and uniforms
for his troops and, according to Eisenhower, two divisions to help
him to maintain order in the city. In liberating France and putting
de Gaulle in power the Americans had already sustained over 125,-
000 casualties since D-Day. One of their reasons for staging 'Anvil',
the landing in the south of France on 15 August had been to land
French troops to support de Gaulle's government. They were at least
entitled to greater gratitude and courtesy than they got from de
Gaulle. Whether relations would have been more cordial if Patton
rather than Gerow and Bradley had been entrusted with the liber-

ation of the city will never be known but is at least probable. This at any rate can be said: he would have given to the proceedings an air of drama and historical fitness beyond the capacity of anyone other than Churchill himself—and acted de Gaulle completely off the stage to the plaudits of the population of Paris and the world Press. His personal relations with Juin and Koenig, both of whom went out of their way to pay their respects to him on their way to Paris, were excellent. Le Clerc had been thoroughly at home under his command. Above all he loved France after his own country and spoke and read French, accomplishments denied to his fellow American commanders. Admittedly he lacked political sense and on his record, Eisenhower had good reason for keeping him out of Paris at this time. This at least can be said: in doing so he denied history a giant spectacular drama exceeding the wildest dreams of de Mille in the magnificent setting of the Arc de Triomphe, the Invalides, Notre Dame and Napoleon's Tomb.

Although the fighting about the crossings at Vernon and Rouen did not finally die down until the end of the month the fall of Paris constitutes the real end of the Battle of Normandy. In it Patton and the Third Army had advanced over 400 miles in 26 days, fought on two fronts and effectively guarded the southern flank along the line of the Loire by the use of air power combined with close cooperation between the light ground forces and the FFI. In the process they had put out of action in killed, wounded and prisoners of war well over 100,000 Germans and captured or destroyed over 500 tanks and about 700 guns. It can be safely said that if they had been allowed to administer the *coup de grâce* at Argentan, as Patton wished, their contribution would have been much greater. All this had been achieved at a cost of little more than 16,000 casualties, that is less than 13 per cent of the total American losses in Normandy. Admittedly they had not entered the battle until the First Army, Second British and First Canadian Armies and the Allied Air Forces had in eight agonising weeks ground down the Seventh and Fifth Panzer Armies to the verge of exhaustion; admittedly too, many of Third Army's advances had been made in the face of minimal resistance. Eisenhower's other armies could wryly complain with some justification, that although they had borne the burden and heat of the day in the Hedgerows, at St-Lô and around Caen, Third Army got in terms of press adulation more than its fair share of glory. Nevertheless to a considerable degree it owed its low butcher's bill and spectacular advances to the skill to which it had been trained and the brilliance and dash with which it had been led and supplied both by land and air at all levels and to the initiative and daring of all ranks. It now stood, its morale sky high, all its elements magnificently articulated, with sally ports along the line of the lower Seine, 100 miles nearer to the heart of Germany than the rest of the Allied armies, eagerly awaiting the order to spring forward and finally annihilate what remained of the shattered German armies in the West—a veritable thunderbolt capable, if hurled in the right direction, of inflicting a blow which would end the war in 1944.

13

The Broad and the Narrow Front

> The problems of victory are more agreeable
> than those of defeat, but they are no less difficult
>
> *Churchill*

All commanders, unless they are very lucky at one time or another have to fight a battle on two fronts—one to the rear. During August Eisenhower had to face strong criticism from Marshall and the *New York Times* that he was allowing Montgomery too much rope and not keeping a firm grip on the battle. He was quick to reply very forcibly that his critics did not understand his difficulties in the matter of communications, not only with his armies but with the huge air forces, based for the most part in United Kingdom, supporting them. He assured Marshall that 'No major effort takes place in this theatre by ground, sea or air except with my approval . . . no-one in this Allied Command presumes to question my supreme authority and responsibility for the whole campaign.' Nevertheless in these last crucial days in August there were grounds for suspicion that Montgomery and Bradley were being allowed to go the way of their own choosing. Montgomery had made his own plans for the continuation of the pursuit beyond the Seine to start the moment he had got a bridge over the Seine at Vernon capable of taking all classes of traffic. Horrocks and xxx Corps would then thrust without halting by day or night due north-east on Brussels and Antwerp whilst First Canadian Army mopped up the coast of the Pas de Calais and Belgium, destroying en route the sites of the guided missiles now harassing London.

On 25 August, the day Paris was liberated, Bradley summoned Patton to Chartres. He too had made his own plans for the continuation of the pursuit: First Army would now cross the Seine at Melun and Mantes, both of which places had been captured and bridged by Third Army, and make for Lille. Third Army with XII Corps on the right and XX Corps on the left was to burst out of its bridgeheads over the Seine on the morrow and to continue the pursuit generally along the line of the two great highways running east from Paris towards what Patton called 'the Nancy Gap' and Bradley, the line 'Metz–Strasbourg'. Patton's *corps de chasse* now consisted of three armoured and four good infantry divisions all fully mechanised. That this was the line along which the main pursuit should go had been his conviction ever since the breakout at St-Lô and indeed long before. This was the direction in which Pershing had intended to go in 1918: now Patton knew in some strange way that it was his destiny to go this way too, to fulfil the triumph of the American Army which his old and revered commander had been denied. A few days previously his faith had been reinforced by his old instructor at the staff school at Langres in the First War whom he had had flown up all the way from Vannes in Brittany by his aide Codman. Juin too, for whom he had both liking and respect, when he called on 23 August had strengthened his conviction that the main pursuit should be directed towards the Moselle, Worms and Frankfurt.

With the dawn of the 26th both he and his troops were on the move. He personally first drove to XX Corps at Fontainebleau, then on to Nemours to the south-east of Montereau to see the 5th Infantry Division and to congratulate Irwin its commander on their recent achievements. Here he found time to decorate several men with the DSC in the presence of the press cameramen. Like Napoleon he put great stress on the prompt award and issue of decorations for bravery with the maximum publicity, knowing well that if too long delayed the recipients were only too likely to be dead or wounded. In any front-line unit it always seems to be the same men who take the big risks and pay the penalty: the rest follow. Early in the campaign this division, when ordered to ride on the tanks of an armoured division, had complained that they had nothing to hang on to: Patton had told them that any soldier would rather ride 25 miles, no matter how uncomfortably, than walk 15. Now they all knew this to be true and were loud in their praises of the tanks.

He then retraced his steps and crossed the Seine at Melun where the 3rd Armoured Division were rumbling forward. All recognised him at once, stood up in their tanks and cheered. It was not however a day devoted entirely to congratulation and ovations. On arrival at the headquarters of the 7th Armored Division he struck a less cordial note, and in what he described as 'incisive language', told its commander that he was satisfied neither with its turnout nor its progress and that unless it improved, and soon, he would go. It didn't; he went.

Then on he drove to Fontainebleau. Here he took to the air and flew to see the headquarters of XII Corps on the road from Sens to Troyes. It was a fortunate halt. Whilst here, Wood, the commander of 4th Armoured Division came in to report that Bruce Clark with CCA had captured Troyes after a brusque and brilliant action in the face of surprisingly obstinate resistance by security troops and remnants manning the perimeter of the town. Clark had lined up one medium-tank company, followed by two armoured infantry companies and charged with all guns blazing.

Next day XX Corps continued its thrust on Reims while XII Corps made for Chalons. Meanwhile the airstrip at Bricy near Orléans was thick with aircraft landing with loads of ammunition and petrol: no less than half of Third Army's daily consumption of 368,025 gallons was now being delivered by air.

On the 28th Patton's columns were over the Marne at Château Thierry and Chalons and heading east over the First War battlefields unchecked. Now however a project to drop the Allied airborne army at Tournai in advance of Hodges and Montgomery now threatened to take away all the aircraft Patton needed for his supplies. Faced by the unpleasant prospect of having to suspend Patton's air supply, Bradley went to his headquarters about 10.30 with the intention of calling a halt to the pursuit for the time being. Patton protested and it was only after considerable argument that he got permission to press on to the Meuse.

In Third Army's advance there was an element of exultation and emotional release: war may be hell but victorious pursuit is heady stuff. Reconnaissance units and cavalry swept far and wide, clearing the country ahead and on the flanks to enable the main columns to get forward along the main highways. Many of the Germans encountered on the way were leaderless and bewildered: some were even eager to surrender; none were anxious to fall into the clutches of the FFI now assassinating stragglers to their hearts' content. Such resistance as there was came usually at river crossing sites in the form of small battle groups embodying one or two tanks or SP guns and up to a hundred infantry. Road blocks were often perfunctory and easily brushed aside. It seemed that the Germans had abandoned all hope of establishing a stable line anywhere except at the West Wall. Everywhere there were signs of complete German confusion. Patton's tanks closed with trains moving eastwards from Paris loaded with attractive and portable loot in the form of silk, cameras and optical instruments, canned food and truck loads of wine and brandy 'Reserved for the Wehrmacht'. Tank crews found the shooting up of railway engines a rewarding target, in more senses than one. Thirty years later old soldiers would relate with advantages the story of what to them was the high summer of their lives, these halcyon days of pursuit across a continent with 'Roaring George'.

The 29 August was the crucial day; this Patton thought at the time and 30 years later it can be seen that he was right. It was evident to him and indeed to the whole of his army that German resistance had collapsed, and that nothing could stop them if they pressed on, except the doubts of their own higher command. He therefore directed Eddy of XII Corps and Walker of XX Corps on to the crossings of the Meuse at Commercy and Verdun with orders to bounce them before the Germans could blow the bridges up. All seemed to be going well. Then suddenly the blow descended: the 140,000 gallons of petrol due to him that day had not arrived: the C 47s had been withdrawn for the airdrop by the First Airborne Army at Tournai at the northern end of the Allied front. Patton at once indignantly protested to Bradley but got no change. On return to his headquarters he now discovered that Eddy was proposing to halt at St-Dizier, 30 miles short of the Meuse for lack of petrol. All the change he got was a curt order to press on until his tanks ran dry; he could then get out and walk. In the First War in similar circumstances Patton had drawn off the petrol from three-quarters of his tanks in order to keep the remainder on the move. Eddy now could do the same. Cost what it might he must get the crossings over the Meuse with all speed. In the event both leading corps were over the river that evening between Verdun and Commercy. Somehow or other they had got forward with the aid of captured stocks of which Bradley and Eisenhower's headquarters were unaware. Next day, 30 August, provided he got the necessary fuel, he intended to continue his forward drive towards the Moselle between Metz and Nancy. He was less than a hundred miles from the Rhine, 35 miles from Metz and 75 miles from the Saar. In actual fact the West Wall on this day was unmanned. Patton burst in on Bradley. 'Dammit Brad,' he pleaded, 'just give me 400,000 gallons of gasoline, and I'll put you inside Germany in two days.' According to Bradley 'George might as well have asked for the moon.' All available air transport must go to support the airdrop by the First Airborne Army at Tournai—ironically an operation which Montgomery's own advance was making unnecessary at that very moment. Eddy confided to his diary. 'It seems strange to me that we should be sitting here . . . I am convinced that if we could obtain the necessary fuel this war might be over in a couple of weeks.'

The situation of the Germans was indeed desperate. The SHAEF intelligence summary euphorically declared in a momentary lapse into colloquialism: 'The August battles have done it and the enemy in the West has had it . . . (The German Army is) no longer a cohesive force but a number of fugitive battle groups, disorganised and even demoralised, short of equipment and arms.' The Sixth Army Group having landed in the South of France was driving up the Rhone Valley for all practical purposes unopposed. The Eastern Front was reeling back. The Russian Grand Offensive, starting in mid-June, had by this time forced Finland and Rumania to capitulate and Bulgaria to drop out of the war. In the centre East Prussia, with all its memories of Tannenberg, had been overrun: the Russians were now at the gates of Warsaw.

Captured records have since revealed that SHAEF's estimate was not far wide of the mark. On the whole Western Front there were barely 100 tanks fit for action against more than 2,000 with the

Allied spearheads. In the air the disparity was even more astonishing —570 serviceable aircraft against 14,000. In effect the Allies enjoyed a superiority of 20 to one in tanks and 25 to one in aircraft. Speidel, Chief of Staff of Army Group B, described the Allied advance of the last week of August as a foaming torrent in which the remnants of Seventh Army and Fifth Panzer Army were swallowed up or engulfed in a gigantic traffic jam around Mons. According to him there were in Germany no ground forces of any importance that could be thrown in: the ghastly battles in East Prussia and Hungary were at their climax and absorbed all available reserves. Blumentritt, the Chief of Staff in the West, summed up the situation in a sentence, 'There were no German Forces behind the Rhine and at the end of August our front was wide open.' The West Wall was unmanned and no one knew where the keys were to be found. For a fleeting moment the whole German command structure had collapsed. Now was the time, as Patton realised to the depth of his being, for a single thrust deep into the heart of Germany which would bring down the Wehrmacht in irretrievable and immediate ruin.

It was at this climacteric moment that Eisenhower officially took direct operational control of Bradley's and Montgomery's Army Groups thus doubling the role of Supreme Commander and Commander of the Land Forces. He did so in circumstances of very great difficulty. His headquarters at Granville near Cherbourg were 400 miles behind the battle front. The planners and the Services concerned had made inadequate provision for signal communications. To enable Bradley to keep touch with Patton's rapidly moving advance, American signal units designated for SHAEF had been given to Bradley. Even his communications were now limited to radio telephone or laborious code: Eisenhower's communications with Bradley and Montgomery were equally precarious and subject to astonishing delay. It was with this grave handicap that he now faced the most controversial issue of the whole war which has since been debated *ad nauseam:* was it to be the Broad Front, as originally planned by Morgan and his myrmidons for Overlord or the Narrow Front, and if the latter, was it to be in the north under Montgomery as he had been urging for the past ten days, in the centre under Bradley or under Patton towards Worms and Frankfurt? The factors to be considered were many and complex but that of ways and means overrode all others: whichever course was adopted the decision would have to be reached at once as to whom was to be given the limited supplies and transport now coming forward. In other words the logistic factor was the key to the problem.

The original Overlord plan had been made on the assumption that the Germans would withdraw in an orderly manner pausing on the river lines: according to this forecast the Seine would be reached on D plus 90. In fact Patton and Hodges had got there 11 days ahead of schedule. It had also been assumed that the Brittany ports would be working; in fact they were not. As a result the logistic system was completely deranged. It was not so much a shortage of supplies, especially of petrol that was the difficulty—there was plenty in the Normandy beach-head but lack of transport to get it forward. Now Paris had been liberated 55 days ahead of programme and its people were clamouring for food. Bradley therefore was feeding them, using literally 'hundreds of trucks' for the purpose. Why they could not have been told to get on their bicycles and collect their meat and potatoes from the well-stocked farms around the city has never been explained. They all looked well-nourished. Why too Lee, the commander of Com Z, had been allowed to set up a vast cantonment in the Cotentin in Nissen huts, employing an inordinate number of vehicles in doing so is a mystery. He was now on 30 August engaged in moving his horde of back-area barnacles to Paris. As Bradley said 'No one can compute the cost of that move in lost truck tonnage on the front.' Nevertheless 'Pluto', the oil pipe line from the United Kingdom, had now reached France and was working. Even Tedder's demands for airfields could now be met without difficulty. To keep Patton going the 'Red Ball Express', a long-distance through-highway system had been in operation since 25 August. On this more than 100 truck companies were employed in a round trip of 670 miles, moving over 10,000 tons of supplies. Every vehicle ran at least 20 hours a day. It was a justifiable if extravagant gamble, resulting as it did in the abuse of vehicles by excessive speeding, poor maintenance and a high accident rate from driver fatigue. Few who saw them will ever forget the enthusiasm of the Negro drivers, hell-bent whatever the risk, to get

General Patton his supplies. Food was not the main problem: many German dumps were now being captured and there were plenty of cattle, pigs and hens on the farms which could have been requisitioned; there were plenty of potatoes in the fields and the fruit was ripe. A far less constipating diet than K-rations was within the reach of all. The major requirement was petrol, now being consumed by the armies at the rate of 800,000 gallons a day. There is little doubt that with improvisation there was enough transport to back up a single thrust across the Rhine, either by Montgomery in the north or Patton in the south. What was abundantly clear was that a direct advance by all three would soon end in an administrative collapse.

Westphal, as able a professional soldier as any of his grade, German or Allied, who assumed the duties of Chief of Staff to von Rundstedt when reappointed C-in-C West on 5 September, and thus in a position to speak with authority concerning the strength and dispositions of the Army at this time, considered that the direction of the thrust the Allies should have made was less important than that it should be concentrated on a narrow front. He thought:

> The overall situation in the West was serious in the extreme. *A heavy defeat anywhere along the front,* which was so full of gaps that it did not deserve the name, might lead to a catastrophe, if the enemy were to exploit his opportunity skilfully. A particular source of danger was that not a single bridge over the Rhine had been prepared for demolition, an omission which it took weeks to repair. . . . Until the middle of October the enemy could have broken through at any point he liked with ease, and would then have been able to cross the Rhine and thrust deep into Germany almost unhindered.

On the principle therefore that there should be a single thrust delivered with speed in depth three high-grade fighting soldiers, Montgomery, Patton and Westphal were of one mind. This too according to Major-General Sixsmith was the view of Simonds, the ablest of the Canadian commanders at this time. All had that inborn appreciation of the nature of battle, developed by actual fighting experience, that touch of inspiration which makes the difference, as in art or music, between high art and the mere display of technical skill.

There were strong military reasons for backing Montgomery's demand for the single thrust in the north which he had been urging Eisenhower to adopt ever since 17 August. He believed most emphatically that the pursuit could be directed and controlled only by one man devoting all his time and energy to the task—himself. Nevertheless, if he personally was unacceptable to American opinion, he was prepared to serve under Bradley. He claimed that his plan would cause greater confusion in Germany than any other: at the worst he would seize the Ruhr, at the time producing at least 50 per cent of Germany's coal and steel. The West Wall in the north was incomplete. In addition a further consideration forced his hand: London and Southern England had suffered grievously from the V1 weapons, the sites of which were in the Pas de Calais; it was known that the more deadly V2s would soon open up from Holland. He had strong patriotic and humanitarian reasons therefore for pressing his own argument for a single thrust even at the risk of straining the alliance.

There were however formidable American objections to placing the major effort in British and in particular, Montgomery's hands. To have launched a Narrow Front thrust under him would have meant relegating a large part of the United States forces in Europe, now larger than the British and destined soon to rise to 100 divisions, to a static role, whilst handing over all the glory to be gained in the pursuit to the British, and would have been intolerable to American public opinion. It is fair comment to add that Roosevelt's chances of being re-elected for a fourth term in the coming November would have suffered if Montgomery's plan had been tried and failed. Patton's lightning progress had been dramatised to such an extent in the United States that to stop him in full cry would have aroused the Press and public to fever pitch of indignation. Montgomery too, to put it mildly, had ruffled the feelings of the American generals who did not hesitate, then, or later, to express their personal dislike of him. If there had to be a single thrust then it would have to be American.

There were very strong reasons therefore that it should be under Patton. He, more than anyone else, had shown himself capable of exploiting the American genius for exploiting success. He was 'carrying the ball' and 'making the end-run' with the crowd cheering him on: he more than any other general was capable of exploiting the built-in aptitude of the American soldier of World War Two for high-speed mechanised warfare demanding a high degree of initiative and improvisation, their capacity for enthusiasm for a cause in which they believed and their readiness to take big risks for big results. That a thrust on his front through the West Wall to the Saar and to Worms and Frankfurt, would to some extent be a long way round to the Ruhr was a minor consideration. It is not always the blow on the chin which knocks the boxer out. In mechanised warfare it is not so much distance that matters as shrewd timing, good roads and flexible command. The over-riding need therefore was for a single concentrated thrust by Patton, so deep that the enemy would have no chance to rally, on 29 August—the day Bradley arbitrarily reduced his petrol from 400,000 gallons a day to a trickle. Instead, on this day the main effort was in the north with the three northern armies advancing on a broad front and Patton virtually immobilised beyond the Meuse for want of fuel.

On 2 September Eisenhower pulled back Bradley, Hodges, Patton and Hoyt Vandenburg, the new commander of 9th Air Force, 400 miles to Granville in the Cotentin to explain his future plans. On this day First Army was dealing with a big pocket of Germans they had surrounded near Mons. To the north, Horrocks' xxx Corps with Guards Armoured Division on the right and 11th Armoured Division on the left, driving ahead day and night, were within striking distance of Brussels and Antwerp in a spectacular drive of over 200 miles since 29 August. Patton confirmed that 4th Armored Division on 31 August had captured intact the Meuse bridges at Commercy and Pont-sur-Meuse before the German rearguards could set off the charges. At Verdun 7th Armored Division had seized another bridge intact. Both bridgeheads were now solidly held by armour, infantry and artillery. Furthermore he now had patrols on the Moselle in the vicinity of Nancy and the 3rd Cavalry had entered Metz. Cutting off his petrol had not entirely made him immobile or caused him to lose heart. He is said to have blurted out: 'My men can eat their belts but my tanks have got to have gas.' Although cut off officially from normal petrol supplies, Third Army in fact had used their initiative. Over 100,000 gallons had been captured and no necessity had been seen to report the fact. It is also said that Third Army personnel disguised as members of First Army had been able to secure further supplies—an irregularity into which Patton did not see fit to enquire. Third Army too had at its disposal vast quantities of captured champagne and brandy, reserved for the use of the Wehrmacht. It is a principle of transportation that there should be full loads for both forward and return journeys. Third Army did not ignore it. Supply assignments whether by land or air to them were therefore popular.

At this conference Eisenhower initiated what was for practical purposes the first stage of the Broad Front policy. For the moment, he told his army commanders, he was concentrating on a drive by the First Army and Second British Army in the north designed to annihilate the Germans in the Mons Pocket. When this had been completed both First and Third Armies would remain 'generally static' until sufficient gasoline and other supplies could be accumulated for an attack by Third Army and v Corps on the West Wall. They would then seize and hold that line. Patton's impression was that Eisenhower was obsessed with the thought of a great battle now imminent in the north. Patton made it clear that he considered this was most unlikely and that if he was allowed to go on all German resistance would collapse. Bradley followed Eisenhower's statement by giving Patton a future axis of advance calculated to take him eventually across the Rhine to Mannheim and Frankfurt when the supply situation permitted. He went on to promise him two more divisions, the 79th Infantry Division and the 2nd French Armoured Division but pointed out that he would not need them until he was through the West Wall. As a concession he would be allowed now to secure the crossings of the Moselle if he could get fuel. Somewhat mollified but still unconvinced of the soundness of Eisenhower's decision, Patton like a good soldier bowed to his superior's orders. That afternoon he telephoned his own headquarters: Third Army would stand fast on the line of the bridgeheads over the Meuse; cavalry reconnaissances might continue to probe towards the east. His headquarters promptly relayed these orders to Eddy of xii Corps and Walker of xx Corps but there was little point in doing so. The

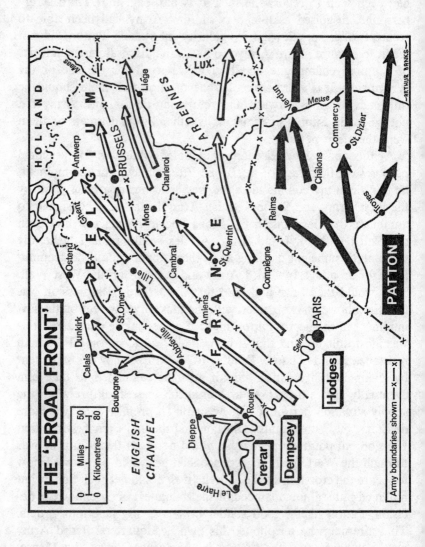

THE 'BROAD FRONT'

ENGLISH CHANNEL

HOLLAND

B E L G I U M

LUX.

ARDENNES

F R A N C E

Antwerp
Ghent
Ostend
Dunkirk
Calais
Boulogne
Dieppe
Le Havre
Rouen
St. Omer
Lille
Abbeville
Amiens
Cambrai
St. Quentin
Mons
Charleroi
BRUSSELS
Liége
Compiègne
PARIS
Seine
Reims
Châlons
Commercy
St. Dizier
Verdun
Meuse
Troyes
Maas

Meas

PATTON

Hodges

Dempsey

Crerar

—ARTHUR BANKS—

0   50
Miles
0   80
Kilometres

Army boundaries shown —x—x

tanks of Third Army had stopped and the guns had ceased to fire. The infantry pulled off the road and bivouacked under the trees or in barns. Headquarters moved into *châteaux* or comfortable farm houses. The mood was still light-hearted: the war would be over in a matter of weeks. Soon petrol would come and all would ride on to further triumphs over the Rhine and beyond.

Thus it came about at the very moment when the morale of Third Army was at its zenith, when every officer and soldier in it was seized with the desire to reach the Rhine and cross it, when they all felt instinctively that provided they pressed on now nothing could stop them, that they were pulled up in their tracks. Most of Patton's staff and his leading commanders were from the cavalry arm, thoroughly imbued with the cavalry traditions of speed and audacity and devoted to, and inspired by their commander. The headquarters, manned for the most part by officers who had been with Patton in Africa and Sicily, was working smoothly and without fuss like a Rolls-Royce. Apart from the 90th and 35th Infantry Divisions, relatively few of the officers and men had been involved in the tedious and bloody fighting in the hedgerows of Normandy. For them battle had been an exhilarating experience of rapid movement and spectacular success. It is said that 'An old soldier is a cautious soldier; that is why he is an old soldier' but the men of Third Army still had that first enthusiasm which comes from early victory before disillusion creeps in. The contents of the celebrated caves of champagne and warehouses of Reims had further raised their spirits; unlike many American commanders Patton had liberal views in matters of this sort. His mode of life was closer to that of Churchill than Montgomery's. The press correspondents, themselves sustained on a diet of K-rations and champagne, were doing him and his soldiers no less than justice. They had passed through the Argonne Forest with its sinister memories of the First War without a fight; Verdun, the very epitome of mass slaughter in World War One, had been carried at a run by the tanks. Without question or disparagement the Third Army, of all the Allied armies, was the best suited to exploit the fleeting moment, dare all and clinch the victory. When Eisenhower pulled back his army commanders to Granville on 2 September it had already been halted for two vital days. Three days later when, with limited supplies of petrol secured somehow or other by Patton, they were able to resume their advance to the Moselle they met with strong resistance. At the end of five days' fighting, though some of them would seize Toul in the Moselle bend others would be repulsed at Pont à Mousson and the rest would be held up about Metz and Nancy. So far as they were concerned the pursuit would be over and the bloody 16-week Battle of Lorraine would have begun. In the fatal five days' lull on the Third Army front the Germans recovered their nerve and somehow or other patched up the front with five divisions of sorts behind the anti-tank barrier of the Moselle between Metz and Nancy. The halcyon days of headlong pursuit were over. No one at Supreme Headquarters had foreseen such a complete collapse as had occurred. In the record of these first few days of September there is a fog, an arrest of action, a lack of clear direction which research does little to dispel. No one, except Montgomery and especially Patton, was mentally prepared to exploit the greatest opportunity of the whole campaign. Sound militarily though Montgomery's proposal was, American interests and American opinion demanded that the choice should be Patton. The situation called for the brutal and simple solution of the man who had the feel and the smell of the battle, not for a compromise which suited no one and inevitably failed.

The price to be paid for halting Patton on the last day of August would be heavy indeed. Two-thirds of the Allied casualties in the North-West Europe Campaign of 1944/45 were incurred after the check in September. The suffering of the civil population of Europe arising from the prolongation of the war was incalculable. Politically the over-riding need of the Western Allies was to finish the war in 1944 before the Russians penetrated Central Europe: by May 1945 they would reach the Elbe and Czechoslovakia and erect the Iron Curtain. Providence had given Eisenhower the greatest cavalry leader and as good an army as his country had ever produced: at the decisive moment he failed to use them.

14

Lorraine

One man and one mind directed all
Polybius on Hannibal

On 4 September Eisenhower gave Patton the green light to resume his suspended offensive to breach the West Wall on the Saar and then advance in the general direction of Frankfurt. Simultaneously 21st Army Group and First Army, as the major effort, were to secure Antwerp, penetrate the West Wall north of the Ardennes and seize the Ruhr. In an office memorandum explaining these decisions he stated: 'The defeat of the German Armies is complete and the only thing now needed to realise the whole conception is speed.' In fact when on the following day Patton broke out of his bridgehead over the Moselle, with XII Corps on the right facing Nancy and XX Corps on the left east of Verdun, he faced a situation which had radically changed during the five days' halt and stepped forward into countryside which would impose restrictions on operations unknown since the breakout at Avranches—the vaguely defined province of Lorraine which lies between the Saar and the Meuse.

It is a land of ominous and bloody memories of the great French disasters of 1870, of the slaughter of Mars-la-Tour, St-Privat and Gravelotte and the capitulation of Bazaine at Metz which brought down the Second Empire. Here in August 1914 the flower of French manhood had gone to their death in the ill-starred offensive which opened the campaign. Immediately to the west lay the Argonne and the memorials of the costly American battles of October and November 1918. Three rivers, the Moselle, the Nied and the Saar, running roughly north and south, with their many tributaries traverse what is, in fact, an undulating plateau with wide open valleys often bottomless in wet weather. The rich agricultural region in the north-east, marked by flat-topped ridges, is dotted with small woods and stone-built villages. The Moselle itself is a formidable obstacle. Climatically, the wet season normally begins in September with October as the month of maximum rainfall: at this time movement of wheeled and tracked vehicles off roads is difficult and often impossible. The pre-1914 frontier fortifications of France and the Maginot Line which straddle the area provide further complications. To sum up, it can be said that the terrain gave the Germans almost every facility for exploiting their flair for the defensive battle. Opposed river crossings and attacks with limited objectives, placing a great strain on the infantry in particular, were to be expected. Opportunities for wide sweeps with armour were likely to be few; inevitably the tempo of operations would slow down.

Patton had been halted at the very moment when the whole German command framework in the West lay in ruins. When Eisenhower authorised the resumption of his offensive on 4 September it had been restored. Hitler had once more turned to von Rundstedt and reinstated him as C-in-C West, at the same time providing him with a young Chief of Staff of great ability, Westphal, who had fought under Rommel in North Africa, and been Chief of Staff to Kesselring in the Mediterranean. Thus control was once more in competent professional hands. These two, briefed by OKW to hold the Allies in the north as far west as possible, to maintain a firm grip on the Netherlands and in due course to counter-attack towards Reims, soon had the normal command machinery functioning with more than a semblance of its traditional efficiency. Immediately opposing Patton was the First Army under von Knobelsdorff, a veteran of the Russian Campaign with considerable experience as an armoured corps commander, a competent, ruthless and unshakeable man. Whilst Patton stood still between 1 and 5 September he had succeeded in building up a front of sorts with seven nominal divisions and a Panzer brigade. They were short of anti-tank guns and artillery; nevertheless they had plenty of *Panzerfausts*—which were as effective as the American bazookas—Spandau machine-guns and 'Burp' submachine-guns with their peculiar emetic sound. For further supplies they were close to the Ruhr where, despite Allied bombing, arms production was now in full spate. Although some of the troops were over-age, of low category and only partially trained there was no shortage of battle-experienced junior officers and NCOs well versed in the technique of defensive fighting which had saved their armies time and time again in Russia. Third Army in fact faced the strongest German army on the whole Allied front.

Experience in North Africa, Italy and Normandy had confirmed the truth of the First War axiom that, despite developments in the air and in armoured warfare, for success the attack required at least a three to one superiority over the defender when based on a well-organised position. One of Patton's major reasons for pressing to be allowed to continue his all-out pursuit at the end of August had been his desire to avoid being faced by the situation which now confronted him on the Moselle. When on a visit to XII Corps on 3 September he drove up via Commercy on the Meuse to inspect the 80th Division at Gironville he was visibly reminded by the huge monument to the American dead at Montsec of the attack 26 years before in which he had personally taken part. He could not help but think that the delay to which he and his army had been subjected would possibly result, in due course of time, in the erection of many other similar monuments for men who, 'had we gone faster would not have died.' The fighting for the crossings of the Moselle would be bitter indeed. The struggle between the 37th SS Panzer Grenadier Regiment and the 5th Division in the Dornot bridgehead was typical:

Time and time again the German grenadiers came forward in close order, shouting 'Heil Hitler', and screaming wildly, only to be cut down by small arms fire from the woods and exploding shells from the field guns on the opposite side of the Moselle. But each attack took its toll of the defenders of the horseshoe. The wounded were forbidden to moan or call for aid so that the Germans would not know the extent of the losses they had inflicted. The mortar crews abandoned their weapons, whose muzzle blast betrayed the location of the foxhole line, and took up rifles from the dead. A lieutenant operated his radio with one hand and fired his carbine with the other . . . the 2/11th Infantry had only two officer survivors in their three rifle companies and their total casualties numbered over 300.

Nevertheless, despite the striking revival in the enemy's morale, by 25 September in a series of fiercely contested battles xx Corps on the left was over the Moselle and within five miles of Metz, xii Corps had taken Nancy and fought its way forward east of the river. On the southern flank xv Corps, once more temporarily under Patton's command, had taken Lunéville. It was now that Bradley had to deliver to Patton what he knew would be a further bitter blow. It had at last been brought home to Eisenhower that, faced by the threat of a complete logistical collapse, he could no longer continue attacking on all fronts. He therefore had decided that until the port of Antwerp could be opened, priority for supplies must go to First Army for their attack on the West Wall towards Cologne and to 21st Army Group in the Arnhem salient. Third Army must go over to the defensive and 'undertake no more aggressive action than is permitted by the maintenance situation'. Thus down-graded, Patton made no attempt to conceal his resentment. According to Bradley, until the day he died he never recanted his contention that, had priority in supply been given to him at this time, he could even at this late hour, have broken through the Saar defences to the Rhine. The transfer of xv Corps to Sixth Army Group added further to his frustration. According to Bradley 'He padded about his Army like a caged tiger.' In the hope of softening the blow Bradley authorised him to make minor adjustments to his lines—latitude which Patton characteristically interpreted as permission to stage a series of minor operations 'to be executed immediately to secure a suitable line of departure so that we can move rapidly when the Supreme Commander directs us to resume the offensive'.

In the actual strategic situation of the Allies at the end of September, there was an element of the ludicrous. With twice as many men as the Germans, two and a half times as many tanks, and air forces 23 times the size of the Luftwaffe, backed by the inexhaustible resources of the United States in men, money and materials, they must, provided they were directed with elementary commonsense, eventually crush the Germans with the inevitability of an avalanche. Now the unpalatable truth had to be faced that the initiative had temporarily been lost, that the German Army was still prepared to fight with its traditional skill and tenacity in country which discounted to some extent the great Allied preponderence in armour and motor transport and that the long winter months lay ahead with their inevitable concomitant—Napoleon's fifth element, mud. On Patton's own front the German backlash was as fierce and formidable as anywhere from the North Sea to the Alps. Manteuffel's counter-offensive about Lunéville on 18 September had been brusquely repulsed but attacks continued elsewhere until the end of the month. How determinedly they were pressed was well illustrated at Gremecy at the end of the month in an incident which also highlights Patton's own reactions in a crisis and the firm grip he had over all ranks of his Army.

On 30 September the 35th Division in the Forêt de Gremecy some two miles east of the River Seille was counter-attacked by XIII SS Corps both frontally and on both flanks and a serious situation developed. Eddy, the commander of XII Corps, had therefore come forward to the command post of the 320th Infantry in a building at Bioncourt, a small village about a mile west of the forest. Here there had assembled, Baade the commander of 35th Division and all his regimental commanders, Gaffey, Patton's Chief of Staff and Grow, the commander of 6th Armored Division which constituted the Third Army reserve. A burst of shell fire suddenly struck the yard outside killing or wounding several of the aides and orderlies who were waiting there. The assembled officers did what they could for the wounded and then resumed their conference.

What now passed between them is not entirely clear. However this much is true: Eddy issued orders for the withdrawal of 35th Division that night behind the River Seille. Gaffey then reported Eddy's intention on the telephone to Patton who forthwith jumped into a light aircraft and flew from Étain to Eddy's headquarters at Nancy and countermanded Eddy's order for the withdrawal of 35th Division; 'Counter-attack with 6th Armored, that is as soon as you can. Tell them (the 35th Division) to hang on.' He then ordered 4th Armored Division on 35th Division's right to stand firm whatever the circumstances. He and Eddy then set off together for the command post of the 6th Armored Division where plans were made for it to attack on the following morning and where, as the divisional *Journal* noted with obvious discretion 'General Patton emphatically stated that he would not give up another foot of ground to the Ger-

mans.' This is one of the more striking understatements in which
the bulky official history abounds. Here it is sufficient to record that
next day 35th Division and 6th Armored Division restored the
situation.

The wildly optimistic hopes of early September that the war
would be over by Christmas now finally vanished as the days shortened and the weather worsened. Until the administrative situation
improved there could be no resumption of the offensive. All the
ingredients were therefore present for a decline in morale. It is per-
tinent therefore to consider at this stage why this did not occur in
Third Army.

No commander in World War Two succeeded more effectively
in impressing his own personality on the officers and men under
his command than Patton. Indeed many actually developed some
of his idiosyncrasies and mannerisms. It was even said that he had
created Third Army in his own image. Almost every day he sallied
forth to the front to praise, reprimand and inspire. He was never
satisfied with issuing orders: he thought it equally important to see
that they were carried out. He sometimes would deliberately take
considerable risks: 90 per cent of these however were carefully calculated for the effect of their example on his command from GI to
corps commander. He thought it necessary 'to show the soldiers that
generals can get shot at'. By day he would go forward by road and
return late in the evening, often at twilight and indeed sometimes
after dark in a small liaison plane, his theory being that a commander should always be seen going to the front but never coming
away from it and 'The more senior the officer, the more time he
has. Therefore the senior should go forward to visit the junior rather
than call the junior back.' During the October lull he drove inces-
santly up and down his army area, radiating optimism and address-
ing troops whenever an adequate audience could be rounded up.
His speech to 95th Division, which had just arrived in the theatre,
illustrates his oft-repeated theme: 'It is 132 miles to the Rhine from
here, and if this Army will attack with venom and desperate energy,
it is more than probable that the war will end before we get to the
Rhine. Therefore when we attack, we go like hell.' When not in
action, units concentrated on training for the resumption of the of-

fensive. All officers and men studied relief maps and models of the
West Wall. He himself and his staff, in what little time they had
to spare, mentally prepared themselves for operations beyond the
Rhine. A multitude of schools worked at high pressure in the back
areas: they included one for the study of floating Bailey bridges
and even one designed to teach staff officers how to write citations
for gallantry and thus gain prompt and adequate awards.

He was not one of those commanders in World War Two who
apparently sought to demonstrate their own efficiency by frequently
sacking members of their staff. On the contrary, his relations with
them were cordial and helpful. He supported and trusted them and
was not slow to praise when praise was deserved. He never inter-
fered in matters of a minor character and having given a man a
task let him get on with his job. On his birthday the heads of staff
sections gave him a party in Colonel Koch's quarters. There were
'Armored Diesels' to drink, field expedient type. The ingredients of
the original were juice of one lemon, sugar to taste, one and a half
ounces of rye or bourbon, one tea-cup of shaved ice; whirl in a
mixer. Neither—unlike other commanders of the period—when members of his staff had the chance of promotion to command did he
selfishly hang on to them to spare himself inconvenience. He thus
got and retained to the end a staff completely devoted both to himself personally and to Third Army—it is regrettable to have to record
the fact that in their zeal to serve their master and get what they
wanted by hook or by crook they sometimes failed to endear themselves to the serried ranks of SHAEF and particularly to Lee, the
Commander of Com Z who, incredibly, managed to create a ciga-
rette crisis about this time. To all who had it in their power to help
Third Army he went out of his way to extend an almost overwhelming welcome: his hospitality could be lavish. When Eisenhower and
Bradley came to lunch with him in October he gave them a new
drink called the 170. It was half brandy and half champagne. Most
thought it was all champagne so the results in Patton's opinion were
good.

Fred Ayer, Patton's nephew and a civilian engaged in counter-
intelligence, and temporarily disguised as lieutenant-colonel, arrived
at Third Army headquarters on a visit in late October. He was struck

by the fact that every man he met was clean-shaven, had polished boots and wore his necktie and helmet. This was the case with all troops of Third Army when not in direct contact with the enemy. The military police were working at high pressure to maintain their commander's high standards of turnout. They even arrested three members of bomber crews shot down over the army area for 'failing to wear helmets, liners and neckties.' There was no truth in the quip of the moment that the Third Army fought well because death came as a happy release: there were some however thought it was better to face a whole Panzer division than their own commander in a rage. All certainly developed a feeling of moral superiority not only over the Germans but all the other Allied armies as well. Any man asked what his unit was, invariably replied 'I'm with Patton.' A quarter of a century later men from one end of the United States to the other, whether rich or poor, would recollect the bond which placed them in a class apart; they had served under Patton in the days when the prestige of the American Army was at its zenith.

His zeal for efficiency in battle and the maintenance of self-respect at all times, whether in action or not, was backed by an administrative drive to ensure that troops when out of the line were not subjected to avoidable discomfort. When in reserve they were billeted in the towns and villages, given clean clothes and, if they were lucky, sent to Nancy, St-Nicolas and other leave centres for a hot shower, coffee and doughnuts, see a movie and perhaps even Marlene Dietrich's show. Supplies of fresh bread were accelerated from the field bakeries and roasted green coffee was issued wherever possible in place of the bitter soluble variety in the K-ration. The large quantities of German beef captured at Reims and Briey added variety to the official rations. Ordnance companies were put under cover to enable them to increase their output; tanks were fitted with 'duck bills' to enable them to compete with the mud. Winter equipment such as blankets, overcoats, new-type sleeping bags and stoves began to come forward but not fast enough for Patton. Realising to the full that the regular delivery of mail from home affects a soldier's morale, Patton had by early October a special daily train carrying 400 tons of letters and parcels running to his army, within which they were delivered with regularity and speed. No commander ever stressed more forcibly the individual officer's responsibility not only for the conduct of his men in battle, but also for their general health and well-being at all times. Mindful of his own experience in the First War he insisted on the provision of improvised drying rooms and the sending up of a pair of dry socks for each man in the front line with the daily rations. On the subject of trench foot and its prevention, he wrote a personal letter for the widest possible distribution, expressed in his own inimitable style. Trench foot, he maintained on sound medical grounds, was a preventable disease: a colonel whose unit had an excessive number of cases got the sack; the number of men going sick with this malady showed an almost startling decline. All these measures helped to maintain the soldier's individual self-respect and strengthened his confidence in the efficiency of those above him. They were in fact a means to an end and not an end in themselves. Welfare as developed in later years would not have had Patton's approval because he held that, by itself, it is essentially soft and that hardship and privation, when necessary, are the school of the good soldier.

Thus in the first week of November, on the eve of the resumption of the offensive, the morale and battle-worthiness of Third Army, despite the incessant rain and enforced inactivity, remained as high as ever. It now comprised six infantry and three armoured divisions besides a large number of non-divisional units. In effective strength it amounted to a quarter of a million men. As a result of the all-out efforts of the staff and supply services, the necessary backing for prolonged operations in arms, ammunition, gasoline, engineer equipment and tanks had been built up. The material foundations for further victories had indeed been well and truly laid.

What exactly Eisenhower's Broad Front policy implied, in the practical terms which set the pattern of Allied strategy for the rest of the campaign, was revealed to Montgomery and Bradley at a conference held in Brussels on 18 October. Brussels appears to have been selected to ensure that the Field-Marshal attended in person and would have no excuse for sending his Chief of Staff instead. The First Army would attack early in November from Aachen and secure a bridgehead over the Rhine south of Cologne. On its left the Ninth Army would protect its northern flank and then drive north to meet a thrust by Montgomery's Army Group south-east from Nijmegen. Having thus closed with the Rhine, Eisenhower then proposed to encircle the Ruhr by moving Ninth Army to the north and First Army to the south. Third Army's role would be subsidiary: they were to cross the Rhine somewhere between Worms and Mainz 'when logistic conditions permit'. Patton had every intention that they would—and soon. By now he had apparently convinced Bradley that the enemy on Third Army front was disposed with all its strength in the front line and that, having disposed of them, he would soon reach the Rhine. In the event, German resistance in the north delayed the start of the First and Ninth Armies' offensives. When therefore on 2 November Bradley called to explain that the British, Ninth and First Armies were not yet ready, Patton promptly told him that he could attack at 24 hours' notice. In fact detailed preparation for the resumption of the advance to the Saar had been continuous ever since September. The two commanders therefore agreed that the Third Army's offensive would begin as soon as the weather permitted the air forces to soften up the enemy; 8 November was therefore fixed as the day on which XII Corps would start operations. Devers of Sixth Army Group agreed to protect Patton's right flank as he advanced north-east.

The weather was appalling: in October twice the amount of rain had fallen as in a normal year. During the first days of November the Moselle rose rapidly, burst its banks and flooded a large part of the countryside. On the 7th one of the corps commanders and a divisional commander arrived at Patton's headquarters to ask for a postponement of the attack until the weather improved. All the response they got was a quiet request: 'Would you care to make recommendations as to your successors?' This put the matter in a new light: both returned to their headquarters to put the final touches to their preparations for the attack on the morrow. That evening, when Patton rose at 10.30 to go to bed he said to Codman 'I think this has been the longest day of my life. There is nothing I can do now except pray.' It was two years since the Casablanca landing. Later, when Blumentritt was asked whether the attack came as a surprise, he promptly replied that it was not: they knew Patton well enough to know that he would commemorate his first battle in the war.

On the 8th he woke up at three o'clock in the morning; it was raining in torrents. He tried to sleep but finding this impossible he got up and started to read Rommel's book *Infantry Attacks*. By chance he hit upon a chapter describing a battle in the rain in September 1914. This was reassuring: what the Germans had done, he could do. He fell asleep to be woken up at 5 a.m. by the din of the opening bombardment. The whole eastern sky was lit up as 700 guns pounded the enemy positions. About 8 a.m. both Bradley and Eisenhower rang up to wish him well. It was still raining: there was no prospect of air support until the skies cleared. Accompanied by Stiller and Codman he then drove to the observation post of XII Corps. Owing to the smoke screens over the Moselle there was little to be seen. The rain however soon diminished to a drizzle and then suddenly at about ten o'clock the sun broke through the clouds. Almost at once hundreds of fighter-bombers appeared in force and descended with deadly effect on the known enemy command posts. It was a breath-taking sight. 'I'm almost sorry for those German bastards!' Patton exclaimed. He then set off on a lightning tour of the command posts of the three attacking infantry divisions and the 4th Armored Division. By late afternoon XII Corps could report that practically all their units were on their day's objectives. Unfortunately that night the rain came down once more in a veritable deluge. Next morning the front presented a disheartening sight: many of the bridges were down; everywhere trucks and tanks were marooned in the floods. A magnificent attack by 1,476 aircraft on the defences of Metz greatly heartened the troops. That night the rain came on once more: every bridge over the Moselle except the one at Pont à Mousson collapsed. The Seille increased in width from 200 to 500 feet.

The attack of XX Corps on the northern flank was now in full swing. For the next five weeks, in weather going from bad to worse, the Third Army fought a continuous battle, reminiscent of Normandy at its worst, rather than the lightning drive of the late summer across western France. The Germans had taken the maximum possible advantage of the October lull to re-organise and re-equip;

their morale had conspicuously revived now that they stood on the very fringe of the Fatherland. Between 1 September and 20 December Third Army took only 10,000 more prisoners than they had captured in August. Occasionally an attack on the whole army front, reminiscent of the full-scale battles of the First War, was mounted; the majority of the operations however were of necessity separate attacks on relatively narrow fronts supported by the maximum possible artillery fire. Patton was thus able to keep casualties down to an acceptable figure: he never threw men's lives away unnecessarily. Despite the bad weather XIX TAC was able to give considerable support in the early stages but thereafter in the very poor flying weather of December could do little to help. Of necessity operations now proceeded at the pace of the infantry: the limited road nets and the all-pervading mud inevitably reduced the power of the tanks to exploit their mobility and shock effect. The fortress of Metz capitulated to XX Corps on 22 November as a result of converging attack although some of the outlying forts hung out for a further three weeks. It was the first time, as Patton, with his keen sense of history, was not slow to point out, that it had been taken by assault for 400 years. As the weather grew even wetter and the nights grew colder the enemy abandoned the wooded areas for the shelter of the stone-built villages: operations thus assumed the character of small advances by minor units. Within the ugly and grimy built-up areas of the Saar, German battle-groups were able to fight many an obstinate battle with all their traditional skill in this type of action. On interrogation, some captured German generals went out of their way to criticise the slowness of the American advance at this time. This type of comment should be accepted with greater reservation than has been the case with some writers lacking personal experience of battle under these conditions. In the Hürtgen Forest in the north, First Army had re-created conditions of squalid horror reminiscent of the Meuse–Argonne Battle of October/November 1918; Third Army experience on the Saar was equally sordid. Nevertheless by mid-December they had much to show for their courage and fortitude. They had thrown the enemy back from three formidable defensive positions on the Moselle, the Neid and the Saar rivers—and closed with the West Wall. In the process they had deprived the

German war economy of the production of most of the factories
and rolling mills of Lorraine and the Saar basin that were based
on the coal mines, and had attracted to themselves and badly mauled
troops needed farther north. Despite the ghastly weather, morale
from top to bottom remained high; preparations were well advanced
for a final attack through the West Wall and on to the line of the
Rhine and Frankfurt, timed for 19 December, and to be preceded
by four days' intensive bombing by Ninth Air Force and the RAF.

For this operation Koch had managed to collect an amazing
amount of detail for XIX Tactical Air Force had flown innumerable
photographic missions, the results of which had been meticulously
interpreted. He then had one of those windfalls rare in the history
of the Second World War—a German officer with detailed knowledge of the West Wall defences who was willing to talk. This man
knew that Hitler would never give in: he therefore had reached the
conclusion that it was his duty to do what he could to save what
was left of Germany and to bring the war quickly to an end by
telling Koch all he knew of the secrets of the West Wall. With astonishing accuracy he pin-pointed on air photographs all the field fortifications and gun emplacements with their fields of fire—including
machine-gun positions undetectable by air photography. All this information after verification Koch, with Patton's approval, had over-
printed on large-scale maps for use in the coming attack. This
information when exploited later by Seventh Army proved to be
invaluable.

Then, at the very moment when all was ready Eisenhower ordered Patton to suspend his offensive on the Saar. Developments
on VIII Corps front in the Ardennes had taken not only him, but
Bradley and Montgomery, completely by surprise.

Koch and his staff had not confined themselves to the study of the
enemy situation on their own front. Ever since October they had
been worried by the ever-increasing evidence that the Germans were
building up reserves on the front of the First Army. They included
Panzer divisions, Panzer Grenadier divisions and Parachute divisions—élite troops and not mere run-of-the-mill Wehrmacht. The
puzzle was: to what end? Were they intended for counter-attack
in the Aachen area, where First Army was still attacking, or were

they destined for use as a spoiling attack against Third Army's northern flank when it advanced beyond the Saar? If they were not for use on either of these axes where was it intended that they should intervene? What was the explanation of the heavy rail movement on both sides of the Rhine? On their own army's northern flank in the Ardennes, Middleton's VIII Corps was holding a 75-mile front from Monschau to Echternach, with four and two-thirds divisions, two new to battle and two which had been badly mauled in the Hürtgen Forest. Bradley after the war described this as a 'calculated risk'. The more Koch thought about it the less he liked the situation on the army's immediate northern flank. He therefore, at a briefing on 9 December, pointed out to the assembled staff that the situation here gave cause for concern if not anxiety. On the front of VIII Corps he explained to Patton and his staff, according to his calculations, there were two and a half more divisions than against the entire Third Army, three and a half divisions more than against the Seventh Army on their immediate right and only one division less than the equivalent strength of all the enemy divisions then in contact on the rest of First Army front. The enemy now had a rested and refitted fighter air force capable of putting 1,000 aircraft into the air for a limited period of time. The terrain on VIII Corps' front, Koch went on to say, was not unfavourable for enemy offensive operations: none of the streams were major obstacles, there was plenty of cover from observation, and there were no organised defensive positions. He summed up by reiterating that the enemy had a two and a half to one advantage on the Ardennes front, that he had achieved a gradual and unobtrusive build-up in the area, and that in his opinion a successful diversionary attack here would be a 'shot in the arm' for the Germans. It was a possibility which should not be ignored.

Koch's briefing made a marked impression on the assembled staff: after he ceased speaking there was silence for several minutes. In the discussion which then followed it was agreed that, whilst nothing must be allowed to interfere with the preparations for the big attack on the 19th, planning should start at once to deal with the situation which would arise if the enemy staged an attack on VIII Corps' front; furthermore plans must envisage not only the protection of Third

Army's northern flank but also a counter-stroke in a northerly direction. Patton closed the conference with the words: 'We'll be in a position to meet whatever happens.' Within a week Eisenhower, Bradley and Montgomery would be completely taken by surprise. Patton, like Bradley, believed in taking calculated risks but he also, unlike Bradley, always covered his bets.

15

Ardennes

Damn with faint praise, assent with civil leer,
And without sneering teach the rest to sneer

Pope

Dawn on 16 December came with low-lying cloud, beneath which mist and fog completely hid the deployment on the VIII Corps' front from Monschau to Echternach of the 13 infantry and seven armoured divisions, followed by a further 10 and supported by 2,000 guns which together comprised the Fifth and Sixth Panzer and Seventh Armies. Suddenly at 5.30 a.m. an artillery and mortar bombardment reminiscent of the heaviest barrages of the First War lit up the front: salvoes of V1s hissed overhead flying west. Then as the darkness faded the infantry came forward with the Panzer divisions following close upon their heels. Low cloud all day prevented the Allied air forces from giving any form of close support or information of the enemy's movements. Model had achieved surprise on a grand scale equalled only by Napoleon at Waterloo or Robert E. Lee at Second Manassas.

Early that morning, unaware of developments on VIII Corps' front, Bradley had set off by car from his headquarters at Luxembourg for SHAEF headquarters at Versailles to discuss future plans with Eisenhower and it was not until late afternoon, when in conference, that they were made aware of developments on VIII Corps' front. Bradley's first reaction was to brush the news aside as a mere spoiling attack staged in the hope of forcing Patton to suspend his attack on the West Wall. He was in fact in a far more critical position than he realised: he had no reserve behind the Ardennes sector and his own headquarters in Luxembourg were out on a limb on the southern flank of the breakthrough. He did however decide to reinforce VIII Corps with two armoured divisions, the 7th from Ninth Army in the north and the 10th from the Third Army in the south.

Patton at the time was holding the 10th Armored Division at Thionville, ready to exploit his attack at Saarläutern. Inevitably therefore the order to despatch it at once to Luxembourg brought a violent protest. For some time he had feared that, if he failed to achieve a breakthrough on the Saar in the near future, Montgomery would succeed in persuading Eisenhower to mass all available forces for the offensive in the north and relegate Third Army to a defensive role. He urged that his men had paid a heavy price for their advance to the Saar; they would feel that their sacrifices had been in vain if his offensive was hamstrung by taking 10th Armored Division from him. As he saw the situation, the aim of the Germans was to throw his army off balance and force him to abandon his offensive at the very moment when his immediate enemy was on his last legs. Bradley managed to end the conversation by saying that although there was something to be said for Patton's point of view, he did not himself see the situation in quite the same light: anyhow it was too delicate for further discussion on the telephone. His order must stand; Patton obeyed. Within the hour 10th Armored Division was on the road heading for VIII Corps' front.

Next morning low cloud once more ruled out return to Luxembourg by air. Bradley did not get back to his headquarters at Luxembourg until the afternoon. Going at once to the map room he saw that the map showed no less than fourteen enemy divisions on VIII Corps' front, half of them armoured. That morning, Baron, the commander of 4th Infantry Division, holding the line of the Sauer river 20 miles north of Luxembourg, had only just held the enemy, throwing his last reserves of cooks, bakers and clerks to stop the gaps in his front. He now had warned Allen, Bradley's Chief of Staff, that, if 10th Armored Division did not arrive soon, 12th Army Group's headquarters itself would be faced by the alternative of being in the firing line or packing up for a move elsewhere. The enemy's opening barrage and rapid penetration of VIII Corps' front had completely disrupted communications. Much of the information coming through was obviously exaggerated and in any case, owing partly to the lack of air reconnaissance, unverified and confusing. The outlook in fact seemed worse than it actually was. Unknown to the staff at Army Group headquarters many junior officers of formations and units which had been over-run or bypassed were holding on to isolated key points, blocking roads and blowing up bridges: the survivors of VIII Corps' four divisions were fighting a hundred unrecorded battles with skill and courage and slowing down the German advance. Nevertheless the situation was highly critical—much more critical than Patton realised at the time as he frankly admitted later. He did however on this day summon Millikin, the Commander of III Corps, to Nancy to discuss with him the action which would be necessary, if orders were received, to counter-attack the southern flank of the enemy penetration, soon to be called 'the Bulge'. Fortunately, it was on this day too that Eisenhower decided just in time to despatch his only reserve, the 101 and 82nd Airborne Divisions, from Reims to the key road centre at Bastogne.

Next morning, the 18th, Bradley summoned Patton to Luxembourg where he arrived in mid-morning. Despite the overcast skies a clearer picture of the situation in the Ardennes was now beginning to emerge. The penetration was much greater than either had thought; the shoulders however were holding firm. Sepp Dietrich's main thrust with the Sixth Panzer Army in the north was being held at Malmédy: 7th Armored Division had arrived in time to hold St-Vith. North of Luxembourg the prompt arrival of 10th Armored Division had temporarily stabilised the front. In the centre however Fifth Panzer Army was heading all out for Bastogne, as yet held only by elements of 9th and 10th Armored Divisions but 101 Airborne Division in a mad rush from Reims was on its way with orders to hold the place at all costs. Bradley said that his general intention was for the First Army to hold firm in the north and to move a corps of three divisions from the south to help VIII Corps. Patton must call off his offensive on the Saar. He then asked him what he could do. Without a moment's hesitation Patton replied that he could start to concentrate the 4th Armored Division near Longwy by midnight, pull the 80th Division out of the line and put it on the road to Luxembourg at first light and get the 26th Division moving north within 24 hours. He then returned to his own headquarters to see that these orders were carried out with the normal promptitude of Third Army.

That night at 23.00 hours Bradley spoke to him on the telephone: Eisenhower was on his way to Verdun where he would hold a conference at 11.00 hours on the morrow, the 19th, to be attended by Patton and Devers of Sixth Army Group. Before going to bed, Patton ordered his Chief of Staff to arrange a staff meeting next morning at 08.00 hours to include not only all members of the General Staff but also Weyland of XIX TAC and his staff as well.

The meeting began in true Patton style. Plans, he informed them, had been changed; while he knew they were accustomed to rapid movement, they were now to have the privilege of moving even faster. In general he explained that he proposed to strike due north to hit the underbelly of the German penetration where it hurt, using VIII Corps and III Corps on any two of three possible axis: the first due north from Diekirch, the second from Arlon on Bastogne and the third on the Neufchâteau–Bastogne road against the tip of the Bulge—wherever that might be. In the next hour he and his staff planned in outline three distinct operations and arranged a simple code using which he could telephone Gay, his Chief of Staff, from Verdun to say which was to be implemented. Pleased with his handiwork he then set off for Verdun arriving at the rendezvous 15 minutes ahead of the appointed hour.

It was a distinguished gathering of higher commanders which assembled in the stone-cold barracks: Eisenhower, who had travelled all the way from Versailles in a heavy bullet-proof car because it was rumoured that Skorzeny had despatched a hand-picked squad of gunmen to assassinate him; Tedder, his British deputy—ready as ever to offer if possible advice differing from Montgomery's—Bradley and Devers. Major-General Strong, ordered to bring the assembled generals up to date with the situation, opened the proceedings by painting a picture of almost inspissated gloom. This prompted Eisenhower to put matters in their true perspective by saying with emphasis: 'The present situation is to be regarded as one of opportunity for us and not of disaster. There will be only cheerful faces at this conference table.' Patton at once burst out 'Hell, let's have the guts to let the . . . go all the way to Paris, then we'll really cut 'em off and chew 'em up.' This raised a laugh. They then proceeded to business.

All agreed that a counter-attack must be delivered at the earliest possible moment. All agreed that it must be against the enemy's southern flank; all agreed that Patton was the man for the job. Asked by Eisenhower when he could get to Luxembourg and take charge of the battle he replied, that afternoon. He could make a strong attack, he said, with III Corps, with three divisions striking north up the road from Arlon to Bastogne; 4th Armored, 26th and 80th Divisions would be ready to this end by 22 December. He added that he could not attack with a stronger force till several days later and that to wait till then would be to forfeit surprise. This forthright statement touched off a ripple of astonished satisfaction. All agreed that for the moment Hodges in the north, with his whole front in a state of flux, was in no position to stage a counter-offensive just yet and that the rest of the Allied front must revert to the defence. The conference then proceeded to adjust responsibility south of the Moselle so that Patton could pull out his XII Corps and switch it north and north-east of Luxembourg. Devers quickly agreed to take over Patton's front on the Saar up to Saarläutern. Patton however refused to give up that part of it held by his XX Corps: he wanted it as a rest area and, looking farther ahead, because he would need it to take Trier later on and thus make possible the campaign through the Palatinate on which he had set his heart. He refused to hand over any bridging equipment as well. Eisenhower finally summarised the day's decisions in a telegram to the Chiefs of Staff: 'The general plan is to plug the holes in the north and launch a coordinated attack from the south.' The details he, Tedder and Bradley were more than happy to leave to Patton. According to Bradley he was itching to start. Lighting a fresh cigar he pointed to the Bulge where it pierced the blue lines on the map and exclaimed: 'Brad, this time the Kraut's stuck his head in a meatgrinder.' Then with a turn of his fist he added: 'And this time I've got hold of the handle.' Raising the telephone to speak to Gay, his Chief of Staff, he told him to get the 26th Division and the 4th Armored Division moving on Arlon via Longwy and the 80th Division on Luxembourg via Thionville. The main effort he said would be by III Corps up the Arlon–

Bastogne road; XII Corps would take over north of Luxembourg. This done he set off for the headquarters of XX Corps where he proposed to spend the night; on arrival here he set in motion the 5th Division, at the time engaged in an attack at Sauerläutern, towards the north. Within 24 hours they would be in an assembly area north of Luxembourg.

On arrival at 12th Army Group's headquarters at Luxembourg next morning he was shocked to learn that Eisenhower on return to Versailles had taken a decision which deprived Bradley of the First and Ninth Armies and placed them under command of Montgomery. This left Bradley one army, Patton's Third. The Bulge had split Bradley's Army Group irrevocably into two parts—Patton and the Third Army plus a fraction of First Army to the south of the great salient and the greater part of First and Ninth Armies to the north. Bradley with his headquarters in Luxembourg was in no position to control the two northern armies. He was unwilling to transfer his headquarters to Namur on the grounds that it would have a bad effect on the morale of the troops. Eisenhower, after some heartsearching, had therefore on purely military grounds—and on military grounds alone—decided to place all forces north of the line Givet–Prum under Montgomery, who was much better placed to exercise command with, incidentally, a very strong corps in reserve behind the Meuse between Liège and Namur. To Bradley this was a bitter blow: in protesting to Bedell Smith, Eisenhower's Chief of Staff, he said 'Certainly if Monty's were an American command, I would agree with you entirely' and later he wrote 'There was ample justification to the Army Group in the north taking temporary command on the side of the penetration.' It was most unfortunate that there should at this time have been so much antagonism towards Montgomery at both SHAEF and on the part of Patton. There was some justification however for their resentment at Eisenhower's apparent bias towards the British. Fully aware that they were responsible for the far-larger share of the campaign, they felt strongly that British influence at SHAEF was out of proportion to their contribution to the combined effort. The Supreme Commander's Deputy and the naval and air commanders were all British. In the event Bradley took what was in fact a reduction in status with dignity; neither did he at any time interfere with Patton's operations, as he might well have done, since his was the only army in his Army Group. As for Eisenhower, nothing enhances his reputation more than his courage in taking in the cold light of military necessity a decision which placed Allied interests before national prestige, and probably his own personal feelings. Furthermore, knowing only too well Patton's impetuous character and tendency to get the bit between his teeth, he made it quite clear that for the present his counter-attack must not go beyond Bastogne.

From Luxembourg Patton drove on to Arlon to get from Middleton of the unfortunate VIII Corps a first-hand picture of what was going on in the Bulge. Here he found Gaffey of 4th Armored Division and Millikin of III Corps already there. The remnants of the corps were still fighting well. Within Bastogne, now surrounded by three divisions of Fifth Panzer and Seventh Armies, were 101 Airborne Division plus a combat command of 9th and another of 10th Armored Division, the 705th Tank Destroyer Battalion and some coloured artillery and quartermaster units—all clearly resolved to fight on if necessary to the end. From here he set off for the eastern flank, visiting in succession the headquarters of 9th and 10th Armored Divisions and the 4th and 80th Infantry Divisions north-east of Luxembourg. As a temporary measure, pending the arrival of XII Corps to look after this flank, he placed Major-General Morris temporarily in charge. Having thus sorted out the command problems on his new front he then proceeded to order forward self-propelled tank destroyer battalions, hospitals and miscellaneous units to stiffen further his new front. The 20 December, even for Patton, was indeed a hectic day; only an army staff of exceptional resilience could have competed with such an apparently chaotic situation and, incidentally, so dynamic a commander. A major part of Third Army was now making a gigantic 90 degree wheel and driving north at full speed, to complete the redeployment now rapidly taking shape with, on the left, VIII Corps consisting of 101 Airborne Division, 28th Infantry Division and 9th Armored Division; in the centre about Arlon, III Corps with the 4th Armored, 26th and 28th Infantry Divisions and on the right, in the north-east of Luxembourg, XII Corps comprising 4th and 5th Infantry and 10th

Armored Divisions. xx Corps were still in the line on the Saar front. Provisionally Patton had prescribed 00.40 hours on 22 December for iii Corps to start its advance to relieve Bastogne and open the way to St-Vith. No commander in World War Two, except perhaps Rommel, had a greater capacity to get the real feel of a situation: to defeat the unforgiving minute he was prepared to violate almost every tenet of the teaching of the Staff College at Fort Leavenworth, to improvise from day to day, to stretch the capacity of the available roads and to exploit the individual initiative and offensive eagerness of his officers and men to the full. He had every justification for turning on the heat for this was the very day when von Rundstedt, with Sepp Dietrich stalled in the north at Malmédy, switched his main effort to von Manteuffel's Fifth Panzer Army now surging around what remained of the American defences anchored on St-Vith and Bastogne.

Patton's switch of the Third Army from its bridgehead on the Saar to the Ardennes by any standard can stand comparison with advantage with any similar manoeuvre achieved under much easier conditions by Rommel in North Africa and von Rundstedt in France in 1940. Within less than 48 hours after receiving Eisenhower's orders at Verdun he would have two divisions attacking towards Bastogne. Within a week he would move the bulk of his army a quarter of a million strong and including 133,000 tanks and trucks between 50 and 70 miles to the north in damnable weather and over icy roads. Bradley in Luxembourg looked out of his office window on the serried columns of the Third Army, double-banked, relentlessly moving north round the clock. The troops in their muddy greatcoats huddled together as the bitter east wind swept through their canvas-topped trucks. The tank commanders, in the turrets of their Shermans, muffled to the eyes in woollen scarves, guided their clumsy vehicles over the cobblestones. All day and all night with blazing headlights the vast array moved relentlessly on. On 21 December a heavy snowfall deadened the noise of the grinding trucks; tanks skidded on the ice. The sky was still overcast: there could be no help from the air. Throughout 12th Army Group the tension reached its climax.

Patton's main anxiety, although he did not betray it, concerned

4th Division at Echternach now, after five days' continuous battle in a fighting withdrawal of four miles from the Sauer River, believed to be nearing the end of its tether. Although Eddy himself had already arrived in Luxembourg and taken charge, the earliest date he could mount a counter-attack with the 5th Infantry and 10th Armored Divisions was the 24th. Fortunately the 10th Infantry Regiment would soon arrive to stage an impromptu attack immediately after a 75-mile drive from Saarläutern which would stabilise the front. Meanwhile no one realised better than Patton that if the enemy now put in a full-scale attack on this part of his front, his own offensive with III Corps would at best be completely put out of gear: that is what he himself would have done had he been in the enemy's position. His continual admonitions to 'drive like hell' can therefore be understood. Fortunately the enemy had not an inkling that the Third Army was on the move.

At a final coordinating meeting on the 21st at Luxembourg for the attack on the morrow with the staffs of III, XII and XX Corps, sensing the stress under which all were labouring, he rose from his seat after the briefing and, glaring into the anxious faces before him, roared 'This will get the bastards out of their holes so we can kill all of 'em—now go to work.' By a lucky chance the Christmas cards prepared for distribution before the attack on the West Wall and written on 11 December contained a prayer for fine weather for the battle and a blessing from the army commander; these were now issued. He personally had no doubt whatever, despite his anxiety with regard to the situation on the 4th Divisional front, that the III Corps attack would succeed. During the night Millikin, the commander of III Corps, requested postponement of H-Hour from 04.00 hours to 06.00 hours; his wish was granted.

The country astride the Arlon–Bastogne road is as rugged as anywhere in the Ardennes. It is criss-crossed by small rivers and streams, many with deep gorges; dense woods alternate with rolling fields and clearings. Bastogne dominates the road net. There are many roads and tracks of dubious quality linking up the isolated farms. The main roads from Arlon to the north-west and from Neufchâteau to the north-east offer some, but not many, possibilities for manoeuvre. There is only one lateral—the main road from Arlon

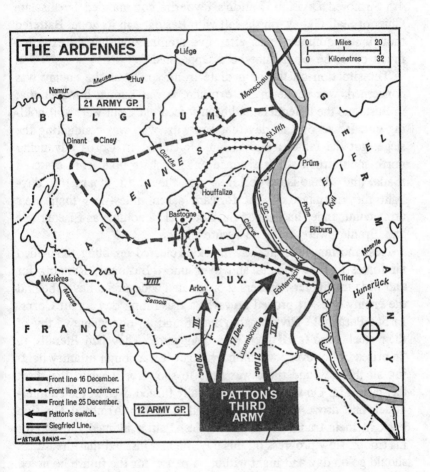

THE ARDENNES

Miles 0 — 20
Kilometres 0 — 32

Liége

Meuse

Huy

Monschau

Namur

21 ARMY GP.

B E L G I U M

Dinant   Ciney

St.Vith

Prüm

A R D E N N E S

Ourthe

Houffalize

Bastogne

Clerve

Prüm

Kyll

Bitburg

Moselle

Mézières

VIII

L U X.

Arlon

Echternach

Trier

Hunsrück

Semois

III

17 Dec.

Luxembourg

III

21 Dec.

N

F R A N C E

20 Dec.

Front line 16 December.
Front line 20 December.
Front line 25 December.
Patton's switch.
Siegfried Line.

12 ARMY GP.

PATTON'S
THIRD
ARMY

— ARTHUR BANKS —

G E I F E L   F R O M   G E R M A N Y

to Neufchâteau. It was from this start line that III Corps stepped off at 06.00 hours on the 22nd, on time despite the fever heat in which it had been mounted. Millikin, with his headquarters in Arlon, had 80th Division on the right, the 26th Division in the centre and 4th Armored Division, Patton's favourite commanded by his late Chief of Staff Gaffey, on the left with Bastogne in its zone. Battered though its equipment was after five months' fighting he expected much of it: he would not be disappointed.

The situation on the immediate front, so far as the enemy was concerned, was vague in the extreme. It was known however that in Bastogne the defenders had been forced back but were still holding out. It was on this day that Luttwitz, who was conducting the siege, got the famous reply from McAuliffe. III Corps advancing north soon struck stiff resistance and much trouble from cratered roads and demolished bridges. In the short hours of daylight they managed to get forward seven miles—less than their army commander had hoped but nonetheless notable as Eisenhower and Bradley were quick to assure him.

Next morning at long last the skies cleared enabling the Allied air forces to take a hand and to resupply Bastogne. Ranging far and wide the fighter-bombers soon created widespread havoc behind the enemy lines. It proved however a frustrating day for III Corps. In 5th Parachute Division they had found an opponent worthy of their steel—hard-faced men who died game. They had literally to be prised out of every wood and village: it was tough infantry fighting all the way and there was little to show for it when the short day closed in. On the 24th they actually turned over to the counterattack and drove Combat Command B of 4th Armored Division back in their tracks for several miles. Patton blamed himself for his troops' slow progress on this day: he had insisted that the attack should go on day and night without a pause; for the future he noted that whilst this is feasible for two nights on end, thereafter the toughest men faltered through fatigue. Twice he went to the length of apologising to Eisenhower for the slowness of his advance—quite unnecessarily, under less-determined leadership than his own and that of Millikin, Eddy and Gaffey, there would probably have been no progress at all, so close was the country, so damnable the weather and so bloody-minded the enemy.

By now XII Corps on the right south of the Sauer had started its offensive against the right shoulder of the Bulge in country at least as intricate as that on III Corps' front. Here the enemy artillery and *nebelwerfer* fire on both sides reached a crescendo. By now Patton had built up his supporting artillery to the impressive total of 88 battalions of 1,056 guns of 105mm. calibre and over, in addition to the divisional artilleries.

Within Bastogne the defence perimeter had now shrunk to 16 miles. On Christmas Day the enemy launched his supreme effort against the heroic garrison, only to be thrown back time and time again. On the east flank XII Corps broke through and forced the enemy back to the Sauer. On III Corps' front it was however another frustrating day. Millikin faced apparent stalemate. He therefore decided to attempt to work round the west flank on the morrow in the direction of the Neufchâteau–Bastogne road. Early in the afternoon Gaffey of 4th Armored Division asked permission to take a big risk with Combat Command R for a breakthrough to Bastogne. It was granted. At 18.45 hours, working round the edge of the village of Assenois, they at last made contact with 101 Airborne Division, opening a corridor three hundred yards wide. That night the light-tank company of the 37th Tank Battalion escorted 40 trucks of supplies and 70 ambulances into Bastogne.

Both sides at the time recognised this day, 26 December, as the Day of Decision, the turning point of the Ardennes battle. There is no need 25 years later to dispute this view. Von Manteuffel's Panzer divisions, bypassing Bastogne, had reached Celles five miles from the Meuse at Dinant; on Christmas Day Collins' VII Corps with the British 29th Armoured Brigade under his command had struck back and thrown the Germans out of the village. With clear skies, so complete had the Allied dominance of the air become that from the 26th all the Panzer divisions were forbidden to move in daylight. Only at this late hour did Hitler at long last give permission for the rest of the reserves of tanks supplies and ammunition to be given to von Manteuffel but now they could not be moved for lack of petrol. On Third Army's front, XII Corps had by now on the Sauer completely eliminated the shoulder the German Seventh Army had been ordered to create. Admittedly Bastogne was still linked with Third Army only by a tenuous and precarious corridor; it had none the less been relieved. The news put fresh heart into all the Allied armies. Much hard fighting around the place still lay ahead; before it was over it would suck into the maelstrom no less than nine German divisions and two corps headquarters, more often than not thrown in piecemeal in response to frantic orders from Hitler and his hangers-on. It was a soldiers' battle in bitter cold and biting wind; never did 101 Airborne Division and Third Army fight with greater determination. By 2 January they had pushed the Germans back between four and six miles from the centre of the ruins of the little town. Next day, far too late according to von Manteuffel, the Germans short of men, weapons, petrol and ammunition called off the attack.

On 27 December Patton put forward in forthright terms a plan for amputating the great salient—now 40 miles wide at the base— from the shoulders of the Bulge with strong armoured forces, his own army pushing direct toward Bitburg and Prüm on what his staff called the 'Honeymoon Trail'. Bedell Smith, Eisenhower's Chief of Staff, thought there was much to be said for the concept despite the awkward lay-out of the roads in the north. To let Patton's army loose in this way, however, would inevitably have distorted Eisenhower's plans for the Broad Front. Patton, at this time too, continued to press Bradley to try to get back control of the whole front into American hands. Bradley therefore, after a visit to Montgomery on Christmas Day in the vain hope of accelerating the counter-attack in the north, did his utmost to try to persuade Eisenhower to give him back the First and Ninth Armies. He failed to get his way despite the fact that Montgomery, with almost incredible lack of tact, had chosen this very moment to revive the proposal that there should be a separate commander for the ground forces. Controlling his justifiable irritation Eisenhower made it unequivocally clear that the existing arrangements for command would hold good for the moment. Furthermore the First and Third Armies would get on with the reduction of the salient by attacking respectively from north and south mid-way through the Bulge towards Houffalize. Meanwhile he made it unequivocally clear that he would stand no further argument from Bradley, Montgomery and Patton. His admirers can thus draw comfort from the fact that at this time of crisis, unshaken by the suggestions of others, he proceeded serenely on his chosen way like the great von Moltke; others can regret that once again a great opportunity was missed to exploit the talents of Patton and Third Army to the full.

Undeterred by discouragement from above, the enemy and the appalling weather Third Army and its ebullient commander thrust forward, this time towards Houffalize, four days ahead of Montgomery—VII and xxx British Corps in the north. His Order of the Day of 1 January had the true Napoleonic ring:

> To The Officers and Men of the Third Army
> and
> To our Comrades of the XIX Tactical Air Force.
>
> From the bloody corridor at Avranches, to Brest, thence across France to the Saar, over the Saar into Germany, and now on to Bastogne, your record has been one of continuous victory. Not only have you invariably defeated a cunning and ruthless enemy, but also you have overcome by your indomitable fortitude every aspect of terrain and weather. Neither heat nor dust nor floods nor snow have stayed your progress. The speed and brilliancy of your achievements are unsurpassed in military history.
>
> Recently I had the honour of receiving at the hands of the Twelfth Army Group Commander, Lieutenant General Omar N. Bradley, a second Oak Leaf Cluster to the DSM. This award was bestowed on me, not for what I have done, but because of what you have achieved. From the bottom of my heart I thank you.
>
> My New Year wish and sure conviction for you is that, under the protection of Almighty God, and the inspired leadership of our President and the High Command, you will continue your victorious course to the end that tyranny and vice shall be eliminated, our dead comrades avenged, and peace restored to a war-weary world.
>
> In closing, I can find no fitter expression of my feelings than to apply to you the immortal words spoken by General Scott at Chapultepec when he said: "Brave rifles, veterans, you have been baptized in fire and blood and have come out steel."
>
> G.S. Patton, Jr.,
> Lieut. General, U.S. Army,
> Commanding.

Better evidence of his own personal morale at this time it would be hard to find. Whether inspired by his literary efforts or not it is small wonder that he infected all under him with his own indomitable spirit to fight on through fire, ice and snow, cost what it might, to ultimate victory. Here was no cold-blooded strategist, remote from the battle driving his men to their deaths. In his innermost heart he knew that he was one of them: he shared their emotions and felt their suffering to the depth of his being. In driving to the headquarters of the III Corps on 7 January he

> passed through the last combat team of 90th Division moving up for battle. These men had been in trucks for a great many hours with the temperature at six degrees below zero and were thoroughly chilled. On the opposite side of the road was an endless file of ambulances bringing men back—wounded men; and yet, when the soldiers of the 90th Division saw me they stood up and cheered. It was the most moving experience of my life, and the knowledge of what the ambulance contained made it still more poignant.

The burden of command in battle is indeed heavy and bitter, for success inevitably is bought at the price of the lives of one's fellow men. There is a hint too of Patton's own realisation of the ultimate cruelty of war in the macabre parody he wrote when his army linked up with the First Army on 16 January at Houffalize:

> *O little town of Houffalize, how still we see thee lie;*
> *Above thy steep and battered streets, the aeroplanes sail by.*
> *Yet in thy dark streets shineth not any Goddamned light,*
> *The hopes and fears of all the years were blown to Hell last night.*

First Army went on to capture St-Vith on 23 January and four days later Third Army reached the Our river in the south. The Ardennes battle was over.

The Battle of the Bulge has been the subject of as much bilious criticism as Waterloo, Gettysburg and Alamein. As a result only three reputations have emerged with almost unqualified acclaim— those of Eisenhower, the Allied air forces and the American soldier. Justice demands that to these should be added the name of Patton.

In the tense days before Christmas the knowledge that a fighting commander of repute was taking positive action sustained many far beyond the heroic garrison of Bastogne to as far back as Paris and indeed Washington. In the faint praise given in *Crusade in Europe* for his part in the battle there is a hint of condescension which comes ill from the pen of one who despite all his talents and virtues was an unblooded soldier. There is truth in its commander's claim that Third Army in its lightning deployment to the north at the critical moment to relieve Bastogne 'moved farther and faster and engaged more divisions in less time than any other Army in the history of United States.' It had been the bloodiest battle in the Third Army's career; the enemy's toll of casualties had been higher still. Above all his men had responded magnificently to his leadership. He could write with pride and conviction immediately after the battle: 'No country can stand against such an Army.'

16

Triumph West of the Rhine

Mobilitate vigemus
(In mobility lies our strength)
Cavalry Motto

Few will quarrel with Chester Wilmot's comment soon after the war that by now Eisenhower, despite British objections and criticism from Patton and Bradley, had taken a firm grip of his command. The Germans still had 85 divisions west of the Rhine; on his past form it was virtually certain that Hitler would allow no withdrawal on their part. Eisenhower therefore decided to destroy them where they were and in the process close with the whole length of the Rhine. He would thus, with this defensive barrier in his possession, be able to forestall any counter-offensive the enemy might care to stage. Furthermore by closing with the river along the whole front he would have a choice of crossing places from which to develop his attacks in support of his main effort against the Ruhr. In particular the possibilities of an advance through Frankfurt and Kassel seemed more attractive than through the rugged country between Cologne and Bonn—a self-evident fact to every German worker on his holiday in the seventies, as he drinks his beer in the sunshine on the deck of a boat proceeding up the Rhine to Koblenz and Mainz. Accordingly, as a first step, he directed Montgomery's 21st Army Group with Ninth United States Army under command to seize the western bank of the river from Nijmegen to Düsseldorff by converging attacks, one by First Canadian Army from the Reichswald ('Veritable') and the other from the Roer river by the Ninth Army ('Grenade'). In this phase First Army was to take the Roer dams and at the same time protect the southern flank of Ninth

Army. When Ninth Army reached the Rhine, First Army would strike towards Cologne and, after taking the city, move south and cut off the enemy west of the river. Patton and Third Army meanwhile, on the grounds that the flow of reinforcements could not support a simultaneous offensive by Ninth, First and Third Armies, were condemned to a virtually static role. No course of action could have been less congenial to its commander, already absorbed in a series of minor offensives politely called probing attacks, than thus to be relegated to a back seat when the news was broken to him at a conference held at First Army headquarters at Spa on 2 February.

The assumption that the Allied policy underlying Eisenhower's orders was still based on his directive of 1 January, which specifically stated that on reaching the Rhine 'the main effort would be north of the Ruhr', still held good: the British in fact would remain under this delusion for a further two months. Indeed the ponderous logistic preparations necessary in Montgomery's Army Group to carry it not only across the Rhine but right through thereafter to Berlin were already in an advanced planning stage. What a bitter pill to swallow this was for Bradley and Patton never seems to have been realised by Montgomery and others at the time and, indeed, since. On patriotic grounds alone it seemed to them that a fair share in the final victory and the glory going with it, now obviously not far off, was being denied to their country. The American contribution to the Allied cause in men, money and material was now more than three times as great as that of the British; since November their armies had borne a higher proportion of the casualties. It seemed less than fair that the laurels now to be gained should go above all to Montgomery who had in the Ardennes battle so recently outraged American sentiment by an ill-timed and ill-worded statement to the Press. As professional soldiers they would have been less than human had they not resented being deprived of what seemed to them their fair share of personal advancement and acclaim. If the thought that the ultimate aim of the Allies should have been the achievement of the political end most acceptable to the United States, Great Britain and Western Europe ever entered their heads is more than doubtful, subscribing as they did to the doctrine of their generation of regular soldiers, that their task was to destroy the main forces of the enemy. Once the Wehrmacht was destroyed all other objectives would fall into their laps like ripe plums from a tree. The rest could be left to the politicians. On purely topographical grounds they were on a better wicket: the plains of Northern Germany were not the ideal romping grounds for tanks as Montgomery claimed: there was much to be said for a double envelopment via Frankfurt and a thrust towards Kassel. There was something to be said too for continuing the pressure in the centre and the south to prevent the withdrawal of German forces to the north.

Patton's objections to the comparatively passive role now assigned to him were, however, based primarily on more subtle grounds. No American general had a better grasp of the human element in war: no one realised more profoundly that morale is never constant. From his experience in two wars he realised that troops in contact with the enemy should never be allowed to remain quiescent: allow them to sit still and acquiesce in a routine of live and let live with the enemy and they will brood to their own moral undoing; action, and offensive action at that, alone brings release. This, allied with the concept of speed, was the very heart of the Patton approach to battle. With his army already probing the Siegfried defences he had no intention whatever of complying literally with SHAEF's written orders consigning him to the defensive. Fortunately in Bradley he had a most understanding immediate superior who realised his fundamental incapacity to sit still. With Eisenhower's tacit consent he allowed Patton to mount an offensive on his front in the Eifel allegedly designed to prevent the enemy pulling out troops for use in the north against Montgomery. In the process he was 'to pierce the Siegfried defences north of the Moselle and advance quietly to the Kyll', a mountain stream parallel to the Luxembourg border and 12 miles beyond the German frontier. There he was to seize a bridgehead for use later in an eventual advance to the Rhine. The operation, to meet any objections Montgomery might raise if he got wind of it, was officially described as 'aggressive defence'. Few instances in the whole campaign better illustrate the loose rein on which Eisenhower drove his American commanders and the length to which he was prepared to go to maintain the appearance of Allied solidarity, despite the recent provocation by Montgomery and the obvious decline in British importance as the war neared its end. Patton's meeting with him on 5 February casts an intriguing light on their relationship at this time. Summoned to Bastogne, Patton arrived fearing that his impending offensive would be nipped in the bud. To his intense relief he found that the purpose of the meeting was of a routine character including the taking of photographs for the Press—a function he always enjoyed. Although it was the first time they had met since 19 December, in a very different atmosphere, at Verdun, Eisenhower in the course of conversation never once mentioned the Third Army's relief of Bastogne.

On the evening of 7 February Montgomery opened his offensive in the north from the Nijmegen area striking with First Canadian Army, 75 per cent of which was United Kingdom based. First Army duly captured the Roer dams, whereupon the Germans opened the stopcocks and flooded the area thus preventing Ninth Army from playing its part in the pincer movement until 23 February, by which time the waters had subsided. In this fortnight First Canadian Army in its struggle with the German First Parachute Army, whose morale was high, encountered and surmounted almost every bedevilment characteristic of an attack in wet winter weather against fixed defences and with their lines of communication with the rear several feet under water. Patton's so-called 'aggressive defence' in the Eifel proceeded in a strikingly similar setting—mud, collapsed roads, incessant rain, floods and concrete defences plus mines. Some of his forward troops even had to be supplied by air so bad was the going. It took the form of two 'probing attacks' the first directed on Prüm, an important communications centre and key position, and the other on Bitburg 24 miles to the south and also covered by the Siegfried defence system. Here the West Wall had reached a high stage of development. It consisted of a belt of defences, between two and three miles wide, of concrete bunkers, pill-boxes, fire trenches and gun positions, protected by forests of barbed wire, deep minefields and concrete anti-tank obstacles. Some of the amenities were of a most elaborate character: there were water closets, showerbaths, underground barracks and every conceivable convenience, including electricity and an enormous telephone installation. Some of the

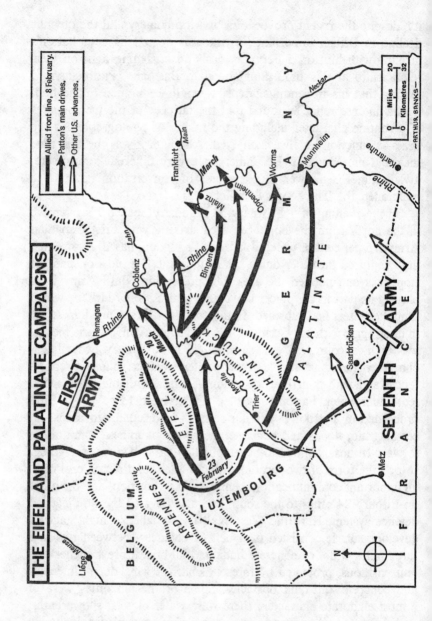

THE EIFEL AND PALATINATE CAMPAIGNS

Allied front line, 8 February.
Patton's main drives.
Other U.S. advances.

Miles 0 20
Kilometres 0 32

—ARTHUR BANKS—

G E R M A N Y

Frankfurt
Main
Mainz
Oppenheim
Worms
Mannheim
Neckar
Karlsruhe
Rhine

21 March

Lahn
Coblenz
Rhine
Bingen
Remagen
Rhine

10 March

FIRST ARMY

EIFEL

H U N S R Ü C K

P A L A T I N A T E

Moselle
Trier

23 February

Saarbrücken

SEVENTH ARMY

F R A N C E

Metz

LUXEMBOURG

ARDENNES

BELGIUM

Liége
Meuse

N

cupolas were ten inches thick and impervious to American 90mm. shells. Alternating frosts and thaws converted the intervening ground into quagmires; the heavy rain turned the streams into roaring torrents. Nothing deterred Third Army. By 22 February almost the whole defensive system on the Army front had been pierced, Prüm had been taken, Bitburg was on the point of falling and south of the Moselle xx Corps had won a small bridgehead over the Sauer south of its junction with the Moselle near Trier. Patton had a poor opinion of fixed defences. 'Pacifists,' he wrote, 'would do well to study the Siegfried and Maginot Lines, remembering that these defences were forced; that Troy fell; that the walls of Hadrian succumbed; that the Great Wall of China was futile. . . . In war, the only sure defence is offence, and the efficiency of offence depends on the warlike souls of those conducting it.' When in the midst of his operations Bradley telephoned to ask how soon he could go on the defensive, he replied that he was the oldest leader in age and combat experience in the us Army in Europe, and that if he had to go on the defensive he would ask to be relieved. Bradley tactfully replied that he owed too much to his troops to do that and would have to stay on. The conversation concluded with a suggestion that it would be a good thing if some of Bradley's staff visited the front to find out how the other half lived. Third Army continued its aggressive defence.

It might have been expected in the damnable weather conditions that the proportion of sick to battle casualties would have shown a marked rise: in fact it did not. Patton personally spent most of the hours of daylight touring his front in an open car: he never had a cold and his face though slightly blistered gave him no trouble. He recorded not without satisfaction that his aides in the back seat suffered more than he did. He was everywhere. The story however that he swam the Sauer in a flood and in face of heavy enemy fire is an exaggeration. In fact he crossed on a partly submerged assault bridge with no hand rails, under a smoke screen. He recorded that on arrival on the far bank 'the men were glad to see me.' The knowledge that he had from his own observation of the dangers and discomforts they had to endure, and his readiness to praise their feats of arms to the skies was equalled only by his unique capacity to deliver unforgettable reprimands where justified. This goes far to explain the high morale of his army at this stage of the war. The bond between him and his soldiers had grown very close. One day early in March in an icy drizzle he noticed that his driver, who was a stranger to him and clad only in an Eisenhower jacket over a brown wool pullover, was turning blue. Reaching forward he tapped him on the shoulder and said 'Corporal, are you cold?' He replied that he was. When asked whether he had a warm sweater he replied that he had none. Promptly Patton unbuttoned his own jacket, pulled off his own sweater and gave it to the man. The devout will recollect that not far from this spot the Blessed Saint Martin, a military tribune, in similar circumstances retained half his cloak for himself.

By the end of February, VIII Corps on the left and XII Corps in the centre were over the Kyll. On 2 March XX Corps took Trier, capturing the bridge over the Moselle intact. The stage was now set for Third Army's Eifel campaign. On their northern flank, First Army was over the Erft which they had bridged in several places; already the Rhine itself was within range of American guns. In the Rhineland, First Canadian and Ninth Armies had linked up at Geldern and were battering to death the remnants of the First Parachute Army as they struggled to escape across the river at Xanten.

Bradley now issued orders for the brief campaign designed to close with the Rhine north of the Moselle on which he, with very good reason, would always look back with the greatest professional pride. In brief the First Army was to take Cologne and then move south-east to link up with a thrust by the Third Army through the heart of the Eifel aimed at Koblenz. On 5 March both armies struck simultaneously. 4th Armored Division burst out and despite rain and mud advanced 16 kilometres before dark, capturing the German corps commander on their front; 11th Armored Division on their left also got forward. Thereafter 4th Armored Division literally streaked for Koblenz through the forests of the Eifel. Within two days they had created a corridor 35 miles long, right through the enemy's position. On 7 March their columns converged with those of 11th Armored Division a few miles west of the Rhine, thus cutting off large numbers of Germans, stranded without a clue, in the rugged uplands of the Eifel. West of the Rhine on both the First and Third Army fronts organised resistance collapsed. As the American tanks rolled into the deserted streets of the towns they found white sheets signifying surrender hung out on every house and all the windows shuttered. Army transport abandoned for want of petrol littered the roads. From the direction of the Rhine came the dull thud of bridges being blown up. Almost at the very moment when 4th and 11th Armored Divisions were meeting near Koblenz, a combat team of 9th Armored Division struck out for the railway bridge over the Rhine at Remagen. Its capture intact before the demolition parties could complete its destruction in itself is one of the epics of the war. It is however part of the history of Hodges' army and not Patton's. So too is Bradley's immediate decision to exploit it, endorsed enthusiastically by Eisenhower, giving him as it did not only an alternative in the event of Montgomery's offensive beyond the river in the north breaking down, but also, whatever happened, a promising route via Frankfurt, Giessen and Kassel for the double envelopment of the Ruhr. The Broad Front plan of October of the previous year, the bible of the logistic staffs, already dog-eared and outdated, would never be the same again. Bradley, still fearful that divisions would be filched from his own army group for Montgomery's benefit, and Hodges and Patton relegated to a minor role in the triumphal march to final victory, now determined to get both so deeply committed that they could not be withdrawn. South of the Moselle from Koblenz to Strasbourg stretched the huge German salient of the Saar Palatinate, a triangle with 75-mile sides with its base on the Rhine, part of it admittedly outside the boundaries of his army group, but it would do. Now that Patton was in possession of all the country north of the Moselle the possibility lay wide open for an attack south-east, taking in rear the West Wall defences holding up the Seventh Army. The prospect not only appealed to Bradley but to Eisenhower too. Bradley therefore took to the air for Patton's headquarters at Luxembourg.

Patton was having his hair cut in the odd setting of a home for the aged and infirm. He called for another barber: Bradley could do with a hair-cut too. As the barbers snipped, the two together hatched the plot for one of the most brilliant and audacious operations of the war. Despite the lack of enthusiasm for it on the part of Devers of Sixth Army Group and the staff of SHAEF, preparations went ahead with the speed normal in Third Army. By 13 March Patton had five divisions on the line of the Moselle from Luxembourg to the Rhine and a further four in XX Corps in the hilly triangle north-east of Trier. Despite the speed with which the operations had been mounted his attack, this time with the infantry leading, got off to time. On the Trier front, progress at first was slow but the attack here did have the merit of attracting the enemy's main reserve, a good mountain division. XII Corps in the centre was thus able to force the Moselle on a two-divisional front with ease. By noon they had four bridges across it, and by nightfall 14 battalions south of the river. Bradley had feared that the wooded Hunsrück Mountains would prove a serious obstacle to Patton's tanks. Here for once he underestimated their dash and skill. Once again 4th Armored Division led the advance and swept all before them. Within two days they had reached the Nahe river which bisects the Palatinate near Bad Kreuznach. Here Patton paused to allow time for further troops to be brought up to strengthen his position in face of the counter-attack his intuition told him was now due. When it came it withered away in the face of XII Corps' concentrated fire. On their right XX Corps' advance from Trier was now well under way. Within six days the armour of the two corps, leaving their infantry to mop up the German units they had bypassed, had linked up south of the Nahe river. Patton now turned them towards the plains of Hesse between Mainz and Mannheim where the Rhine flows between broad level banks and on the far side gives good going towards Frankfurt. Meanwhile in the north VIII Corps had completed the capture of Koblenz and Seventh Army had forced its way through the extensive minefields of the Siegfried defences on their front. By 21 March virtually all German resistance was at an end: what remained of their Seventh and First Armies had been destroyed. Acceptance of defeat was now apparent amongst the regimental officers; the NCOs and men were indifferent. Everywhere the remnants were surrendering, with the exception of a few fanatics, in a state of utter dejection. Over 70,000 prisoners were taken by Third Army alone in four days. All traces of organisation had vanished. German generals were being rounded up on the road by military police. Patton himself driving through the woods between Kaiserslautern and Neustadt witnessed what he described as one of the greatest scenes of destruction in his experience. A German column consisting mainly of horse transport entering the road from the north-west had been struck in flank by a company of medium tanks of the 10th Armored Division:

> The Germans were moving up a rather steep canyon with a precipitous cliff on their left, while the tanks came in between them and the mountain. For more than two miles horses and vehicles were pushed over the cliff. You could see the marks of the tank treads on the flanks and shoulders of the horses, and see powder smoke on the men and horses where they had been shot at point blank range. In spite of my pride in the achievement, I was sorry for the poor creatures.

Without a pause his advance closed in on the Rhine for the crossing by *coup de main* which would be the climax of one of the most successful and complete operations in recorded history. The smell of victory was in the air.

It should not be forgotten that in these final battles Third Army and XIX Tactical Air Command had worked as one. At all times the close cooperation of the airmen with the troops on the ground had been a decisive factor. Their reconnaissance aircraft had been an essential aid in the rapidly moving operations: the fighter-bombers had ruthlessly attacked the enemy's columns as they withdrew and often when the army's advance had been temporarily held up by obstinate rearguards, a quick call to the supporting airmen had loosened the defence and resulted in a quick overthrow. Above all they had completely denied the use of the air above the battlefield to the Luftwaffe. Weyland, their commander, at all times had been in Patton's closest confidence and not far from his side. Now he and his airmen could guarantee unchallenged air supremacy over the Rhine itself.

By the 21st the XII Corps had reached Mainz and was attacking the town with two regiments. The 4th and 11th Armored Divisions were north and south of Worms. In XX Corps 12th Armored Division were closing on Mannheim. Patton and Eddy, the commander of XII Corps, reached the conclusion that the Germans expected then to attempt a crossing at Mainz. They therefore decided to lay a smoke screen there over the river and, without pausing, to make their crossing at Oppenheim about 15 miles upstream. Here by lucky chance, there was a harbour for barges accessible from the town and out of sight of both banks. Here assault boats could be launched unseen by the enemy and slip quietly into the river. Eddy in fact had selected this point months before. In addition Patton had brought forward a naval detachment of twelve LCPs who had rehearsed the crossing at Toul. His Chief Engineer, Major-General Conklin, by almost superhuman effort, had all the bridging material required well forward on wheels. On the morning of 22 March both XII and XX Corps were moving due south; then suddenly 5th and 90th Divisions swung due east. That night at 22.00 hours the 23rd Regiment of the 5th Division in assault boats and on rafts, without artillery preparation, air bombardment or dropping of airborne troops, slipped so quietly into the water that they surprised not only the enemy but the rest of Third Army as well. Before dawn on 23 March the division had six battalions on the far side with the loss of only eight killed and 20 wounded.

That morning sunlight flooded the room in the Château de Namur where Bradley was having breakfast. Suddenly he was called to the telephone. Raising the instrument he heard the familiar high-pitched voice:

'Brad, don't tell anyone but I'm across . . . I sneaked a division over last night. There are so few Krauts about they don't know it yet. So don't make any announcement: we'll keep it secret until we see how it goes.'

In the evening he telephoned again:

'Brad, for God's sake tell the world we're across. We knocked down 33 Krauts when they came after our pontoon bridge. I want the world to know Third Army made it before Monty starts across.'

Next morning Patton himself proceeded to Oppenheim, passed through the town to the barge harbour and then led the way across the low bridge spanning the Rhine. Half-way across he stopped. 'Time for a short halt' he said and, standing on the edge of the bridge, relieved his bladder into the Rhine. 'I have been looking forward to this for a long time' he said buttoning his breeches. He then walked on to the far bank: here he deliberately stubbed his toe and fell to the ground as Scipio Africanus and William the Conqueror had done in similar circumstances saying that they saw in their hands the soil of Africa or England. He now saw in his own hands the soil of Germany. For all eternity he would be in company with his peers. George Patton never under-rated himself. He left that to others: some of them his own countrymen but not of the Third Army.

17

Over the Rhine and Beyond

> In the end it is the result of the manner in which the cards
> are played or the battle fought that is put down on the score
> sheets and in the pages of history. Therefore I vote the skil-
> ful tactician above the strategist, especially him who plays
> the bad cards well
>
> *Field-Marshal Wavell*

The crossing of the Rhine at Oppenheim 24 hours ahead of Montgomery in the north opposite Wesel would be the true apogee of
Patton's career. He had fought his last full-dress battle. Henceforward Third Army's spectacular advance would partake more of the
nature of a triumphal march, punctuated by a number of fanatical
and obviously futile German attempts at further resistance, rather
than the pursuit of a beaten but still unbroken enemy.

Eisenhower had set out to defeat the Germans west of the Rhine,
close up with the river and cross it. In the process, despite criticism
from the British CIGS Alanbrooke, he had realised his highest hopes.
In February and March 21st Army Group had had 23,000 casualties
and taken 50,000 prisoners; 12th Army Group had suffered the
highest losses (nearly 40,000) but had captured the largest number
of prisoners (over 185,000); for Sixth Army Group the figures were
33,000 with 47,000 prisoners. Of these totals Third Army's share
is impressive—about 25,000 casualties and about 100,000 prisoners,
that is, about double the number in each case captured by 21st and
6th Army Groups. By the evening of 24 March Eisenhower would
have substantial and rapidly expanding bridgeheads at Wesel,
Remagen, Oppenheim and Boppard. Although on paper the Germans still had 60 divisions, most of them were little more than battle

groups; ammunition, petrol and weapons were all lacking. Model with approximately 300,000 faced imminent and inevitable encirclement in the Ruhr.

In Italy, Alexander was on the point of launching the final offensive which was to end a few weeks later in the capitulation of Army Group C in the valley of the Po. On the Eastern Front the Russians had a bridgehead over the Oder only 30 miles from Berlin but had made little progress since February. Eisenhower had scored a decisive victory and it was obvious to the whole world that the Germans were doomed.

The decision he now took has been the subject of high-powered controversy, much of it tinctured with hindsight, ever since. In brief it was this: when the Ruhr was encircled the Ninth Army would revert to 12th Army Group, which thus raised to a strength of 48 divisions would constitute the Allied main effort under Bradley aimed not at Berlin but via Leipzig on Dresden. Here it would link up with the Red Army, thus cutting the remaining German forces in two. Montgomery was to cover Bradley's left flank. Finally Devers' 6th Army Group was to protect his right and be ready to move down the Danube to seize the 'national Redoubt'. This plan Eisenhower, without consulting his Allies, sent direct to Moscow marked 'Personal for Marshal Stalin'.

The complex issues arising from Eisenhower's decision thus to abandon the original Allied intention of making the main effort towards Berlin have since been examined over and over again with great verbal expertise by high-level militarily minded intellectuals with scintillating objectivity leaving Eisenhower's reputation for integrity intact and showing that there is something to be said in justification of the action he took so far as Berlin is concerned; unquestionably he deserved better political guidance than he got. There is far less charitable unanimity however with regard to the wisdom of the tasks which fell to Patton and Third Army as a result of his directives from now on to the end of hostilities.

Nothing could hold back the spearheads of Third Army as they swung forward north-east up the Frankfurt–Kassel corridor, on the right flank of Bradley's great enveloping movement of the southern edge of the Ruhr. On 28 March Patton linked up with Hodges at

Giessen; on the following day Frankfurt fell. At one time on the autobahn north of Frankfurt two of his armoured divisions and two infantry divisions were moving north abreast towards Kassel while in the centre of the same road German prisoners were streaming south unescorted. To coordinate the advance Patton took to the air so as to ensure personal touch with his three forward corps. From the moment when 4th Armored Division erupted from the Oppenheim bridgehead, air supply by the Troop Carrier Command's C 47s began to operate on an unprecedented scale. Daily the 'flying box-cars' delivered approximately half a million gallons of petrol and 150,000 rations: for ammunition there was less need. Kassel fell on 2 April: 48 hours later Patton had several bridgeheads over the Werra, established in the teeth of a futile revival of air attack by the enemy. Here he paused to allow his infantry to catch up with the armour.

With Model irretrievably surrounded in the Ruhr, by 11 April Eisenhower could now begin his final drive eastwards with all his three army groups to the line of the Elbe and the Mulde as agreed with Stalin. Patton's three leading corps once more plunged forward immediately north of the Thuringian Forest, over-running horror camps, releasing Allied prisoners and capturing vast quantities of war stores. By the 15th they had reached Chemnitz 35 miles from Dresden; at Rocklitz they were 20 miles from Leipzig: at Hof they were within ten miles of the Czechoslovak border. On the 17th his patrols crossed the frontier and brought back a large number of prisoners. It was only on the previous day that the Russians had launched their final offensive against Berlin. Ironically for the next three weeks they could have motored to Prague at any time without encountering a single Russian. However Patton was ordered to halt here and regroup for his final mission. Whilst Bradley held the line of the Elbe–Mulde rivers with two armies and Montgomery went for Lübeck, Patton was to thrust due south down the Danube valley to eliminate the National Redoubt within which, incredibly, 100 German divisions were said to be rallying for a final *Götterdämmerung*.

Third Army now comprised four corps of 12 infantry and six armoured divisions and three cavalry groups making a total of

437,000 men, its greatest strength in the war. Regrouping was completed with normal Third Army speed: on 22 April they were off once more. Thereafter progress was rapid. Thorough reconnaissance and enquiry failed to reveal any trace whatever of the National Redoubt or its garrison, the existence of which Koch had long since written off as the myth it proved to be. The whole border of western Czechoslovakia had been reached by 25 April. On 4 May 4th Armored Division passed through Linz in Austria to meet Mark Clark's Fifth Army coming up from Italy. At this time there was no danger of a clash between American and Russian forces for the Red Army was over 70 miles away from Prague and still encountering obstinate resistance from the Germans. Eisenhower therefore on 4 May told Bradley to order Patton to occupy the line Karlsbad–Pilsen–Budejovice roughly 20 miles within Czechoslovakia and to be ready to advance to Prague. This decision duly communicated to the Russians immediately produced a violent protest. Eisenhower, as ever anxious to keep on good terms with his allies, accordingly ordered Patton to halt his xii and v Corps on this line. On the morrow the partisans in Prague rose against the German garrison and called upon Eisenhower for help, asking in particular that the Czech Brigade which was part of Bradley's Army Group should be sent at once. They also appealed to Patton too for help. It was all in vain. Despite the fact that the operational situation justified American intervention in force in Prague, Eisenhower confined himself to telling the Czechs that he had halted Patton's forces at the request of the Russians and that applications for assistance should be addressed direct to them.

At the very climax of the war Eisenhower had ready America's finest army nearly half a million strong, superbly equipped and supported by overwhelming air power under the ablest and most dynamic commander in the West, all straining at the leash to reap the fruits of their victories by occupying the strategic centre of Europe. For the fifth time, and at the most crucial moment of all, Eisenhower failed to use it to get a decision. Stalin, who once asked how many divisions had the Pope, would at least have understood the force of an argument such as this.

Four times since the breakout at Avranches Patton and his army had given Eisenhower opportunities which might well have proved decisive, shortened the war, saved thousands of lives and left the West in a better strategic posture than it would be more than a quarter of a century later. It will be recollected that firstly on 13 August his xv Corps led by 5th Armored Division and Le Clerc's French Armoured Division had been ordered by Bradley, with Eisenhower's approval, to abandon its thrust on Argentan to meet the First Canadian Army at Falaise and thus close the gap. To his dying day Patton would be convinced that given a free hand at this time he could have ensured the complete destruction then and there of the German armies in Normandy. Secondly, when he reached the Seine and got a crossing at Mantes–Gassicourt on 20 August his proposal, if implemented, that his 5th Armored Division should thrust along the north bank of the river to seal off the exits from Rouen would in all probability have seen the end of Army Group B. Speidel, their Chief of Staff, who was on the spot, at any rate thought so.

Thirdly, if Eisenhower at the end of August when Patton reached the Meuse had not cut off his petrol for five vital days it is highly probable that he could have bounced the Rhine and got a bridgehead before von Rundstedt resumed command and restored some sort of order to the front. Patton himself thought that if he had not been pulled up in his tracks he could, by penetrating deep into Germany, have produced such a state of chaos that recovery would have been impossible.

Fourthly in the Ardennes battle, immediately after he relieved Bastogne, he had proposed that his army should be the right pincer of a great counter-attack designed to slice off the Ardennes salient at the base instead of bisecting it in the middle. In retrospect it does seem that action on these lines might well have shortened the agony and cut down the cost in terms of American life.

The bitter truth is that Eisenhower, great and good man though he was, never really got the feel of what went on at the front end of his armies. Never having personally been through the fire of close combat he deferred too much to the advice of others less qualified than Patton. Fate had given him an army commander of genius, in no whit inferior to Guderian, Manstein and Rommel and a great army as good as any the Allies—or for that matter the Germans and Russians—ever produced in Europe, and he failed to grasp their potential fully. Now ironically his ingenuous trust in Russian good faith would prevent him using that very army and its commander to complete his victory. Regrettably gentlemen, if there ever were any, had been extinct in Russia since 1917.

Nevertheless the history of war shows few instances of a single army having such a great effect in deciding the major issues of a campaign. Third Army's record is peerless by any measure and in the strictest sense of the term. In terms of statistics alone it outclasses anything achieved by any other Allied army as its final casualty report of 8 May 1945 shows:

Third Army		Enemy	
Killed	21,441	Killed	144,500
Wounded	99,224	Wounded	386,200
Missing	16,200	Prisoners of war	956,000
Total	136,865	*Total*	1,486,700

Non-battle casualties		
	111,562	Unknown

Material Losses			
Light tanks	308	Medium tanks	1,529
Medium tanks	949	Panther and Tiger tanks	858
Guns	175	Guns	3,454

It remains to be decided therefore what was behind the flamboyant facade of its commander, created partly by himself, partly by the Press and the mountebanks of Hollywood and partly by some of his contemporaries in the Allied armies.

Fundamentally he was a profoundly religious man, an Episcopalian who read the Bible daily. He was a good son, a good father and a good husband. He was indeed fortunate to find in his wife a woman, like Lady Spencer Churchill, big enough to appreciate, help and hold a man on the grand scale. As with all serious soldiers he had to face the continual and ever-recurring clash between Christian ideals and the grim work he often had to do. The sight of the dead on the battlefield and the severely wounded in hospital moved him deeply to the very end. Above all he loathed the bombing of the centres of cities and the suffering of refugees including the Germans. As he saw it from the earliest days the best elements in the Church had striven to mitigate some of the horrors of war. He nevertheless realised to the full that it is un-Christian to remain neutral against evil—and that, if ever there was an evil thing, it was the Nazi regime and all it stood for. He believed from the bottom of his heart all he wrote in his 'Soldiers Prayer' of 1 January 1944.

> God of our Fathers, who by land and sea has ever led us to victory, please continue your inspiring guidance in this the greatest of our conflicts.
>
> Strengthen my soul so that the weakening instinct of self-preservation, which besets all in battle, shall not blind me in my duty to my own manhood, to the glory of my calling, and to my responsibility to my fellow soldiers.
>
> Grant to our armed forces that disciplined valour and mutual confidence which ensures success in war.
>
> Let me not mourn for the men who have died fighting, but rather let me be glad that such heroes have lived.
>
> If it be my lot to die, let me do so with courage and honour in a manner which will bring the greatest harm to the enemy, and, please, Oh Lord, protect and guard those I shall leave behind.
>
> Grant us the victory, Lord.

He sincerely believed that 'a citizen's proudest privilege is to bear arms under his country's flag.' From his boyhood, perhaps to some extent as a result of his family's distinguished military tradition, he never had any other ambition than to be a great leader on the battlefield with all the glory and adulation that goes with it. This is the theme of his whole life. Nevertheless he managed to combine personal ambition with unswerving loyalty to the Army as a whole and to serve cheerfully under Bradley and Eisenhower who were younger and considerably his juniors in service. Like Churchill he was a late developer and, like Churchill too, he overcame by sheer force of will a physical handicap to leadership, in Churchill's case a stutter and in his a high-pitched voice. Indeed he trained and disciplined his life from the earliest days for the role he always in some strange way knew he would have to play. Like Mountbatten, whatever the sport or other activity in which he engaged, he had a built-in compulsion to excel in it whether it was pistol shooting, swordsmanship, sailing, polo, fishing, shooting, hunting or steeplechasing.

Unlike many inordinately ambitious men who have no interests outside their profession and who on social occasions cast a gloom over the proceedings, he managed to combine his overwhelming zeal and enthusiasm for whatever he undertook with great personal charm. Alexander had a great regard for him as had he for Alexander. His smile was most attractive: his British liaison officer in Morocco found him courteous and urbane off duty. His staff were devoted to him: once under his command they never wanted to serve under anyone else. He loved life, good food and drink, cheerful and civilised society, the quiet countryside and the sea, the joy which comes after hard exercise, and the pages of a well-written book.

He was generous in an unobtrusive way. In France his Chief of Staff told him of a Red Cross girl in trouble: in fact she was pregnant outside wedlock and needed money to have the baby, return to the United States, and start life again. Having satisfied himself that he personally would not be implicated in the case he handed over $800 without further comment: according to Semmes not half a dozen people ever knew of this compassionate act. In this respect he resembled Suvorov, Catherine the Great's general, a man in similar mould: after his death it was discovered that he was the unknown donor of large sums of money sent to the prison in Moscow every Easter for the redemption of debtors. With him too, Patton shared a sense of humour rare amongst generals: Cromwell, Napoleon, Frederick the Great, Stonewall Jackson and Haig certainly had none. In both cases it sometimes took a Rabelaisian turn: for example, when one of his social circle had recently given birth to a son, told him that it was wonderful to be able to roll over and lie on her stomach again, he is said to have replied in a voice that could be heard all over the hospital, 'Why, my dear young lady, had you retained that position in the first place, you would probably not have been in your recent unenviable condition.' Closely allied to his sense of humour was his capacity for concise and forceful expression. Ayer, his nephew, relates that in the Palatinate campaign they came upon a column over a mile long held up nose to tail, jammed at a turning under a railway bridge and presenting a perfect target to an enemy behind a 155mm. gun. The officer in command was about half way back in the column and apparently at a loss as to what to do. The conversation between him and Patton was brief and one-sided: 'Colonel, you can blow up the goddam gun. You can blow up the goddam bridge, or you can blow out your goddam brains, and I don't care which.'

His experience in the First War had taught him how men react to enemy fire and convinced him like Montgomery that morale is the most important factor in war—hence his unrelenting efforts to see the battle personally from the front and not through the eyes of his staff. Daily he missed no opportunity of emphasising to regimental officers their personal responsibility for their men. He realised that hot food in battle is often as important as ammunition. He showed himself to the troops as often and as impressively as possible. Like Allenby 'his imperious bearing radiated an impression of quick decision and steely discipline.' A firm believer in discipline at all costs his approach to the soldier who was doing his duty was kindly: to offenders his irascibility was blistering and never forgotten. He was quick to praise where praise was due and quick to reward. He understood his men's weaknesses: he was certainly no kill-joy in the matter of drink and he regarded with contempt the official policy of non-fraternisation with the women and children of the defeated enemy. His addresses to his troops, couched in a vernacular which they understood, read somewhat strangely today: nothing is so outdated as yesterday's slang, which may well have jarred the nerves of intellectuals at the time. It should be borne in mind however that such men are rare at the cutting edge of armies. With the majority they unquestionably struck home. What generals say to soldiers before or in battle should, like communications between husband and wife in matrimony, not be used in evidence against them.

So far as he personally was concerned, the day had not gone when generals could put themselves at the head of their men in a crisis, as Napoleon did on the bridge of Lodi, or Lannes at Ulm, who, placing himself at the head of the storming party, led them forward in the teeth of enemy fire saying 'I was a grenadier before I was a Marshal of France.' Semmes relates a typical instance of Patton's personal courage under fire.

It was proposed that tanks with their turrets closed should attack, supported by artillery fire bursting in the air immediately above them, thus neutralising the enemy infantry and artillery. Semmes arranged a demonstration of this technique just before the Sicilian landing. To his consternation, Patton announced that he proposed to act as a gunner in the leading wave. Luckily he was not killed, but the tanks suffered considerably from the artillery fire and needed extensive repair and replacement, particularly of the antennae and the gun sights which in Patton's tank were shot away. He himself had a wonderful time firing the cannon from his own tank. Like the legendary Freyberg, the New Zealander, who was wounded 26 times, he seems to have thought that a little shell fire did everybody good; like Freyberg too his medical record showed an impressive number of fractures and similar accidents resulting from World War One wounds and from falls at polo, in the hunting field and in steeplechasing: this may to some extent explain his occasional irascibility. Wavell thought what he called 'robustness', the physical and mental ability to stand up to prolonged strain arising from the responsibility of dealing with men's lives, an essential quality in a good commander; Patton certainly possessed it. After two and a half years of almost continuous action he was still at the top of his form in May 1945.

Eisenhower said of him: 'His emotional range was very great and he lived either at one end or the other of it.' Whether this is an overstatement or not, he was like Nelson, Suvorov and for that matter Churchill a highly emotional man. There was a spontaneity about him, as with Churchill, characteristic rather of the eighteenth than the twentieth century: his indiscreet outbursts, especially to the Press sometimes distressed his greatest admirers and indeed in the end would prove his undoing. He sometimes said things on the spur of the moment which he later regretted and for which he apologised. The slapping incident in Sicily certainly did his reputation great harm and caused Eisenhower much embarrassment. Nevertheless these pent-up forces within him may well have been responsible to some extent for his power to inspire men to supreme effort, part of the secret of the immense drive he gave to Third Army and of its unconquerable will to close with the enemy. Great victories, like great works of art, have seldom been the work of unemotional men.

As in Churchill too, and for that matter Goering, there was in him a highly developed histrionic streak. As early as 1927 he was caught looking in a mirror practising what he called his 'war face'. As with most actors of his generation, both professional and amateur, everything he did had to be a little larger than life. Hence the flamboyance, the elaborate uniforms and the pomp and circumstance with which he surrounded himself. He longed for applause not only from the stalls, but regrettably from the gallery as well. He revelled in the adulation of the Press. These foibles to a considerable extent explain his almost pathological dislike of Montgomery who, in his own austere style, could carry any audience of British troops off its feet and who also loved to hit the headlines with equal relish. Not surprisingly they both gave Eisenhower most of the worries of an impresario trying to run a ballet with two highly temperamental stars in it who hate each other's guts and make no attempt to conceal the fact.

Denied the opportunity in long periods of peace to practise their craft, commanders have almost always exercised their minds in the study of military history. Patton for his part brought to it an exceptionally lively mind and vivid imagination—so vivid in fact at times that he could visualise himself as actually living in the age of Caesar, Belisarius or Napoleon. His library of over 500 volumes dealing with history, biography and military memoirs attested the breadth of his humanity and the extent of his reading. To him history was the essence of a thousand military biographies. His wife had been educated in Europe and spoke fluent French: hence to some extent his love of France. In much that he did and said can be caught echoes from Marbot's version of the campaigns of Napoleon. Between the wars his contributions to the *Cavalry Journal*, written it seems often to clear his own mind, have a clarity, stress on which has been one of France's contributions to Western Civilisation. When the time came for him to lead an army for her liberation, he knew the lie of the land like the back of his hand, and the problems it had presented to commanders of armies since the days of Caesar. In the hours of peacetime reading and reflection which he had spent in his study lies part of the explanation of his speed of decision when these very problems arose again in a new form.

From this military and cultural background he approached the problems raised by the advent of the tank and the aeroplane in the light of the great cavalry tradition dating back to the invention of the stirrup about the time of the advent of the Dark Ages: surprise, speed, mobility, flexibility, wide outflanking movements and relentless pursuit, regardless of the exhaustion of man and horse. And, above all, willingness to take risks and indeed great risks to get a final unequivocal decision. As Napoleon said: 'If the art of war consisted in not taking risks glory would be at the mercy of very mediocre talent.' He thus had ready a doctrine on which to train the newly raised armoured divisions when the opportunity came in 1940. He brought to it his own originality and flair for the unorthodox. With the advent of armour he saw that chances of flank attack could be taken more readily than with infantry for the tank is not as vulnerable to small-arms fire and the air can give timely warning. In due course they would be quicker to profit from their experience in Tunisia than the British.

In his bearing and style of inspection he owed much to the example of Pershing. He stood no nonsense from his subordinates: so far as he was concerned an order was an order and not a basis for discussion. Hence too his insistence on the outward and visible signs of discipline as evidenced by smart turnout. Nevertheless he had a happy headquarters: he never tried to do the work of his staff but having given them clear instructions left them to get on with their job. Unlike Rommel and the brilliant but erratic Wingate, he was predictable to his staff. He realised the importance of logistics but he never regarded them as an over-riding factor. Whilst he showed no mercy to the inefficient, like Churchill he never forgot an old friend; no one, given the chance of serving under him, ever wished to serve under anyone else despite his readiness in a crisis to violate every orthodox rule of procedure.

Patton was unquestionably the outstanding exponent of armoured warfare produced by the Allies in the Second World War. In terms of blood and iron he personified the national genius which had raised the United States from humble beginnings to world power: the eagerness to seize opportunities and to exploit them to the full, the ruthless overriding of opposition, the love of the unconventional, the ingenious and the unorthodox, the will to win whatever the cost and, above all, in the shortest possible time. As Speidel, Rommel's Chief of Staff and later Commander-in-Chief, Allied Forces Central Europe, said: 'He was the only Allied general who dared exceed the safety limits in the endeavour to achieve a decision.' He added that he earned little thanks for his generalship.

Where therefore does he stand in the lists of fame? He never exercised independent command: he therefore does not fall into the category of the great supreme commanders—Hannibal, Scipio, Marlborough, Frederick the Great, Napoleon and, perhaps, MacArthur —the men who could see their war as a whole, relate sea power (and later air power) with land power and their operations with their political needs. He had even less political sense than Montgomery and that is saying much. It is with the great commanders on the battlefield itself that he stands comparison: with Murat, Sherman, Forrest, Stonewall Jackson, Manstein and Rommel. His friend and admirer Field-Marshal Alexander, whose combat experience in both world wars, both in victory and defeat, was greater than that of all other British and American generals spoke of him as 'a dashing steed' and as a genius on the battlefield itself. A quarter of a century later it can be confirmed that in mobile operations he outshone with startling brilliance in imagination, technique and achievement his Allied contemporaries.

Epilogue

The arrival of the Third Army on the frontiers of Czechoslovakia and Austria where the Roman Legions too had halted in the heyday of their power and the end of the fighting in Western Europe provide the climax to Patton's career. A later generation, however, will wish to know what happened to him afterwards.

VE-Day brought with it direct responsibility for the government of Bavaria, a task which called for the maximum possible diplomatic skill and knowledge of civil administration. In particular at a time when the overriding need was to get the German economy on its feet the Allied policy of de-Nazification demanded that all officials with Nazi affiliations should be removed from positions of authority including the running of the railways, the power stations and the hospitals. To saddle a great fighting soldier with political problems of this sort was unjust and, in view of his past record for outspoken and indiscreet comment, inexcusable. His soldierly instinct to treat his defeated enemy with generosity soon exposed him to hostile comment in the Press and his unrestrained criticism of his own government's policy damaged his own reputation with them beyond repair. In particular his blatantly hostile attitude to the Russians was widely reported. The climax came at a Press Conference on 22 September. To use his own words: 'This conference cost me the command of the Third Army, or rather of a group of soldiers, mostly recruits, who then rejoiced in that historic name; but I was intentionally direct, because I believed that it was time for people to know what was going on. My language was not particularly polite, but I have yet to find where politic language produces successful government.'

Three times his friend Eisenhower had saved him from the wrath of the politicians: now it was beyond his power. He had no alternative other than to order him to hand over his command to Truscott.

He did however save his face to some extent by transferring him to the command of the so-called Fifteenth Army, a headquarters still in Germany with little to do except compile a record of the operations since D-Day.

On Sunday 9 December he and Gay, still his Chief of Staff, set off down the Frankfurt-Mannheim road for a day's pheasant shooting. Both were sitting in the back of the car. Suddenly an army truck from the opposite direction turned left in front of them to enter a side road. Both cars swerved to avoid a head-on collision and struck each other a glancing blow. Patton was thrown forward so violently that his head struck either the back of the front seat or the roof of the car. The vertebrae of the upper spine were crushed, resulting in almost immediate paralysis from the neck downwards. Tragically he who dreamed of a soldier's sudden death in his last battle lingered on for twelve days.

He lies buried in the American Cemetery at Hamm in Luxembourg still at the head of the men of the Third Army who fought and died in the Ardennes. As Napoleon said 'the boundaries of a nation's greatness are marked by the graves of her soldiers'.

Bibliography

Allen S., *Lucky Forward*, Macfadden, 1965

Ambrose S., *The Supreme Commander*, Cassell, 1971

Ayer F., *Before the Colours Fade*, Cassell, 1965

Blake R. (Ed), *The Private Papers of Douglas Haig*, Eyre and Spottiswoode, 1955

*Blumenson M., *Breakout and Pursuit*, Department of the Army, 1961

*Blumenson M., *Rommel's Last Victory*, Allen and Unwin, 1968

*Blumenson M. (Ed), *The Patton Papers 1885–1940*, Houghton Mifflin, 1972

Bradley O.N., *A Soldier's Story*, Eyre and Spottiswoode, 1951

Bryant A., *The Turn of the Tide*, Collins, 1957

Bryant A., *Triumph in the West*, Collins, 1959

Butcher H.C., *Three Years with Eisenhower*, Heinemann, 1946

Butler A.J. (Trans), *Memoirs of Baron de Marbot*, Longmans, 1907

Carell H.M., *Invasion They're Coming*, Harrap, 1962

Carver M., *Tobruk*, Batsford, 1964

*Chandler A. and Ambrose S., *The Eisenhower Papers*, 5 Vols, Johns Hopkins Press, 1970

Churchill W.S., *The Second World War*, Vols IV and V, Cassell, 1951

Codman C.R., *Drive*, Little, Brown and Co, Boston, 1957

Coffman E.M., *The War to End All Wars*, OUP, New York, 1968

*Cole H.M., *The Lorraine Campaign*, Department of the Army, 1949

* Denotes a book of unusual interest recommended for further reading.

*Cole H.M., *The Ardennes*, Department of the Army, 1964

*Ellis L.F., *Victory in the West*, 2 Vols, HMSO, 1962 and 1968

Eisenhower D.D., *Crusade in Europe*, Heinemann, 1948

*Esposito V.J., *The West Point Atlas of American Wars*, Praeger, 1959

Essame H., *Battle for Germany*, Batsford, 1969

Essame H., *Battle for Europe 1918*, Batsford, 1972

*Farago L., *Patton, Ordeal and Triumph*, Barker, 1966

Fergusson B., *The Watery Maze*, Collins, 1961

Galante P., *The General*, Leslie Frewin, 1969

Gillie M.H., *Forging the Thunderbolt*, Military Service Publishing Company, Harrisburg Pa, 1947

*Greenfield K.R. (Ed), *Command Decisions*, Methuen, 1960

Harmon E.N., *Combat Commander*, Prentice-Hall, 1970

*Henriques R., *From a Biography of Myself*, Secker and Warburg, 1969

Horrocks B., *A Full Life*, Collins, 1960

Jackson W., *Alexander of Tunis*, Batsford, 1971

Koch O.W., *G2 Intelligence for Patton*, Army Times/Whitmore, 1971

Lewin R., *Rommel as Military Commander*, Batsford, 1968

Lewin R., *Montgomery*, Batsford, 1971

Liddell Hart B., *The Rommel Papers*, Cassell, 1953

*Liddell Hart B., *History of the Second World War*, Cassell, 1970

Long G., *MacArthur as Military Commander*, Batsford, 1964

Macmillan H., *The Blast of War*, Macmillan, 1967

Montgomery B., *Normandy to the Baltic*, Hutchinson, 1946

Montgomery B., *El Alamein to the Sangro*, Hutchinson, 1948

Montgomery B., *Memoirs*, Collins, 1958

Nicholson N., *Alex*, Weidenfeld and Nicholson, 1973

*Patton G.S. Jr, *War as I Knew It*, Houghton Mifflin, 1947

Pearl J., *Blood and Guts Patton*, Monarch Books, 1961

Pershing J.J., *My Experiences in the World War*, Hodder and Stoughton, 1931

Rommel E., *Infantry Attacks*, Combat Forces Press, 1956

*Semmes H.H., *Psychology of Leadership*, Appleton-Century-Crofts, 1955

Sixsmith E.K.G., *Eisenhower*, Batsford, 1973
*Speidel H., *We Defended Normandy*, Herbert Jenkins, 1951
Strong K., *Intelligence at the Top*, Cassell, 1965
Tedder A.W., *With Prejudice*, Cassell, 1966
Westphal R.S., *The German Army in the West*, Cassell, 1951
Westphal R.T., *Fatal Decisions*, Joseph, 1956
*Wilmot C., *The Struggle for Europe*, Collins, 1952

Index